To Tricia

If you [...] what was Roderick's mind, this book will give you some of the answers.

Love,
Margaret
Oct. 28, 1989

FALSTAFF
THE ARCHETYPAL MYTH

FALSTAFF

THE ARCHETYPAL MYTH

RODERICK MARSHALL

A NADDER BOOK
ELEMENT BOOKS

First published in Great Britain 1989 by
Element Books Limited
Longmead, Shaftesbury, Dorset

Printed and bound in Great Britain by
Billings, Hylton Road, Worcester

Designed by Clarke Williams

Jacket designed by Max Fairbrother

British Library Cataloguing in Publication Data
Marshall, Roderick
Falstaff, the archetypal myth.
1. Literature. Characters
I. Title
809'.027

ISBN 1-85230-089-2

Contents

To the compelling richness of Silenos,
Bes, Enkidu, Abu Zaid, Kuvera, Ganeśa,
Li Po, Ilya, and Merlin as woven into
the character of Falstaff.

Preface

In *The Fortunes of Falstaff*, published in 1944, J. Dover Wilson says that already in the eighteenth century, Dr Johnson saw the character of the fat knight so steadily and whole that nothing important remains to be said, even by Mr Wilson. To be sure, he does go on to write a book which goes far to advance his thesis that Falstaffian criticism put to port in a happy haven, or perhaps a dead end, some two hundred years ago.

Grudgingly Mr Wilson acknowledges the existence of a contrary-minded group of writers from Morgann to Bradley who hold that in Falstaff Shakespeare created an extraordinary being who at the expense of king, prince, and country dominates both *Henry IV* plays and casts a cosmic shadow across even *Henry V* – a being whose ponderous significance remains as yet ungauged and perhaps unmanageable. Yet these admirers of Falstaff, really "idolators", Wilson dismisses as a parcel of feverishly imaginative and emotionally frustrated professors. They may or may not be, like Bradley, of a "shy, gentle, refined, subtle, hypersensitive, entirely moral, almost otherworldly personality, at once donnish, a little old-maidish, and extraordinarily winning",[1] but there is something decidedly wrong with them. Why, otherwise, should they apotheocise a figure whom Dr Johnson correctly characterised as an "obsequious ... agent of vice"? Let us face the truth, says Wilson, about these academic heretics: for them to thieve and guzzle and gourmandise, to whore and blaspheme and boast in the company of old Jack Falstaff is vicariously to consummate a typical professor's day-dreams and purge the straitjacketed academic mind of its fear of "conduct unbecoming a teacher", its pity (of self, that is) induced by constant knuckling under to Old Father Antic the Law in the form of college presidents and boards of trustees. Thus they enjoy in Falstaff not what the text permits but what the context suggests – a most immoral escape from the responsibilities of a campus life that is real and earnest. Well ...

Thirty years ago I saw no more – in fact, rather less – in the Falstaff–Hal stories than Mr Dover Wilson. Today I find his Johnson-Redivivus almost wholly superficial. During the decades I speak of, I have not merely grown older, more frustrated, and more irresponsible; I have also been rifling the literature and mythology of Oriental countries with some application and, like so many other distracted people of our time, I have dabbled in the findings of the anthropologists, the theories of the folklorists, and the speculations of the psychologists and psychiatrists, especially as these promise to throw light on problems connected with the creation and enjoyment of art.

Some ten years ago, after neglecting the Bard for years, I was called on to give a course in his comedies. That semester I never got beyond the Falstaff plays because the story of the planetary knight and his adventures, in which I had once seen nothing particularly engrossing, now showed themselves crammed with unexpected meaning and undreamt-of fascination. I was immediately impressed by the fact that the three plays in which Falstaff appears, along with *Richard II*, in which his advent seems called for, and *Henry V*, in the mouth of which his death is squarely set, constitute a great drama or pentology embedding more myth, legend, and fossilised religion, also more up-to-the-minute psychological insights, than I could possibly hope to do justice to, or even try to do justice to. Speech after speech can be used to illustrate hundreds of icons, carved, painted, or cast in ancient Egypt, Greece, Babylon, India, and China, in medieval Islam, in old Russia or the Celtic countries, and among present-day Africans, Amerindians, and South Sea Islanders. It was when I was beginning to get a hold on these things that I read *The Fortunes of Falstaff* for the first time and found it impossible to agree that Shakespeare criticism reached its zenith in the Johnson–Wilson school or that the apotheosis of Falstaff by other critics was the mere aberration of frustrated professors.

I must confess here to feeling often and often, as I felt when reading Wilson and his many followers, that much of the criticism of our major poets and writers is thickening towards stagnation. What can be learned from the study of influences, that is, of the measurable degree to which some books have been affected by others, has pretty much been learned, while whatever light that the facts of an author's life and times can throw on his art has pretty much been thrown. His place in clearly defined literary traditions has been clearly defined. As for the so-called aesthetic approach to literature, here we remain where we have always been: in the realm of imponderables, every pondering of which seems either to gild the flower or to crush it. Aesthetic Geiger-counters brought into the sphere of radioactive beauty not only begin to rattle but cause their carriers to rattle. The self-plotted cardiographs of the critic's reactions to a given work of art furnish little clue to most of the forces – religious, mythic, somnambulistic – which must often, perhaps on an unconscious level as the psychologists tell us, set the heart vibrating when a supreme creation begins to upheave ancient crusts. In fine, most of the usual strategies by which scholarship and criticism seek to ensnare the essential life of great works of literature seem to have been applied to the point of vanishing returns.

In this book I would like to try a new approach to a surprising work of art, seeking in the process to demonstrate, roughly, the methodology as well as to describe the results that such an approach may be expected to yield. The methods and fruits of comparative literature in the usual sense of the word have been known to us for a long time and are not essentially different from any study of the literary influence of one author or group of authors upon another author or group. What I propose here is a study, as it were, in the history of a *dramatis persona* or character type – the Falstaffian, if we may call him after his most illustrious example – in which I shall bring together samples of this figure from the literatures of many countries and many epochs, quite irrespective of any direct influence, or even of the possibility of influence, that they may have exerted upon each other or upon Shakespeare's incomparable creation. Assembled together, I hope they will shed useful light on each other.

The character is a grotesque, fat, feral, oversexed, crapulous, witty, profane, old–young creature who in times of trouble undertakes to misrule–rule a waste country and educate the heir of its sick and dying monarch in practices calculated to restore peace and prosperity. When the prince has learned his lessons, usually two battles are fought. In the first of these the tutor–buffoon, with a following of bizarre recruits, helps the prince to win a notable victory over demonically powerful adversaries. After this victory the prince is crowned and the teacher rejected, imprisoned, and sometimes killed. Following the tutor's death the king, now fully initiated into the exercise of superhuman powers, goes on to win the second battle in his own right and establish joy and fertility in his kingdom.

For the purpose of examining and interpreting the character of the tutor and the events in which he is involved, I intend to use stories and plays exemplifying this pattern collected from countries and periods widely separated in space and time, my hope being that they will shed from opposite ends of the earth antiphonal radiance on the significance of the age-old myth here involved and still highly favoured in folklore, literature, and art. Some of the characters I intend to examine seem to stress one aspect of the Falstaff temper or syndrome at the expense of the others. In any given example some traits and adventures may be entirely wanting, but this does not happen frequently. My hope is that when these accounts, along with icons I reproduce to illustrate them, are gathered together, the true inwardness of the Falstaffian character will appear. As we read widely, the resulting empathy which brings a glad acceptance of worldwide responsibilities seems less hopeless when we realise that in different parts of the world the human mind has, in its art and literature, evolved concepts, images, and values so similar that a literally identical parenthood for all men could not possibly have made them more brotherly.

In the eighteenth century, the heyday of the deists, the first modern citizens of the world, the author of the first full-length book about Falstaff, Maurice Morgann (*An Essay on the Dramatic Character of Sir John Falstaff*, 1777), had glimpses of his fat subject as a figure far transcending the politics and social life of Shakespeare's England or, indeed, of western countries generally – a figure whose dimensions and mysteries are on the scale of nothing smaller than the Pyramids and Stonehenge – while in our own time the late H.C. Goddard discerned in Falstaff "the proportions of a mythological figure. He seems at times more like a god than a man. His very solidity is solar, his rotundity comic."[3] Lord Raglan could not help feeling "that Shakespeare had at the back of his mind the idea that Falstaff was a holy man",[4] whose piety could be understood only in relation to the ceremonies, myths, and religious beliefs of the ancient Greeks, Semites, and Hindus – only with the help of the legends and folklore of medieval Russians, Celts, and Scandinavians.

For my part, I find it difficult not to see something mysteriously awful in a figure the events of whose life I cannot now, after getting some acquaintance with the world's art, dissociate from dozens of poems and hundreds of icons which have fascinated man from the moment when he began to leave a tangible record of his hopes and fears. It is my hope that a study such as the following may, like Falstaff himself, woo "both high and low, both rich and poor, both young and old, one with another" and help bring the peoples of the world together in a hierogamos worthy of being presided over by a genial demon of his global dimensions.

I trust that this study may put bees in the nightcaps of other comparative literaturists, religionists, or whatever we may call ourselves. We are always telling each other that we have, as students of humane arts and letters, a moral responsibility to society to sift, synthesise, and interpret the tremendous amounts of data now available in such a way as to offer people a little guidance out of the bog through which they often seem to be dragging their feet in a death march. The present study demonstrates, perhaps, one way in which this moral debt can be repaid. When I speak of bees for professors' nightcaps, I mean perhaps hornets, for the preparation is considerable and the thinking onerous. Those who would carry out such a task need to feel for the world's art and literature not merely love but bulimia, described as "excessive hunger, often suddenly at night".

I

The "Magnificent Irrelevance" of Falstaff?

If the Falstaff dramas can be satisfactorily accounted for, as Dover Wilson insists, as a great Morality Play in the tradition of *Everyman*, then Johnson–Wilson criticism has indeed long since defined their scope and exhausted discussion of them; but if they can be more satisfactorily treated as a great Mystery Play, in a sense which I shall soon define, then it is time to break up the critical ice-crust that threatens to bring fishing in these deep waters to an end. There is, I think, an opportunity and a necessity to bring to the interpretation of these plays some of the manifold discoveries that modern interrelated and often correlated studies in anthropology, myth, religion, and psychology have been turning up during the past half-century. If we seize this opportunity, make a virtue of necessity, we may find not only plenty of mystery-religion in these dramas but also more morality than can ever be discovered in the Johnson–Wilson venue.

The Morality, of which he takes the Falstaffian plays to be the latest and grandest example, Dover Wilson defines as a drama "which exhibited the process of salvation in the individual soul on its road between birth and death, beset with the Snares of the World or the Wiles of the Evil One".[1] He notes with satisfaction that in the Morality Play, "however many capers the Devil and his Vice may cut on Everyman's way" to salvation, "always the powers of darkness are withstood finally and overcome by the agents of light".[2] The struggle between these opposing powers he takes to be the heart of Shakespeare's Falstaff–Henry cycle. But this struggle in Shakespeare's plays is not, Wilson concedes, a contest on the grand scale reaching into the manifold hiding places of human depravity or summoning up unlikely and even astounding resources of moral strength. With the coming of humanism and the Tudors, he says, the long Moralities like *Everyman* gave place to shorter and lighter interludes "dealing not with human life as a whole but with youth and its besetting sins",[3] plays in which the Devil was parcelled among personifications of Riot, Pride, Lust, and Revenge. It is superficially in such interludes that he finds the source and theme of the Falstaff–Henry dramas. As an example of an interlude that deals specifically with what he takes to be the main subject of Shakespeare's plays, Wilson cites *Youth*, written about 1520, in which a young man, inexperienced and somewhat contemptuous of things spiritual, is introduced by Riot to Pride and Lady Lechery, who lead him down a primrose path which in time sprouts thorns enough to drive him to such repentance that the play may end, as Wilson notes with satisfaction, in "the most seemly fashion imaginable".

Now I submit that it is simply impossible to find as little subtlety of intent or so trite a moral in the Shakespeare plays as this analogy suggests.

Wilson himself is well aware that the figure of Falstaff is compared by Shakespeare not only to the Vice of the Morality or the Riot of the Interlude but also to the Fiend of the Miracle Plays. Now the Miracles, which preceded the Moralities, not only brought Hell-Mouth itself on to the stage but provided sufficient fiends, led by their Grand Master, to stuff its fatal jaws with the unrepentant. Hal, playing the role of his own father in a rare piece of Boar's Head extempore, calls his old preceptor not merely "that reverend Vice" but "that old white-bearded Satan".[4] Throughout the three plays in which he appears, Falstaff is continually called, whether in jest or earnest, the Devil or the Fiend. I am not suggesting, however, that these Shakespeare plays be looked on as a tremendous Miracle Play designed with the usual purpose of discomfiting Satan. That would, by the very definition of a Miracle as a drama based on Holy Writ, be impossible. I am suggesting that Falstaff's physical and psychic origins may with profit be looked for in a type of play that preceded the Miracle itself, a form of drama reaching back into pre-Christian times, which used – or itself constituted – the holy writ of an earlier faith, and gave a large role to a deity identified in Christian times as the Devil in accord with the principle that the "God of the old religion becomes the devil of the new". This kind of drama is itself often called a Mystery because it dealt with mysteries or non-Christian miracles such as the rebirth of the sun's power at the winter solstice or the upsurge of vegetation after the vernal equinox. Such mystery plays did not merely allegorise these natural events but were intended actually to aid and abet them. These plays have a thousand times been traced back to primitive rites intended to help the fertilising passion of sun and earth in their eternal obsession of the yearly battle with drawn-out darkness and frozen furrows – with winter's sadness. We have a heritage, sometimes fragmentary, of such plays from ancient Egypt, from all parts of Asia and Europe, and indeed from Amerindia and Indonesia, dating from times both ancient and modern.

In England the most impressive body of such Mysteries left to us are the Folk Plays still performed at winter or springtime festivals. It is in the recoverable material of such plays, it seems to me, that we do well to look for the more immediate origins of our old white-bearded Satan. If a case, not of identity but of analogy, of shared spirit and point, between this kind of Mystery Play and Shakespeare's dramas can be established, we may then feel free and justified in roaming through the familiar Mystery literature of the world in search of rotund characters whose functions and adventures may throw light on the meaning of Falstaff.

It is perfectly possible, of course, to read the Falstaff–Henry plays quite literally, as we do other chronicles by Shakespeare and his contemporaries, and see in the Falstaff material merely comic relief for the serious business of wars and conquests transacted by kings and princes. This is the typical approach of a Johnson or a Wilson, the latter of whom divides his book into chapters in which the bawdy Falstaff escapades are antiseptically separated from the majestic sickness of the Court, and the stories of Hal and his tutor are developed as uncompromisingly independent of each other. They meet only at those points where Hal and Falstaff come physically into contact. Indeed Wilson insulates the Boar's Head witchcraft so thoroughly from the Star Chamber statecraft that he nullifies his own definition of the plays as a grand Morality in which youth overcomes the temptations thrown in the way of his accession to the throne of righteousness by a fiend who seeks to discredit all spiritual values. At one end of the town all is drunkenness, debauchery, and levity while at the other all is grave policy and high-toned moralising upon the heavy duties of kingship. From such a dichotomising of the material of the plays Hal cannot help emerging a half-hearted reveller, a dishonest prig, or a coldly calculating politician, in none of which roles does he ever suggest for a moment the fallen and repentant sinner of a Morality Play. (Though there are passages in the plays that lend a little colour to the view of the Falstaff–Henry dramas as a great Morality in which the prince stands for Everyman battling valiantly with an old grey-bearded Devil for the salvation of his soul in this world and the next.) The very material of the plays – the rite-like acts, the tableaux-scenes, the peculiar imagery, and especially the rich-textured and scintillating language, often hieratically authoritative in the case of Falstaff – forces us to look for deeper meanings in the characters and, as we might expect from our greatest poet, more organic relations between the tavern and the palace scenes, between the episodes of apparently low-minded vice and those of apparently high-minded policy, than Wilson will allow.

Unless such relations can be established, the Falstaff of these plays becomes exactly what F.L. Lucas calls him, "a magnificent irrelevance", whose presence in the *Henries* helps make of them "an ill constructed monstrosity".[5] The Falstaff of this school of thought is entirely expendable, being introduced into the plays as an avatar of the Miles Gloriosus of Plautus because Elizabethan audiences liked military uproar[6], or as a broken-down Lollard – all for comic relief to serious business – even Wilson's Falstaff has much of this in him since it is admitted he is not much of a tempter, or as a survival of the medieval Vice whose role was partly to be silly and slapped about.[7] Even those who hold, like Wilson, that Falstaff is a wicked tempter needed to clarify the nature of the good life for Hal find little horrifying sinfulness or malignant purpose in that "tun of man".

Yet who, reading or seeing these plays, can doubt that the "episodes" in which Falstaff capers are really the heart of the dramas on which all the other scenes depend for such significance as they may have? Who has ever really felt that the Falstaff incidents provide, chiefly, comic relief to the main action or that these plays, with the Falstaff scenes removed, would have any more meaning in them than *Hamlet* without Hamlet? If Falstaff be at the beginning a corrupter of youth and Hal a true hero at the end, then the reader must conclude, it seems to me, both from the interweaving of scenes and from the tone and the style of all Falstaff's deportment that Hal has become heroic by – not in spite of – the hours spent roistering with him and the other corrupters of youth at the Boar's Head. As Lord Raglan writes in *The Hero*:

> It is quite clear that Shakespeare and his predecessors regarded Henry as a great hero, and it follows that they regarded association with a man of disreputable character, such as Falstaff was, as being in keeping with the character of a great hero. ... It seems clear that to Shakespeare's audiences the proper way for a budding hero to behave was to roister with a drunken buffoon.[8]

Raglan never suggests why such improper behaviour was "proper" for a prince, but he notes in the chapter on "Myth and the Historic Hero" many examples of such a belief obtaining at many times and in all quarters of the globe. Raglan also points out, as have many others, that such facts as are known about the historical Henry bear no relation to the picture of him as the crony of highwaymen, pickpockets, and whores, the madcap who, according to Thomas Elyot's *The Governor* (1531) and Edward Hall's *Union of the Noble Houses of Lancaster and York* (1542), gave the face of Chief Justice Gascoigne a slap which resounded unforgettably down the years. As Raglan says, these two highly respectable authors sought to tell the truth about Henry and had no reason whatever to try to give his history comic relief, especially by the introduction of ribald stories. Simply, they did not find it possible to ignore or cut through the tight integument of a tradition which had begun to weave itself around the story of Hal within fifty years of his death. Raglan recalls that in his *History of England* Sir Charles Oman declares that Hal, who became his father's deputy in Wales at the age of thirteen and spent the next seven years of his life in almost continuous warfare with Owen Glendower and his allies, devoting his entire adolescence to military strategy, statecraft, and the liquidation of Lollardy, was

> grave and earnest in speech, courteous in all his dealings, and an enemy of flatterers and favourites. His sincere piety bordered on asceticism. ... His enemies called him hard-hearted and sanctimonious. ... The legendary tales which speak of him as a debauchee and idle youth, who consorted with disreputable favourites, such as Shakespeare's famous Sir John Falstaff, are entirely worthless.[9]

The *Dictionary of National Biography* says of Hal that "the popular tradition (immortalised by Shakespeare) of his riotous and dissolute conduct is not supported by any contemporary authority." To quote Raglan again,

> It is difficult to imagine who could have transmitted the stories of Hal's debauchery with knowledge and safety, and they are quite out of keeping with Henry's activities as king, all of which suggest a long apprenticeship to war and statecraft. An idle and dissolute scapegrace transformed in an instant into the first soldier and statesman of his age would indeed be an astonishing spectacle.[10]

The only conclusion we can draw from all this is that because Henry's statesmanship and victories caused him to be regarded as a recipient or vessel of divine favour and the guarantor of national prosperity, there came inevitably to be attached to his life a whole series of incidents and stories appropriate and indispensable, at least in the folk imagination, to such a character. It thus becomes highly likely that Shakespeare's Falstaff–Henry plays, while having an air of realism about them and passing as dramatised chronicles of fact, fall into the class of Mystery dramas mentioned above, for it is chiefly in these, especially in the English Mummers' Play and not in the old Moralities, Miracles, or Interludes, that we find definite analogues to the characters, incidents, actions, and morals so grandiosely set forth in the two *Henry IV* plays, *The Merry Wives of Windsor*, and *Henry V*, with their pointing prologue in *Richard II*.

Let me try, as well as I can, to outline the action and indicate the significance of a tiny Mummer–Mystery of the type that may have furnished a seed for Shakespeare's gigantic overgrowth. One can say without exaggeration that some kind of drama of this type exists or has existed in every part of the world, and the brief account I intend to give will be synthesised from material drawn from many times and places.*

---

*For detailed information on a fascinating subject, I recommend:

(1) A. Moret, *Rois et Dieux d'Egypte* (Paris, 1922);
(2) A.M. Hocart, *Kingship* (Oxford, 1927), one of the best studies;
(3) F.S. Marvin, *Kingship in India* (London, 1928);
(4) S.H. Hooke, ed., *Myth and Ritual* (Oxford, 1933);
(5) S.H. Hooke, ed., *The Labyrinth* (London, 1935);
(6) Lord Raglan, *The Hero: a Study in Tradition, Myth, and Drama* (London, 1936);
(7) A.M. Hocart, *Kings and Councillors* (Cairo, 1936);
(8) I. Engnell, *Studies in Divine Kingship in the Ancient Near East* (Uppsala, 1943);
(9) T. Irstam, *The King of Ganda: Studies in the Institutions of Sacral Kingship in Africa* (Stockholm, 1944);
(10) R. Patai, *Man and Temple in Ancient Jewish Myth and Ritual* (London, etc., 1947);
(11) H. Frankfort, *Kingship and the Gods: A Study of Near Eastern Religion as the Integration of Society and Nature* (Chicago, 1948);
(12) T.H. Gaster, *Thespis: Ritual, Myth, and Drama in the Ancient Near East* (New York, 1950);
(13) W.E. Soothill, *The Hall of Light: A Study in Early Chinese Kingship* (London, 1951).

Since the publication of Frazer's *Golden Bough*, the first two volumes of which appeared in 1890, there has appeared an imposing literature dealing with the ways and means resorted to by early or so-called primitive men in order to facilitate the regular and fruitful functioning of nature upon which their well-being very largely depended, not only in long-ago times but down to our own days. Almost every important civilisation of which we know, including those which have survived to colour our present world, evolved elaborate religio-political systems with complex ritualistic ceremonies performed at seasonal festivals. Professor S.H. Hooke, speaking of his special area of expertise, sums up the case for every part of the world when he says that a study of Near Eastern religion, with its associated myths and seasonal rites, shows "a community seeking to bring under control by means of an organised system of ritual actions the order of nature on the functioning of which its well-being depends".[11]

Ancient men believed that a god or a congeries of deities controlled sunshine, rainfall, and the growth of crops. They also frequently believed that their leader or king was the offspring of the intercourse of natural powers rather than of human parents, had great influence with his father the sun and with his mother the earth, and could persuade them by means of prayer and filial love expressed through ritual actions to bless his people with abundant harvests and animal and human offspring. It was obvious, however, that at certain periods of the year this leader's powers waned as his parents' powers became desperately endangered by cold, darkness, drought, or destructive floods. It was therefore necessary for the so-called Divine King not merely to please and propitiate his parents but to do everything in his power to ward off their enemies and defend them from cosmic melancholia. In many parts of the world the king was considered an incarnation or avatar of a fertility god, especially of his father the sun, and therefore strictly a deity though in human shape. As a human being, however, his powers were subject to decay and death, and it was believed that only at his physical peak could he operate with maximum benefit to his people. In his declining years he was frequently killed, or a Substitute King or Interrex was seated on the throne during periods of seasonal danger or crisis. After performing the ritual ceremonies, the Substitute King was himself, the danger having been averted, often sacrificed. The death of the real king seems to have served the purpose of strengthening the declining sun by returning to it what was left of the filial energy, while the killing of the Substitute or Mock King was thought to strengthen the actual monarch in his declining years for reasons which I am about to discuss.

The process of choosing a Substitute or Mock King presents a fascinating problem. It is not to be supposed for a moment that any strong young man could take the king's place. Often the chosen individual seems not to have been young at all – or, rather, he was both old and young at the same time, a mature man of undiminished vigour enjoying a shape which approximated to that of the sun itself. The most important qualification seems to have been that he be descended, however uncouth, wild, or even deformed, from the Divine King stock of a dynasty or people long in possession of the soil though now deprived of sovereignty and honour. Nearly every known state or civilisation in the world shows signs of having been built upon the conquest, and having adopted the achievements, of a conquered people who may themselves have been conquerors of still earlier organised groups. It is also true that, of old, conquering dynasties were for generations uncertain of their power to win or compel the co-operation of the deities of the land, the Earth Mother which they had, as it were, raped, or of the male sun and rain gods who could successfully woo her womb. Would they feed the invaders? Thus the problem arose of finding a substitute for the monarch in times of seasonal crisis or the search for a scion of the displaced royal line. It can readily be imagined that the heir of a subjugated people, a degraded leader living in forest exile, may easily have been uncouth, wild, or deformed, as I have said, and so, it seems, he frequently was. Once captured, this king for a day, a week, or an indefinite period of atmospheric danger had to perform rites of overeating, overdrinking, and excessive coupling with some representative of Mother Earth, perhaps a priestess or a degraded Divine Queen of the earlier group or the wife or concubine of the King himself – rites intended, by the potency of sympathetic magic, to reinvigorate the reproductive powers of nature and made more efficacious, it seems, by ritual cursing of the powers-that-be, the usurping kings and deities whom the Substitute King is actually (but probably unwillingly) seeking to serve.

But the Interrex had to do more: he had to fight off the threatening powers of infertility in a battle or battles in which he often led a contingent of his one-time subjects, now as degraded from their former high status as himself; these battles were, like his feasting and lovemaking, essentially ritual acts designed to influence the course of nature. And one more duty he had, especially when the real ruler lay old and dying; he had to initiate the ruler's heir into the meaning and performances of the rites prescribed from of old for the flourishing of the conquered soil. His chief duty indeed was that of educating the crown prince in the arcana and practice of fertility stimulation, the secrets that the usurping father had perhaps never properly understood or was no longer able to practice. The rude Mock King may be witnessed teaching his pupil to drink, dance, and copulate for the stimulation of the soil, and may even be seen fighting with him against the powers of cold and darkness. Only after these lessons had been learned and the preliminary skirmishes against the enemy won was the second danger considered averted and the rite brought to an end by the dismissal, imprisonment, or killing of the Mock King. Sometimes he suffered successively all three of these fates. It is imagined that for the various incidents of the ritual performance outlined above there came, in time, to be detailed and traditional spoken parts; that this seasonal play, at once symbolic and deathly real – especially for the Mock King – came to be mounted as frequently as a given people felt the need of springlike renewal; and that this sequence of acts and speeches became at least one of the sources of secular drama in all countries.

The question arises whether a Kalidasa in India or a Shakespeare were close enough in time to the ancient rituals of their countries (supplanted respectively by orthodox Hinduism and Christianity), to a version of such ritual drama, as to understand their significance. We forget, I think, that nothing the human mind has ever prized because of its material utility or its spiritual serviceability is allowed easily to die; also that the greatest poets and dramatists seem often to have been among the most sensitive folklorists, with an uncanny interest in the uncanny.

Scholars have often been impressed by the fact that the great ages of Indian (third to seventh century) and Elizabethan drama were equally fond of "the learned fool", who appears on the stages as a confidant, tutor, and protector of the prince or king – a somewhat impudent fellow whose values are strictly eating, drinking, lovemaking, and – wisdom. In both great ages of drama, perhaps the most "golden" the world has ever known, these jesters (in India: *vudysakas*) rail at society's false values such as honour, war, hunting, and gambling, and do their utmost to promote love and love-making. In old India they were a common feature in life as well as on the stage, and a *vidusaka* or jester is defined in an Indian work of about A.D. 300 as one who knows something of ancient magical arts and songs yet "is without wealth and has nothing but his own person, or is maimed and is a native or a foreigner [foreign to the conquerors?] and can no longer lead his former mode of life: *an amazing person and a confidant ...*"[12]. This, it seems, is a pointed description of the degraded monarch of a conquered civilisation who has to be propitiated and kept around for ritual purposes. In addition, certain schools of modern psychology claim that they can on purely psychic grounds account for the artist's attachment to mythical kings and degraded gods, but we cannot go into the Jungian theory of archetypes here.

What we can say about Shakespeare is that he seems to have believed wholeheartedly in the ancient idea that nature, with the sun in its brow, and society, with the king at its head, were analogous, interpreted, and mutually interacting and dependent worlds functioning according to a single principle, loosely definable as "the love which makes the world go round". If this principle is violated, especially in the moral realm of society, and more especially if the life or health (spiritual or physical) of a king or ruler is threatened or destroyed, then physical nature becomes involved in disorders and disasters. Everybody remembers the "civil strife in heaven" caused by Caesar's murder, the men "all in fire" who paced the streets of Rome by daylight, the lion that glared on Caesar in the Forum, the owl that sat hooting and shrieking in the noonday marketplace[13] – pictures that haunt high-school freshmen – or those equally portentous horrors that seize on seniors when they read in *Macbeth* that the murder of Duncan troubled the heavens, causing night to strangle the short-travelled lamp of the sun, a mousing owl to kill a falcon, and the royal horses, "a thing most strange and certain", to break from their stalls as they would make war with mankind and end by eating each other.[14] Shakespeare seems also to have believed, conversely (or at least his Ulysses in *Troilus and Cressida* did), that human troubles may begin in heaven when things go wrong with

> the glorious planet Sol
> In noble eminence enthron'd and spher'd
> Amidst the ether; whose med'cinable eye
> Corrects the ill aspects of planets evil
> And posts, like the commandment of a king,
> Sans check, to good and bad: but when the planets
> In evil mixture to disorder wander,
> What plagues, and what portents, what mutiny ...
> Divert and crack, rend and deracinate
> The unity and married calm of states
> Quite from their fixture![15]

However, the argument seems about as circular as the course of the sun itself and usually ends by fixing the responsibility for heavenly disorder on earthly kings. Microcosm and macrocosm flourish or run amok together because like affects like, but it is almost always the leaders of men who mislead the light of heaven. In line with this belief Shakespeare presents nearly all his kings as *rois soleils*, sons of the sun whose acts affect their fathers. None of his monarchs is more a sun-king in this sense than Richard II, with whose story, it seems to me, the Falstaff–Henry plays properly begin, for the sickness of the state which Henry V cured for a time began under Richard and was much aggravated by his sickly murderer. In life Richard had a sun-and-cloud cognisance which in the play impresses even Bolingbroke with his rival's *roi soleil* pretensions:

> *Bol.:*   See, see King Richard doth himself appear
> As doth the blushing discontented sun
> From out the fiery portal of the East
> When he perceives the envious clouds are bent
> To dim his glory and to stain the track
> Of his bright passage to the Occident.[16]

But because Richard is more of a landlord than a husbandman, or husband, to the demi-paradise set in a silver sea, his fortunes decline fast:

> *King:*   Down, down I come, like glist'ring Phaeton,
> Wanting the manage of unruly jades.
> In the base court? Base court, where kings grow base
> To come at traitors' calls and do them grace!
> In the base court? Come down? Down court! Down king!
> For night owls shriek where mounting larks should sing.
> (*Exeunt from above.*)[17]

As everyone remembers, III, iv consists of an elaborate symbol designed to make clear the nature of Richard's fault: that he has neglected the rites due his father sun and mother earth and to till the fair plot of England:

> our sea-walled garden, the whole land,
> Is full of weeds, her fairest flowers chok'd up,
> Her fruit trees all unprun'd, her hedges ruin'd,
> Her knots disorder'd, and her wholesome herbs
> Swarming with caterpillars.

But, bad gardener though he was, it did England no good to pass "from Richard's night to Bolingbroke's fair day". When Richard, like "a mockery king of snow", melted in streams before "the sun of Bolingbroke" and the face that "like the sun did make beholders wink" sank into darkness, no spectacular spring returned to bless this England. Two oddly named servants of Richard, Bushy and Green, had been treacherously murdered and Richard, impotent sun-surrogate that he was, had apparently contracted a not-incompatible marriage with the English earth. When he asks the soil to curse his enemies, she responds as readily as if he had been a better lover with a better command of sex symbolism (for "mother with her child" read "husband with his wife"?):

> *King*:   Dear earth, I do salute thee with my hand,
> Though rebels wound thee with their horses' hoofs.
> As a long-parted mother with her child
> Plays fondly with her [his?] tears and smiles in meeting,
> So weeping, smiling, greet I thee, my earth,
> And do these favours with my royal hands.
> Feed not thy sovereign's foe, my gentle earth ...[18]

In Henry IV's time there was – accordingly, we must suppose – such poor weather and such desperate blight that the usurping monarch was thought to be cursed and persecuted by witches, vulgarly supposed capable of affecting fertility adversely:

> The King had never but tempest foul and rain,
>   As long as he lay in Walie's ground
> Rocks and mists, winds and storms ever certain;
>   All men troed that witches made that stound.[19]

In Shakespeare Henry IV appears only as an ailing, querulous, apparently cowardly and dying man, under whom the kingdom falls, as Richard had predicted, from weediness to desolation because he, even more than his predecessor, lacked the Divine King's touch. Henry IV had no purity of title or power of *mana* that would have helped him to hold sun and earth and society in harmony and "married calm". The very nature of things raised against him "armies of pestilence in every cloud".

The real problem of the Falstaff–Henry plays is to recover, insofar as a usurping dynasty may, the lost peace, fertility, and good government which had made of Englishmen "a happy breed". The very first words of *1 Henry IV*, spoken by the ailing and pallid would-be sun ruler,

> So shaken as we are, so wan with care,
> Find we a time for frighted peace to pant ...
> No more the thirsty entrance of this soil
> Shall daub her lips with her own children's blood;
> No more shall trenching war channel her fields,
> Nor bruise her flowerets with the armoured hoofs
> Of hostile pacers,

are merely a pious and impotent hope; for the period covered by both the plays, spent by this monarch in a long-drawn-out dying, is filled with continual battles which, fought between enemies whose "opposed eyes" flare and wink "like the meteors of a troubled heaven", threaten to burn Gaunt's blessed "nurse, this teeming womb of royal kings" to a cinder.

That the island does not go entirely to ruin is due, I submit, to the fact that in the East End of London there lives a great, round torch of a man with a great, round, red-hot face, a ray-bearded devil or fairy, not exactly young but not old either – a "latter spring", an "All-hallown summer" – feasting, jesting, overdrinking, overcoupling (though "not more than once in a quarter – of an hour") with fair hot wenches "in flame-coloured taffeta", weaving spells against the insurrectionary powers of darkness, and trying to initiate a somewhat ungrateful and impercipient young prince into the mysteries whose proper performance will help the perishing land. From time to time Hal calls this cosmic creature his tutor, but like many another pupil, especially if princely, he is seldom pleased to acknowledge the indebtedness he truly owes. While always careful to attend his classes at the Boar's Head, he undergoes his education with a bad grace, and does not hesitate to becloud his true relation to the solar elves and oafs of the Boar's Head – those living tapers whose noses flame like any hell. What Shakespeare himself meant by the soliloquy with which the prince brings to a close I, ii of *1 Henry IV* we shall never know, but the whole speech in scorn of his dissolute companions smacks of the post-coronation omnipotence and omniscience of the Rejection Scene at the end of *2 Henry IV*:

> I know you all, and will a while uphold
> The unyok'd humour of your idleness;
> Yet herein will I imitate the sun,
> Who doth permit the base contagious clouds
> To smother up his beauty from the world,
> That when he please again to be himself,
> Being wanted, he may be more wond'red at
> By breaking through the foul and ugly mists
> Of vapours that did seem to strangle him.

That Hal should undergo foul and debasing associations simply in order to stage a dramatic sunburst at the end of *2 Henry IV* is implausible, especially when we examine what transpires throughout these two plays when considered as a form of initiation and education in true sun-king wisdom.

Morgann, first and greatest of Falstaff's interpreters, was probably right. We cannot properly estimate the character of Falstaff by "understanding" or ordinary ratiocination, but must rely on our "impression", on what the words and atmosphere of the play make us feel, on intuitive sympathy. When we do, "Falstaff's seeming delinquencies, cowardice, lying, and so forth are only apparent, and are, in a way, the instruments wherewith Falstaff shows himself to be possessed of the very virtues which are the counterparts of the vices he seems to have".[20] The fundamental basis of Morgann's "argument is not to be destroyed", says Charlton, "merely by labelling it 'romantic', as does Mr Stoll; it seems indeed to rest on a plain human and aesthetic truth".[21]

We shall see, on the basis of analogies from all parts of the world which I expect to draw in the ensuing chapters, that the Falstaff–Henry plays are indeed the dramatisation of a kind of seasonal ceremony and perhaps followed closely actual ritualistic performances of this type still extant in Shakespeare's day. I refer to the English folk plays – the Christmas Mummers' Play, the Plough Tuesday Play, and the Sword Dance Play, examples of which Shakespeare could have seen in the Stratford of his boyhood. Surviving evidence even suggests he could have seen the customary St George of these plays replaced by a mummer bearing the name of Henry V and playing an obviously mythopoeic and ritualistic role. When Shakespeare came to rewrite and reshape the Henry Chronicles, it may have been memories of a Mummers' play as well as a few uninspiring passages in Elyot's *Governour* or *The Famous Victories of Henry V* which led him, profound folklorist that he was, to see a truly dramatic, that is to say an organic, relationship between the roistering of Hal with his old white-bearded Satan and Hal's great triumphs as a "sun-soldier" at Shrewsbury and sun-king at Agincourt. That he was able to blend history with myth, achieving that art which conceals, and thereby most effectively reveals, spiritual truth is only what we would expect of the author of most of the plays from *A Midsummer Night's Dream* to *The Winter's Tale*.

Let us try to string together a garland of folk plays (we have only the few lately recorded ones, of course, but they may have existed in somewhat this shape for centuries) of the kind that Shakespeare may have witnessed year after year on overshadowed days reeking with winter's sadness but brightened by the magic (in all senses of the word) of the crude theatrical performances into a season of hope according to a pattern laid deep down, it would seem, and operative over untold centuries, in the human semi-consciousness.

II

Presenter of the English Folk
Plays as Shakespeare's Model

The largest number of English season-rite plays gathered together in any one place is found in R.J.E. Tiddy's *The Mummers' Play* (Oxford, 1923). Here are some thirty-three folk dramas, all intended for midwinter performance, chiefly from Christmas to the first Tuesday after Epiphany – i.e., from two to three weeks after Christmas – called Plough Tuesday. All of them follow very similar patterns and are often so close in the very wording that they have clearly descended from a common source. Tiddy collected these plays personally during the early years of the twentieth century, often from old people who had taken part in them or from younger people who were contemporaneously acting in vestigial versions of these seasonal rites. All of the plays show literary degeneration and suggest that they derive from a form of drama once richly ceremonious, if not grandly symbolical. As Tiddy says:

> At a very early period English literature, like all literature, was entirely of the folk and entirely communal. Like the literature of the Greeks, it originated in religious ceremonies. In the Norse mythology vegetation gods can clearly be descried behind the splendid panoply of heroism with which a later ... imagination has invested them, and the agricultural religion of England was no doubt a primitive form of the Norse mythology. ... Various means were used to secure the fertility of earth and flocks and tribe ...[1]

What these means were I shall try to indicate by reconstructing from

Tiddy's many examples of the Mummers' Play, supplemented by a few plays reproduced in Chambers (*The English Folk Play*, London, 1933), what we may think of as, perhaps, an original rich form. The overall plot, the speeches, the indications of costume and stage business are all taken from Tiddy's book but do not all occur in any one play. Tiddy thinks that the archetypical play from which his many "degenerate" instances derive attained its highest literary expression some time in the seventeenth century. The beginnings of the play could easily reach back another hundred or two hundred years, as Chambers says. It may not be going too far to imagine that something like the plays we are about to reconstruct, using always the very words of actually surviving dramas, were seen by Shakespeare many times during his Stratford boyhood, leaving impressions which were later introduced into a series of conventional Chronicle Plays in such a way as to transfigure whatever real history they embodied into the grandest and most grandiose mummers' rite ever witnessed by Englishmen. These would have been so familiar with their folk drama and so steeped in its folklore themselves that many of them, unlike us, would not have missed the ritual significance of the speeches and actions which their greatest dramatist had chosen to bring upon the boards of the Globe.

The cast of characters of our play includes the following:

1. The Presenter, who introduces the other characters and presides over the whole performance as a half-serious, half-jocular master of ceremonies. In the Mummers' Play he is usually called Father Christmas. In the Plough Plays, presented on Plough Tuesday, he sometimes appears simply under the designation of Fool or Clown. At other times he is a bombastic boaster called the Recruiting Sergeant. Many of the Mummers' Plays contain a character called Beelzebub, who sometimes plays the role of Father Christmas and is a kind of uncouth double for this bluff character.

2. The motley rout of minor characters who cluster around Father Christmas or who are impressed by the Recruiting Officer, yet remain somewhat detached from the play, includes Johnny Jack, Little Wits, John Finney, Little Devil Don't, and Old Tossip who, Bardolph-like, spends all his time drinking his nose into the look of a fiery furnace. In the rout occurs frequently a woman known as Dolly or Molly or Lame Jane or Old Bet, who is represented as being the paramour or outrageous wife of Father Christmas, and is sometimes called Mother Christmas. She is clearly the mistress of the scene or stage-space where the performance is taking place, and this may be readily associated with an inn or public house because the Mummers talk of and, when they can get it from their patrons, consume wine throughout the performance.

3. Next to Father Christmas in importance stands St George, a knight who sometimes is called King George or is given the name of kings and heroes from English history. For example, he is called Henry V in the "Cornwall … Play for Christmas". He is represented as Father Christmas's joy and pride, and is sometimes called his son.

4. Finally, there is George's opponent, called most frequently the Turkish Knight, the Black King of Morocco or of Egypt, but also Gold Slasher or Captain Thunderbolt and even Valiant Soldier or King of France. George always mows him down, of course, but frequently he is revived in order that a second battle may occur, where he is easily and definitively demolished.

The character in whom we are most interested as a possible prototype of Falstaff is, of course, Father Christmas, and it is therefore important to learn as much as we can about his dress and appearance.

The first point to be noted is that he is enormously fat and is referred to again and again as Old Hind-before.[2] In the few plays where we get any notion of how he was dressed, he is said to wear a cloak "with pieces of wadding sewed on it"[3] or to have straw stuffed inside his coat both in front and behind, giving him the appearance of a pot-bellied hunchback.[4] Often he wears a mask which seems, in one case at least, to have had bull's horns attached to it, "a wooden thing for a head with bullock's teeth",[5] and whiskers. This description makes us think immediately of "the Dorset Ooser", a famous mask which it describes almost exactly (the original disappeared around 1900, it is often thought in the direction of America). There is also evidence that he sometimes, like the Fool who led the Morris dancers, wore a calf's tail and carried a bladder with which he stirred the audience as well as his own motley followers to noisy mirth and action. When the bewhiskered animal mask covered the whole face, it seems to have been painted red; when only a part (here we must assume that the actor had a beard of his own), the exposed portion of the mummer's face was daubed with this colour.[6] More frequently than a bladder, the actor carried in his hand a sword, in all likelihood a simulacrum of the Vice's sword of lath, indicative of the fact that Father Christmas was comparable to, perhaps in origin a predecessor of, the Devil of the Miracle Play with his descendants, "the Vicious" of the Morality and the Vice of the Moral Interlude. There is also evidence in the surviving plays to indicate that with this sword Father Christmas at one time played a combatant's role in the mummers' rite.

A debt of Elizabethan drama to the Mummers' Play is perhaps to be noted in the fact that the chief member in every famous acting company was Father Christmas's stand-in, the Clown or Fool, the most famous actors such as Tarleton, Wilson, and Kempe (who possibly created Falstaff) all having been in the first place clowns. Tiddy says that "to me it is impossible ... not to believe that the Morris Fool, ... Beelzebub, the Fool of the Mummers' Play, the Clown of the Sword Play, the Devils of the Morality and the Interludes are all ... ultimately one and the same".[7] As Beelzebub, Father Christmas carried a club rather than a sword, and also "a dripping pan" or "tallow-catch" for a candle, a greasy article to which Hal compared his tutor.[8] In the account of the Mummers' Play in *The Return of the Native* (Chapter IV) Father Christmas, as we have said, seems usually to have worn a long beard, false or otherwise, is always referred to as old, and announces the theme of the Mummers' Play again and again as a mystery involving "activity of age, activity of youth".[9] He is a remarkably vigorous old fellow, in many ways a bearded child who, though "just now turned into his 99 years of age ... can hop and skip and jump like a blackbird in a cage".[10]

Of Father Christmas's wife we have no particular details except that she seems often to be as plump as her husband and is sometimes referred to as "Lame Jane with a neck as long as a crane",[11] though elsewhere she refers to herself as "a lady bright and fair: my fortune is my charms".[12] Evidently the original character, if there was one, of Mother Christmas gradually split into two roles, that of the mistress-of-the-inn and that of the loose lady, both of whom are as fond of drink as Father Christmas (but I am anticipating). Tiddy notes that in the Ampleforth play the character corresponding to this woman or women is called the Queen, and it is likely that in early Christmas dramas sexual by-play between her and Father Christmas was more pronounced than in any of the extant plays, and corresponded to the business between fat Friar Tuck and jolly Maid Marian of the springtime folk plays presented, it is thought, long before the Miracle and Morality Plays came into existence. In a play such as *Robin Hood and the Friar*, printed by William Copeland about 1560 in an edition of the *Gest of Robin Hood* but thought to have been presented in its preserved form by mummers for at least a century before it was printed, fat Tuck describes Marian as follows:

> Here is a huckle duckle an inch above the buckle.
> She is a trull of trust, to serve a friar at his lust,
> A pricker, a prancer, a tearer of sheets,
> A wagger of ballocks when other men sleeps.[13]

George, who is needless to say dressed as a knight in shining armour, is once called Sun George,[14] and often fights with a broad-axe, a weapon equated from Minoan times with the sun and thought to be represented on one of the upright sarsens of Stonehenge. George frequently boasts that in the past he has overcome other Black Knights, such as the King of Egypt, and married their daughters, with whom he made fertility magic; in the Cornwall play at least, in which as Henry V he fights the King of France, this once-important aspect of his role is preserved. His famed act in once slaying a dragon also gives him confidence that he can dispose of his present enemy, the Turkish Knight. All that needs to be said of the Turkish Knight is that he seems to have had his face blackened and to have worn black armour or "a black tunic and a turban".[15] In a few of the plays he is compared rather poetically to an eagle darkening the sun[16] or to the bleak "evening Sun" of winter marking the death of a fearfully foreshortened day. Somehow one gets the idea that Hardy could have made even more, symbolically, than he did of Eustacia Vye when he had her take this role in his Egdon mummers' play.

With these aspects of the chief characters in mind, let us try to reconstruct what we may call the Stratford-on-Avon Mummers' Play (this is one town from which no popular drama of this type has actually come down to us) as Shakespeare may conceivably have seen it.

The Mummers' Play

(All the speeches, actions, and stage directions are taken from Tiddy's book. I note the pages from which I quote but not the names of the individual Mummers' Plays used.)

Father Christmas:	In comes I, Old Hind-before,
	I comes fust to open your door. (174)
	In comes I to make the fun.
	My hair is short, my beard is long ... (229)
	Welcome or welcome not
	I hope old Father Christmas will never be
	forgot. (163)
	Christmas comes but once a year
	And when it comes, it brings good cheer,
	Roast beef, plum pudding, strong ale, and
	mince pie,
	Who likes that better than I?
	I am here to laugh and cheer
	And all I ask is a pocketful of money
	And a cellar full of beer. (163)
	Now I have brought some gallant men with me
	That will show you great activity.
	Activity of youth, activity of age. (189)
	Was never such acting
	Shown upon Christian stage ... (186)

The stage being set for, it seems, a pagan entertainment, he may propose Christmas chess, Old Hind-before or George and the Turkish Knight, or he may – this occurs comparatively rarely – introduce his motley followers. These consist first of all of Father Christmas's double, old Beelzebub. Like Father Christmas, he is fat,

	With a head like a pig
	And a body like a sow, (146)

the last three words being those with which Falstaff describes himself in *2 Henry IV*, I, ii.

Beelzebub:	In comes I, old Beelzebub.
	On my back I carries my club,
	And in my hand a dripping pan.
	I thinks myself a jolly old man.
	Round hole, black as a coal,
	Long tail and little hole. (167)

(In at least one of the plays Beelzebub is known as "the old woman" and is swathed in a frock, which may make one think of Falstaff playing the Witch of Brainford in *The Merry Wives of Windsor*.) Next comes in a Bardolph-like character, his clothes in rags.

Old Tossip:	Oh the next that steps in is Old Tossip, you see.
	He's a gallant old man, you will now agree.
	He wears a pig-tail: can't you see how it cocks?
	And he spends all his time in drinking old ale
	... (236)

Next comes Little Devil Don't, who is a notable petty thief, possibly the father of Pym and apparently the descendant of great Merlin, who in the popular Elizabethan play called *The Birth of Merlin* is represented as a mischievous sprite – "a little antic spirit"[17] – who picks pockets to the huge amusement of the audience.

Father Christmas's crew is a noisy lot, blowing tin whistles, twanging the Jew's harp and usually headed by a character called John Finney or Father Scrump, who "carries the humpenscrump made with a tin with wires across the bridge and a stick with notches for a bow and also a sheep bell on his rump" (173):

John Finney:	In comes I as ain't been yit
	With my big head and little wit.
	My head is so big and my wit is so small,
	I play you a tune as will please you all. (173)
	Green sleeves and yellow leaves [face].
	Now, my boys, we'll dance a pace.
	Hump back and hairy wig,
	Now my boys, we'll dance a jig. (253)

Though John Finney never comes on the scene till the end ("ain't been yit") there is no reason to suppose that in earlier versions of the seasonal mystery there was not hobnobbing, eating and drinking and dancing by Father Christmas and his crew at the beginning as well as at the end of the play. A note to the Camborne (Cornwall) play tells us that all through the entertainment "Father Christmas was accompanied by two merrymen or Clowns who were making funny faces while Father was talking and singing old songs at intervals" (147).

It is now time to introduce St George and his adversary. Of these two, Father Christmas usually introduces the Turkish Knight first. He is a tremendous boaster:

Turkish Knight:	Here comes I, the gold Turkish Knight.
	I come from the Turkish land to fight.　　(144)
	My head is made of iron,
	My body is made of steel.
	My hands are made of knuckle-bone,
	I challenge thee to feel ...　　(87)
Father Christmas:	Bold talk, my Childe, bold talk I am sure –
	But St George is coming through the door.　(144)
St George:	Here comes I, St George,
	A man of courage bold.
	If thy blood is hot,
	I soon will make it cold,
	As cold as any clay.
	I will take thy blood and life away.　　(144)

(Of course, this kind of thing is hardly to be compared with the word-wrangling by Hal and Hotspur.) The contestants begin the fight by crossing swords. After three leg-cuts and three head-cuts, St George strikes a blow at the Turkish Knight and fells him. Father Christmas, concealing some red ochre in his hand, goes to the fallen boaster and rubs it on his neck or groin. Sometimes he or Beelzebub picks up the Turk, throws him across his shoulder, and carries him about the stage, saying:

> I have a fire that is long lighted
> To put the Turk that was long knighted.
> Here I goes, old man *Jack*
> With the Turk upon my back.　　(146)

(This can hardly help reminding us of another "old man Jack" who carried Percy after stabbing him in the groin, from the field of Shrewsbury like "luggage" on his back.) Sometimes Father Christmas takes a hymnal from his pocket and makes fun of the burial service of the Church:

> We will sing a tune to him.
> You will find the hymn 120 – pound beef –
> If you can't find it there, turn over a leaf.　(147)

(This does not exactly constitute hallowing and singing of hymns such as Falstaff claims to have made himself hoarse with, but it suggests his sacrilegious note.)

Doctor:	Now take a few drops of my belly compain
	And rise to fight St George again.　　(146)

In the second battle the Turkish Knight is often summarily slain again, and again carried or dragged offstage in an action that is decidedly anti-climactic. We have what is almost a *da capo* performance recalling the frequent description of *2 Henry IV* as a reprise of the first *Henry*.

The rationale of the revival and second slaying of the Black Knight is to be found, I think, in both a desire to prolong the fun and a need to underscore the death of darkness. It is possible that the fullest version of I, ii of the Christmas plays is to be found in the springtime mumming ceremony, which appropriates any and everything it chooses from the winter ritual but the name of Father Christmas. Here Father appears, like Falstaff in the second *Henry*, as a Recruiting Sergeant or even as Robin Hood gathering men for an outlandish army with which to launch a final attack on bad weather. This stage business would have been quite appropriate in the Christmas celebration, as would the enlarged role of Mother Christmas as Moll–Doll–Marian found in the May Day goings-on. It is only in *2 Henry IV* that Doll Tearsheet contributes her flame-coloured taffeta (I suppose the hot-skirt of the first *Henry* must forecast Doll) to the horseplay which subdues infertility, and enthrones "Sun George". Also it is in the spring plays, more often than in the winter ones, that the bright Saint is replaced by various military heroes from English history, a Cromwell or more particularly Henry V, as in Tiddy's Cornwall play.

In spite of these more or less constant points of difference between the written plays, there is no sufficient reason to split the Mummers' drama into halves, one in which the fight between George and the Turk is umpired by Father Christmas, who sometimes takes part in it, wielding his sword of lath, while in the other the Master of Ceremonies is the boastful Recruiting Sergeant, who makes flagrant public love to a coarse mistress and joins with his motley recruits in the fray before St George (or Henry V) succeeds in slaying for good and all the dark-skinned Turk (or the weakling King of France). In the available remains there is no clear distinction between any two such forms of the Mummers' Play. All the characters and incidents characteristic of one type can and do appear in the other, and in Tiddy's plays free-whirling fragments of both kinds apparently fuse in every possible combination. The simplest way to explain the extant phenomena is to suppose that in a great prototype of these fragmentary plays the second and conclusive battle between George and his sable adversary took place at Christmas too, but not before the old, fat, bearded master of ceremonies had recruited fresh followers and indulged in ceremonial licentiousness with a "lady". It may even have been necessary, as the action of two or three of the remnants indicates, for him to die or to be killed by George himself before the now truly irresistible hero could deliver the seasonal *coup de grâce*.

Assuming, then, that the archetypal play we are trying to reconstruct was an entity intended for Christmas performance but also suitable, with a few changes, for a whole which combined in an ordered ritual pattern the various fragments now scattered through the bare and paltry remains, we may now resume the reconstruction of the folk drama at the point where the comic doctor has successfully revived the sinister Turk.

Father Christmas, having adopted a change of clothing but by no means diminished in stature, appears as a boastful Recruiting Sergeant preceded by a "lady" who introduces herself.

Dolly: In comes I, Mother Dolly.
                    Drinking gin is all my folly.   (157)

(This character was played by a man in woman's clothes; in the Ilmington (Warwickshire) play, where she is called Molly, she refers irreverently to the hero George as her son.)

Molly: Ladies and gentlemen all, my son has lately come home
                    In a silver-buttoned waistcoat, three-legged hat,
                    Spats yellow; calls the cat a bitch ...   (226)

(Molly has obviously had so much gin that her thoughts as well as her rhymes are hopelessly disordered.)

Recruiting Sergeant: In comes I, the Recruiting Sergeant
                         I've arrived here just now with orders from the King
                         To test all you jolly fellows
                         That follows horse or plough,
                         Tinkers, Tailors, Peddlers, Nailers,
                         Does anyone advance? ...

Farmer's Boy: In comes I, the Farmer's Boy,
                         Don't you see my whip in hand?
                         Straight I go from end to end
                         Scarcely make a baulk or bend,
                         To my horses I attend
                         As they go marching round the end,
                         Gee Woa!   (257)

In the Oberton (Hampshire) play and some others the Recruiting Sergeant, perhaps in ironical reference to his great size and bellowing voice, is called Little Twing Twang and usually announces himself:

                    In comes I, Little Twing Twang,
                    Headman in this press gang ...
                    Although I am so short and small,
                    I think myself the best man of you all.   (198)

After Twing Twang has impressed a group of ploughboys, tailors, and tinkers to help "King" George against his enemy, George picks a quarrel with him for his bumptious boasting.

King George:	Stop, stop my little feller: I knowed thy father years and years before: bought pigs off him ... Who doest think thee bist going to kill? Dead mouse?
Twing Twang:	No. Thee. Thee and I had better have a rap or two. (*They fight.*)
King George:	Oh, dear, oh, dear, see what I've been and done, Killed my poor old Father, Abraham Brown. All hear: I sits on that is his; Ladies and gentlemen, give me what you please, Money in the box and God save the King. (198)

If such a scene is in any way to be connected with the famous rejection of Falstaff, the king who quarrels with his recruiting officer, kills him, and sits on "that is his" seems to have gone to extremes of ingratitude never charged against Henry V even by Hazlitt or Bradley.

   Among the extant Mummers' Plays the Cornwall play, already frequently mentioned, is very much to our purpose here. In it St George, after defeating the Turkish Knight, is metamorphosed into Henry V in order to finish off another adversary, the King of Fraunce. In his army Henry numbers recruits like "Little man John with a sword in my hand" and a boastful soldier whose unintelligible eloquence suggests Ancient Pistol's.

Bloody Warrior:	Here I am this Bloody Warer. I have spent my time in bloody War; slash cornary, dam the Ribals carse. Sholl I walk ones twoes thrice over the dark with out hat stockin shart? I bow dack to every drunkerd or proud sot? No, by this Eternal sord in hand the man that is not fit to dye is not fit to live. Stand, delever, push your pikestaf by the hyway hoop; that man's neck is not very big that fears a little rope. ... (152)

"My master greets you, worthy sir:
　　Ten ton of gold that is due to he,
That you will send him his tribute home
　　Or in French land you soon will him see."

"Your master's young and of tender years
　　Not fit to come into my degree,
And I will send him three tennis-balls,
　　That woth them he may learn to play."[18]

When the "lovely page" brings Henry the "nuse" of France's insult, Henry "with all my gallant company" immediately attacks the king and beats him to his knees.   (153)

King of France: Oh pardon, pardon, King Henry.
　　　　　　　　　　The Ton of gould i will pay to thee
　　　　　　　　　　And the finest flour that is in all France
　　　　　　　　　　To the rose of ingland i will give free.   (153)

One of Henry's soldiers, perhaps the Bloody Warrior, finally brings this version of the seasonal battle to an end by murdering those lines from the old ballad which recount:

The first shot that the Frenchman gave,
　　They killed our Englishmen so free;
We killed ten thousand of the French,
　　And the rest of them they ran away,[19]

while another warrior charges the audience:

Gentlemen and ladies, all our sport is don;
i can no longer stay; remember still St George
will bear the sway ...   (154)

At this point the collection for the mummers could be taken up, but many of the remaining plays suggest that the archetypal rite ended with a blessing pronounced on the spectators, or perhaps in the drama's earliest form on some actual prince, whose coronation ceremony consisted in his participation in this very play. The Bulby (Lincolnshire) play, in which Tom Fool seems to play the master of ceremonies, ends with a song sung by all the mummers which suggests Oberon and his fairies blessing the house of Theseus in *A Midsummer Night's Dream* – or rather Dame Quickly, so maltreated by Falstaff and his crew, blessing in her unexpected role of Fairy Queen the royal family in the palace at Windsor:

Mummers: Here's a health unto our master,
                            Our mistress also,
                            Likewise the little children
                            Around the table go:
                            Let's hope that they may never want
                            While nature does provide
                            Us happiness and pleniness
                            And attend to the fireside.
                            You hear our song is ended,
                              (*exit Tom Fool*)
                            And you see our fool is gone:
                            We make it our business
                            To follow him along:
                            And we thank you for civility
                            And for what you gave us here:
                            We wish you all good night
                            And another Happy New Year.   (240)

It is remarkable how many of the Mummers' Plays tend to introduce
characters and incidents from the tales of Robin Hood and his crew of
outlaws. There is evidence that still others of these "merry men" plays have
been lost, from one of which a famous scene, worth recalling at this point,
was adapted into Anthony Munday's *The Death of Robert, Earl of
Huntingdon*. Here fat Friar Tuck, carrying a stag's head or perhaps wearing
it with its branching antlers in the form of a mask, dances a merry morris as
he brings to an end a scene in which King Richard, who is an actor in the
play, is complimented and fêted. Tiddy notes that the doggerel lines in
which the king thanks this horned master of ceremonies – probably simply
another version of the bull-masked Father Christmas with whom our
account of the composite Mummers' Play began – may be a copy or parody
of lines from a seasonal Mystery of this kind:

The King: Gramercy, Frier, for thy glee,
                            Thou greatly hast contented me;
                            What with thy sporting and thy game
                            I swear I highly pleased am.[20]

It may even be that the great ritual drama frequently ended in some such
way as this, the newly installed king thus giving thanks to the great, fat,
profane, animal-like master of ceremonies for enabling him to vanquish the
Black Knight and be seated firmly on the throne.

But it should be remembered that there is also good reason to suppose
that, in some instances at least, only the spirit of Father Christmas survived
to the end of the play, his great body having suffered death before George
embarked on his second battle with the Turk. The same man who remem-

bered that Father Christmas in the Bovey Tracey (Devonshire) play wore a "wooden thing for a head with bullock's teeth" also recalled that at one point in the play, perhaps before the second demise of the Turkish Knight, Father Christmas "came out where two were lying dead and said, *I'll lie down and die beside my only son*".[21] Tiddy's text of this play is in such bad condition that it is impossible to tell to whom the phrase "my only son" refers; it is more likely to refer to George, so often in one of his periods of temporary vanquishment, than to the Turkish Knight, who is called "Father's child" in certain probably garbled passages. It may be that the old man's death was needed at this point in order, by a magical transfer of energy, to revive George for his definitive victory.

If Shakespeare may be plausibly assumed to have seen – perhaps many times over – a play such as the one we have synthesised from the synoptic odds and ends bequeathed us from the seasonal drama that is thought to have existed for several centuries before he wrote, and was perhaps first set down in literary form at the very time in which he flourished, we need search no further for an immediate source of the leading scenes and ideas, images which dominate his wondrous pentalogy from beginning to end. We need not hesitate to call the Falstaff–Henry plays a great Mystery rather than a Morality. The ubiquitous imagery of Shakespeare's dramas – the imagery of sun and heat, of overdrinking and potent animals, of recruiting officers and motley armies, of Lords of Misrule and their drunken paramours, of Mock Kings and ungrateful pupils who condemn them to rejection and death – is all to be found in these folk plays. Since we know that the Mummers' Play was, in its origins, an attempt to hasten by sympathetic magic the renewal of nature, the rebirth of spring, we have in it a useful clue, if not to Shakespeare's whole purpose in the pentalogy, at least to the highly patterned, overall meaning, the organic wholeness, of these plays, which makes it quite clear that the figure of Falstaff is by no means an irrelevance; rather, that he is just what most readers always felt him to be: the central figure in a mighty dramatic pageant which is also a rite.

I shall not elaborate upon the relations between the archetypal Mummers' Play I have outlined above and the Falstaff–Henry dramas, but will list some points that they have in common and then try to throw more light on the nature and meaning both of the Mummers' Play and of Shakespeare's pentalogy by examining closely nine or ten figures from world mythology whose traits and stories resemble Falstaff's in all or most of these points. The points I would stress are these:

1. The central character is a fat person, relatively short and sometimes deformed, whose general shape is that of an enormous ball.
2. He is a tremendous eater and drinker.
3. He is continually associated with prepotent animals such as the bull, boar, goat, and buck because of his obesity and sexual prowess.
4. He is simultaneously or by turns both old and young.

5. He is noted for a disordered halo of richly flaming white hair and beard.

6. He is preternaturally wise with a wisdom which contrasts strongly with the values of the so-called great and honourable who dominate his world (or "this world"), leading him to reject and satirise law, order, and the accepted religion.

7. This wisdom and these attitudes he teaches to a prince who is destined to rescue his country from rapine and infertility.

8. Always he is followed about by a group of grotesque or feral creatures who dance to the wild tune of his unconventional piping and contribute in their boisterous way to the education of the prince.

9. These, their number increased by "recruits", help the prince win battles against the forces of cold and cruelty.

10. In the first of these battles the wild tutor often plays a decisive part in helping his charge to overcome the enemy, sometimes killing the chief demon of darkness and/or saving his pupil's life.

11. Later, however, and before the second battle – which the prince, now a king, wins on his own – the tutor is thrown into prison by the pupil who has successfully mastered his lesson.

12. Finally, the rejected but still devoted old tutor is killed or otherwise dies, or seems to die, usually on the eve of the second battle, which is won when the last energies of the fat teacher, passing into the spirit of the ungrateful youth, make him insuperable.

13. The irresistible king in love sports brings back the Golden Time, a Utopia, the world's fairest garden.

All the figures from world mythology that I would conjure up illustrate most if not all of these points. Some of these figures illustrate one or two particular points much better than do the others, however, and it is by examining, for instance, the young–old aspect of the great god Bes of Egypt or Indian Ganeśa's opposition to conventional religion that I hope to throw the greatest light on these particular characteristics or traits as exhibited by Falstaff. As I have said before, I am not here interested in actual influences or even the possibility of such, but in illuminating the mysterious hold on mankind's affections of a character who has made a massive mark on the rites, the arts, and the literature of every great culture in the world – a character whose humour and unconventional values have amused, challenged, and comforted men in many times and places, and whom mankind, as we can see in India's love of Ganeśa and our own devotion to Santa Claus, will not let die. Incidentally, I shall perhaps be able to elucidate further some of the so-called problems that plague Falstaff critics and illuminate fresh facets of his overwhelming fascination.

III
Silenos
a Greek "Bolting-hutch of Beastliness"

Of all the figures I am about to consider, Silenos of Greek mythology is probably the best known to most of my readers. All of us have seen ancient statues and modern pictures of him in museums and books of mythology and art. We do not have to be told at length that he scores on most of the points laid down for a Falstaff-persona. He is enormously fat, short, and round. Always he is characterised by a rich beard, his body frequently being hairy all over, while his animal nature is made still clearer by his possession of a horse's tail or a horse's, sometimes an ass's, ears. Evidently he is a tremendous "bolting-hutch of beastliness" and a heavy drinker, resembling – also like Falstaff – a hogshead or "bombard of sack". He is usually represented followed by a train of dancing companions, also with horses' tails and ears but otherwise human like himself, with broad faces, snub noses, thick lips, and heavy moustaches which blend into disorderly beards and are matched by thick eyebrows that arch upward in a way that suggests horns. He and his train of unruly, boisterous, music-making followers loved to rush through forests or to dance with nymphs and dryads at seasonal festivals, brandishing leafy spears, torches, and bulging phalli. (They were called *silenoi* or *satyroi*, the latter word meaning "the full ones", in reference to their sexually excited condition.)

That Silenos was a preternaturally wise young–old deity is not so obvious until we remember that he was the tutor of the god Dionysos, in whose honour were performed the great dramatic festivals of Greece, never to be forgotten because of the wisdom as well as the beauty of their unmatchably

Masque of Silenos

thoughtful comedies and tragedies. Also he seems to have had an avatar in the philosopher Socrates, who in a famous passage in the *Symposium* is compared to Silenos. In Asia Minor there were stories to the effect that Silenos (or a *silenos*) could, if made drunk and taken captive by mortals, be persuaded to reveal deep moral and cosmic truths. We may not think of Silenos as much of a soldier either, until we remember that he saved Dionysos from his enemies on at least one occasion, and fought with him in a great definitive battle against the powers of darkness. After Alexander the Great had conquered part of India, his victory over the dark Indian king Porus led him to be considered a descendant or incarnation of Dionysos, and resulted in Dionysos' great seasonal battle being transferred to India itself. The most complete account of the adventures of Dionysos and his tutor, stressing at length Silenos' role in the victory over the Indian king, is the *Dionysiaca* of Nonnos, who flourished in the late fifth century A.D. The book, though late, comprises genuine early material never given memorable expression.

It is probable that Pan of Greek myth is a variant of the Silenos figure. Pan is associated with the goat rather than the horse; he has actual horns, instead of merely horn-shaped eyebrows, and feral legs, in contrast to Silenos', which are human. He is not so pot-bellied, but he is clearly plump or fat, and he is followed by a rout of disreputable creatures resembling himself and playing the same role as the *silenoi* or *satyroi*. (We should call Pan's rout *paniskoi* or fauns after the Latin Pan, known as Faunus, but there is a confusing and perhaps irreversible tendency to call these goat-legged follow-ers of Pan satyrs, a word properly applied, as we have seen, only to the followers of Silenos.) Pan, whose name means "all", may have been one of the earliest gods known to the Greek peninsula, and at the end of the Greek religious evolution he seems to have resumed his ancient character as chief or only deity some time before certain frightened sailors heard women bewailing by night the death of Great Pan on the shores of the island of Lemnos. This episode, perhaps invented by Christians, was used by them to celebrate the triumph of a new all-deity of fertility and love who, like Pan, fought the powers of darkness and, after apparent death and defeat, was resurrected with the coming of springtime and flowers at the vernal equinox. Like Silenos, Pan imparted his ancient wisdom to a god of the conventional Greek pantheon, Hermes, who is perhaps remembered by us as more wily than wise but is nevertheless associated with good crops, large herds, feasts, good business, and the invention of ecstatic music. Like Pan, Hermes is sometimes represented as a phallic god of gardens or fields, the herm being a kind of auspicious boundary stone. The following song to Pan by Beaumont and Fletcher could with equal appropriateness have been addressed to *Silenos*:

> He is great and he is just;
> He is ever good,
> And must
> Be honoured.

Daffodillies,
Roses, pinks, and lovèd lillies,
Let us fling, while we sing
Ever Holy! Ever Holy!
Ever honoured! Ever young!
The great Pan is ever sung.[1]

Other Graeco-Roman figures of the Silenos–Pan ilk, ancient, fat, feral, and
pedagogical, include Chiron the Centaur who tutored rural Aristaios, "the
best god", as well as Asklepios the beloved physician; satyr Marsyas, who
taught Apollo to flute the greenery-evoking songs of spring, only to be
flayed alive; Priapus, the garden-god who instructed Mars in field- and
battle-lore; and Kedalion, the obese dwarf, the Greek Mimir, who taught
Hephaistos the incandescent craft of the smith.

Greek and Roman myths make it quite clear, I think, that the Pan–Silenos
figure is a kind of personified–animalised symbol of the sun itself, the squat,
hot, enormous, ball-shaped figure – or red-faced head – of the deity
inevitably suggesting the sun. There are other ways, too, in which Silenos
makes us think of the flaming star. He is, for instance, fearfully overheated
and seems often to be on fire. In ancient art, especially Roman, his sculptured figure was often used to support a torch, while in Shakespeare Falstaff
is compared to "a wassail candle".[2] To keep his internal furnace blazing he is
a great eater but more especially a tremendous drinker. Lest he cool down
for even a moment between drinks, he is constantly engaged in dancing.
Since he enjoys almost unceasing sexual fulminations, his grey or white
moustache, beard, bushy eyebrows, and sometimes flaring hair are signs not
so much of old age as of coronal power poured out in hair-like rays and
never flaming more dramatically than at times of momentary eclipse. We
may assume that the form of wisdom which he taught his pupil Dionysos
had to do with sun-stimulation of the growth of the soil, and when he helped
his pupil overcome the dark Indian king he fought, we are told, less with the
thyrsos than with his fat, hairy legs, beating the earth in a dazzling sun dance.
In Nonnos' description of Silenos' dance in the *Dionysiaca* we have perhaps
the classic (in both senses of the word) treatment of the sun-figure dancing
itself into "dissolution" as it "sweats to death./And lards the lean earth".[3] As
described by Nonnos, this dance is clearly a ritualistic one in which Silenos
pours out his hot vitality, pisses his fructifying tallow at the cost of his life,
for the victory of his pupil. In the epilogue to *2 Henry IV* it is suggested that
Sir John, if he lives to accompany Henry V to France, perchance "shall die of
a sweat" in the field of combat. Shakespeare may actually have had the end
of Silenos in mind when first dreaming of a play on Henry's victory at
Agincourt.

In the "mystic mazes" of this death-dance Silenos seems to have transferred
his remaining *mana*, his last ray of solar energy, to his pupil Dionysos.
That fructifying rain should fall on the parched earth from the very sun itself
is an odd conception to us, but there is plenty of evidence in the world's
literature that even highly sophisticated people have held rain to be either

the regurgitation or the sweating-out by the sun of water which he drinks up from lake and ocean. Consider these lines from Mayura, an Indian poet of the seventh century A.D.:

> In summer the rays of Martanda [Surya, the sun], having become, as it were, wearied from continually wandering over the universe, and as if drying up with their own heat,
> Repeatedly suck water from the earth, like [men, who drink water when] heated by a forest-fire;
> But in the rainy season, as if [they had been] made sick by excessive drinking, they vomit out [this] water,
> And in winter are, [in consequence], feeble.[4]

Thus the sun itself can be a creature of seasonal if not continual thaw. Nonnos' famous description of Silenos' dance runs, in a rather heavy translation, as follows:

> So horned Silenos wove his [choreographic] web with neat-handed skill … fixing his gaze on the sky, he leapt into the air with bounding shoe. Now he clapped both feet together, then parted them and went hopping from foot to foot; now over the floor he twirled, dancing round and round upright upon his heels, and spun in a circling sweep. He stood steady on his right foot holding a toe of the other foot, or bent his knee and caught it in his clasped hands, or held an outstretched thigh with the other knee upright, the heavyknee Silenos! He lifted the left foot coiling up to the side, to the shoulder, twining it behind him and holding it up until he brought the sole round his neck. Then with a quick turn of the back-swerving dance, he artfully bent himself over, face up, in a hoop, showing his belly spread out and curved up toward the sun, while he spun round and round in his wild caperings. [Sweat poured from him.]
>
> At last his knees failed him; with shaking head he slipped to the ground and rolled over on his back. At once he became a river: his body was flowing water with natural ripples all over, his forehead changed to a winding current with the horns for waves, the turbulent swell came to a crest on his head, his belly sank into the sand, a deep place for fishes. As Silenos lay spread, his hair changed into natural rushes, and over the river his pipes made a shrill tune of themselves as the breezes touched them.[5]

It will be seen that Nonnos has given Silenos horns here, and elsewhere he shows that he and perhaps his readers conceived of the satyr as having not only a horse's tail but very little about him but his face that was human. He had "the shape of a bull" with a bull's horns clasping a disc, probably representing the sun, between them; "the skin of a mountain goat was thrown over his body" while "he shook a pair of long ears like the ears of an ass beside his two cheeks, and he was covered with hair, with a self-wagging tail"[6]. At the sight of this messenger from Dionysos, the dark Indian king

> checked the steps of his towering elephants, and laughing spoke to the Satyr in words of raillery: "What double-shaped men bull-form Dionysos sends to Deriades! What playthings for a soldier!" Monsters,

not creatures having a wholly human shape! They have the form of
beasts! for with a double shape they are bastards, bulls and men [and, he
might have added, goats, asses, and horses] at once ...[7]

It is quite unnecessary to point out, of course, that Dionysos with the help of
his satyrs, fauns, and screaming maenads, a wild army recruited for his
service by Pan and Silenos, won in the end a great victory over the dark
Deriades, apparently because the old tutor himself had given his life in the
way we have seen.

In this and in each of the following chapters I shall stress some particular
aspect of the Falstaff-persona. Here I shall consider especially the significance of the fat man's many animal traits and associations. Falstaff, we
remember, is compared by Hal to a "Manningtree ox",[8] hailed as "sweet
beef",[9] referred to as "the Martlemas",[10] an epithet usually interpreted as
shorthand for "Martlemas ox", and decried as "the town bull".[11] Elsewhere
he is called a "poor ape"[12] or a whale[13], but more frequently he is compared
to a boar or stag. Hal calls him "that damn'd brawn"[14] and "the old boar ... in
the old frank",[15] while Doll Tearsheet caresses him as a "whoreson little tidy
Bartholomew boar-pig",[16] and Falstaff compares himself to "a sow".[17] On the
field of Shrewsbury Hal calls him "so fat a deer",[18] while in *The Merry Wives
of Windsor*, Falstaff in the guise of "a Windsor stag, the fattest, I think, in the
forest"[19] enjoys a striking epiphany as an antlered avatar of Herne or Horne
the Hunter, whose genealogy has been traced back severally to stag-riding
Merlin and to the stag-horned Neck, a deity of the pagan Welsh, who was
adopted into the Christian scheme of things as deer-riding Saint Nicholas or
Nick. It is this Neck or Nicholas of whom Gadshill claims that Falstaff and
his footpads are devout servants or priests – "Saint Nicholas' clerks".[20] It is
impossible to doubt that Shakespeare's "imagery" for Falstaff is pretty
consistently bestial.

Now we have also seen, when considering the Mummers' Play, that
Father Christmas sometimes appeared wearing a bull mask, and it is well
known that mummers of Europe and England used to dress, as they still
sometimes do, in animal costumes. In various parts of Asia, Africa, and the
Pacific islands men often don animal skins or wear elephant, lion, ape, or
boar masks in festivities clearly religious, to this day. In the west the
iconography of Satan has for centuries continued to show him with animal
hoofs – usually those of a goat, stag, or bull – and, springing from his human
torso, either an appropriate animal head or a human face crowned with
horns appropriate to the hoofs. Representations of this creature are found
scratched on the walls of the Palaeolithic caves of southern France, and it is
pretty widely conceded that he was once, in any of his animal shapes, a great
fertility god whose worship was destroyed only with the utmost difficulty
by the Christian church. Scholars like M. Murray believe that the phenomena
of witchcraft, which continued in considerable force in Europe down into
the eighteenth century and has never entirely died away, were and are

simply manifestations of the worship of this horned god, now generally known as the Devil in accordance with the age-old principle that the god of a superseded religion becomes the arch-fiend of its successor.

Our problem here is to reason a little about the way in which men came, or may have come, to worship their deities, especially their sun-deity, in animal or semi-animal form. The practice has not been so long discontinued in the west that we would find it possible to drop the animal traits from our mental picture of that god we call Anti-god, or to cease finding in him a certain fascination, not perhaps too unlike that exerted by that "bolting-hutch of beastliness", "that old white-bearded Satan", Falstaff. Perhaps the biggest question of all in Falstaff criticism is the necessity to account for the strange attractiveness with which Shakespeare, consciously or unconsciously, endowed this character, and which we consciously feel but cannot readily account for. A lesser one, which we may suggest a solution for here, is that of Falstaff's birth and pedigree.

Resemblances between men and animals, physical, vocal, and temperamental, can be noted by any child visiting a zoo and have impressed people from time immemorial with a sense of pan-zoological kinship. Still, in zoos and circuses city dwellers customarily see noble animals divorced from their natural setting, run-down, dusty, and unhappy, so that it is no wonder that poets and story-tellers have often used them as caricatures, not as exemplars, of human beings.

This was not always the case. Early peoples often regarded animals not only as equal but as superior to themselves – stronger, more handsome, more fearless. How animals came to be regarded as the founders of tribes of men, many of which treasured a particular wild creature as its divine totemic father, is a common theme of the anthropologists and can be illustrated from those literatures that have a strong hold on prehistoric materials.

Greek myth and archaeology give us some clue to the origins of a Silenos or a Pan but not enough, for it seems to have been among the pre-Greek peoples of the Aegean islands, sometimes called Pelasgians, that these figures were born. To be sure, Greeks were fascinated with them and handed them down, especially in the fine arts, to modern man in forms which continue to enthral our waking and sleeping visions, but Greek literature tells us very little of Pan or Silenos other than that they were possibly sons of Kronos, who preceded Zeus as head of the Greek pantheon, and were associated with the heat and fire of the sun; according to certain tales, it was their custom to lead their wild men and nymphs in night-time dances accompanied by drinking, shrieking, shouting, and orgiastic lovemaking which, like the crowing of the rooster, was thought to persuade the sun to rise each day from a sleep which might otherwise have remained unbroken. The capers of both *paniskoi* and *silenoi* began at midnight but the carousing seldom ended before sun-up, at which time, their turbulent duty done, they were free to fade into the forest for much-needed rest.

It is in extant Indian literature and beliefs that we are given, more clearly than anywhere else, some insight into the process by which the divine sun, in the form of animal avatars or incarnations, became the totemic father of the tribes of men. More than most early peoples of whom we have record, the old inhabitants of India (frequently called Dravidians) appear to us as sun-worshippers who rejoiced to call themselves elephants, buffalo, boars, lions, stags, and monkeys in honour of the great beasts which the sun begat upon Mother Earth, either simply by casting his hot love upon her from the heavens or by descending to earth in animal form in times when the fertility of his broad-bosomed lover was threatened by cold and darkness. From time immemorial the earth has been represented as a goddess, but in hundreds of forms and by hundreds of names because to any group of worshippers she must appear necessarily as the personification of their locality or region rather than of the earth itself. For a long time, too, the sun has been thought of as her wooer. One of the oldest names for the sun-god in India is Kasyapa, whose worship was described by Devendranath Tagore, father of the Bengali poet, in his *Autobiography* when depicting his grandmother:

> She was a deeply religious woman. ... Sometimes she used to take a vow of solar adoration, and give offerings to the sun from sunrise to sunset. On these occasions I used to be with her on the terrace in the sun; and constantly hearing the *mantras* (short, traditional prayers) of the sun worship repeated they became quite familiar to me.
>
> I salute the bringer of day, red as the Java flower:
> Radiant son of Kashyapa,
> Enemy of Darkness, destroyer of all sins.[21]

Now the *Visnu Purana* tells us that this Kasyapa, ancient father of our present sun, in his day begat upon two sisters most of the animal creation: upon Krodhavasā all the sharp-toothed creatures that devour flesh and upon Surabhī all the grass-eaters such as cows and buffalo. It is a bit hard for us to imagine just how the earth, fertilised by the sun, gave forth the great births of Indian jungle life, but we must remember that for centuries snakes, moles, and some insects were commonly supposed to have been spawned by the action of sunlight on mud, and it was probably in some such way that the Dravidians imagined their animal fathers to have been generated in the beginning.

Lucretius, however, could imagine the process (*De Rerum Natura*, II, 991–98) and Michelangelo could even depict it in the "Fresco of Creation" in the Sistine Chapel, while as late as *Paradise Lost* (VII, 453 sqq.) John Milton chose to represent the first appearance on earth of animals as due to just such a parturition. Earth (here, of course, at God's command rather than the sun's passion)

> Op'ning her fertile womb teem'd at a birth
> Innumerous living creatures, perfect forms, ...
> The grassy clods now calv'd; now half appear'd

The tawny lion, pawing to get free
His hinder parts, then springs as broke from bonds,
And rampant shakes his brindled mane; the ounce,
The libbard and the tiger, as the mole
Rising, the crumbl'd earth above them threw
In hillocks; the swift stag from under ground
Bore up its branching head ...

The mothers of the tribes of men, if we may believe other old Indian stories such as that of the birth of Sita, heroine of the great Indian epic the *Ramayana* who was found in a furrow, were born directly, without the need of a father, from the womb of earth, perhaps on the principle that like has no trouble in begetting like. Now it was upon these earth-born women that the earth-born sun-animals begat the tribal groups of mankind, each of which continued for ages to hold its founding father sacred and to reverence, as perhaps in some degree superior to itself, the animal brothers who bore more precisely the father's form. Just how the divine animal begot children on an earth-born woman is another hard problem. The whole question must probably be referred to the confusions of a time when men did not properly understand the facts of paternity. Some evidence suggests that the earth-daughter was thought to have won impregnation simply by being near a great animal when it died, its immortal spirit seeking of its own volition reincarnation in her womb. Pregnancies of women less mythical than these earth-girls were for a long time explained in this same way in India, and even when the role of human intercourse came to be understood, the Dravidians often made a distinction between the paternity of the body and that of the soul. The body they were willing to admit might be planted by men, but the soul or life spirit they continued to attribute to the magnificent forest creatures they admired so much. Dravidian women who longed for strong, proud-souled children seem often to have performed symbolic sex acts with jungle animals, as by holding a perishing beast against the pelvis. Even in historic times it was customary at a raja's horse-sacrifice to "bundle" his head-wife in a cloak with the freshly smothered stallion in the hope that her next offspring would be fleet-bodied, strong-souled, and perhaps a vegetarian. We must not ask of these ancient people why the offspring of the woman lost those characteristics of divine paternity such as hoofs and horns. What is important for us to remember is that hoofs, horns, animal ears, and shagginess – in fact, animality – continued far into historical times to be associated with the founder of the tribe, considered divine because born directly from the hierogamos of sun and earth.

Sometimes the sun had begotten the animal-father of the tribes simply, as I have said, by shining on the earth, but in most accounts he accomplished the creation of men by descending to earth and fertilising her womb in the form of a handsome animal, usually represented in art as yellow or white, the colour of the sun – an animal which accordingly became identified with the principle of fertility. This animal, whether identified directly with the sun or simply with the sun's great son, the founding father of the tribe, was the centre of seasonal fertility rites presided over by the priest or king of the tribe (often the same man), dressed in skins, animal masks and horns which made his resemblance to the original sun-animal clear. Often he was thought to be more directly descended from the original father than were the other members of the tribe, and it was precisely this clear sun-lineage that entitled him to be king or priest and preside over the rites. In some cases, it seems, the fiction was perpetuated that these sun-priests or -kings were born, not of the seed of human fathers, but of that of the sun- or totem-animal, and it is established beyond dispute that kings frequently visited their wives for purposes of conception, or coupled with them in public in order to stimulate the growth of the soil, dressed in animal masks and furs. For these reasons the figure whom Frazer taught us to call the Divine King and which has since his day received so much attention from folklorists and anthropologists is found more often than not associated with animal emblems, insignia, and disguises of every conceivable kind. The essence of life, the creative sun-power, was clearly thought to have been entrusted almost exclusively to dynasties of rulers who never forgot to testify to their paternity by cultivating their natural hairiness, dressing in skins, and wearing likenesses of the founding father on their banners and coats-of-arms. It is no wonder that Falstaff, with his many sun and animal associations, was shocked to hear his pupil, "whose chin [was] not yet fledg'd", continually boasting of his royal blood. "I will sooner have a beard grow in the palm of my hand than he shall get one off his cheek; and yet he will not stick to say his face is a face royal."[22] Falstaff, whose own hairiness is unquestionable, seems at times to have seriously considered, in his role of supplanted royal heir, beating his beardless charge from the throne.

When we are trying to envisage the full meaning for ancient or even modern man of the divine totem father of a tribe, the great, fat, glossy animal son of the sun who promotes growth and increase of every sort – human, animal, and vegetable – we must not fail to take the wondrous creature's full measure. Above all, we must remember that fertility, nourishment, and growth were conceived of by our ancestors, as well as by ourselves, as taking place on various and interlocking levels. Thus the early Dravidians worshipped their animal-incarnated sun-god or the sun-god himself not merely as the power which begot and sustains life but as that which leads his children to ever higher forms of health and happiness. Such primitive speculation about unlimited possibilities for the development of life is not necessarily outmoded even in our own day when science recognises the sun as the only apparent source of vitality on earth, by whose radiant energy the inorganic colloids first took on a complexity that resulted in a marvellous new unit – and vista – of life; by whose warmth invertebrate organisms forsook the waters and learned to walk, in time, erect; and by whose chemical wizardry vital energy was finally magnified and subtilised into the thing we call human consciousness.

This benevolent interest of the sun in the health, joy, and unfolding of the human body, mind, and spirit is observable again in Hindu thought and myth, in the stories of the various avatars or descents of Visnu to earth during crises that threatened to destroy the human race. Visnu, known as the preserver-god, is a form of the sun worshipped by Vaisnava Hindus in the form of a round stone called the saligram, which is decorated with garlands of flowers. His name is derived from the root *vis* which means "to pervade", and it is supposed by Indians not only that he has diffused his divine essence through all created things, making all men, animals, and other sentient beings his very children, each as its nature is able to testify to the divine presence, but that he has nine times incarnated his full godhead upon earth in order to rescue men from dangerous crises and to promote, by example, the growth of men in ever more perfect bliss and spirituality. Visnu once appeared as a great fish which advised the Indian Noah, Manu, how to build an ark and save a remnant from the impending flood, and again as a tortoise which descended to the bottom of the sea to recover things lost in the deluge and to dredge up civilising arts and saving medicines not formerly enjoyed on earth.

What is more to our purpose here is that in his third avatar Visnu appeared as a wild boar, always represented in art as a stout man with a boar's head; in his fourth as a man–lion, that is, a man with a lion's head; and in his fifth as a fat dwarf who was nevertheless able to span the entire stretch of the heavens in three strides. Three times he came to earth as a human-shaped messiah called Rama, Buddha, or Krishna, all of whom are associated in one way or another with animals, chiefly the monkey and the elephant, while an avatar still to come, the Messiah of the Future, is expected in the form of Kalki, a white horse. Perhaps nowhere in the mythology of the world is the intimate relation between the sun-power and beautiful, prepotent animals more clearly shown than in the legends of Visnu, the saviour god of India. The moral of the *Bhagavad-gita*, often called the Bible of India and spoken by Visnu as Krishna, must be included in any definition of the kind of fertility which the animal sun-god was thought to stimulate. The oldest and most sacred of Hindu *mantras*, prayer-like spells or charms that seek to tap divine power, is addressed to the sun-god under the name of Savitri (Vivifier) and runs, "Let us contemplate the adorable glory of Savitri, the Heavenly God. May he enlighten our thoughts." Deeper insight into the sun as a catalyst of the spirit as well as a preserver of the body is to be found in the *Suryasataka* of Mayura, a poet of the seventh century A.D., already mentioned in this chapter. In the poem whose title means "A hundred stanzas in praise of Surya" (another name for the solar deity) we have a sustained eulogy of the beneficent activities of the sun. Each of the hundred stanzas ends with a prayer that he may free the reader of the poem from all vestiges not only of disease and pain but of unhappiness, poverty, and sin, and make him ever more perfect in the practice of love and creative kindness. Not a breath of pain or misfortune, not a shadow of privation or death, is allowed to creep into the verses, which are so richly ornamented with figures of speech and lines with two or three different but relevant meanings (an ingenious and peculiarly Indian poetic device) that the effect of mental abundance and spiritual brilliance becomes itself a charm to banish barrenness.

Mayura rejected the accumulation of Hindu gods popular in his time and argued for the idea, popularised by the heterodox Akhenaton of Egypt two thousand years before him, that the sun comprises in his beneficial activities all that man can conceive of deity. It is an ancient conception, I feel sure, and yet a not unmodern one, that the poet so knowingly expounds under the pretence of ignorance when he writes

> It cannot be determined whom the Thousand-rayed one is like,
> Whether he is *a god* or *a kinsman*, or *a kind friend*, or *a teacher*, or *a master*,
> Or *protection*, or perhaps an eye, or a lamp, or *a spiritual preceptor*, or *a father*, or the primary cause, or energy;
> [But it is certain that] under all these guises, and at all times, and in all ways, he bestows benefits on the worlds.
> May the Thousand-rayed one grant your prayer![23]

I have italicised certain words here in order to emphasise that the divine sun-power, the life-force – whether it operates directly from the heavens or in the form of a messianic animal or through a kingly descendant of such an animal or by means of an uncouth, feral, fat one – has for thousands of years been held to nourish the spirit as well as the body, to sharpen moral sensitivity as well as the physical senses. Every one of the Falstaffian figures we shall consider is as much a spiritual tutor, foster-father, and self-sacrificing friend as he is a boisterous figure of fun and beast-shaped orgiast.

To turn back to Silenos, the Falstaffian tutor of Dionysos, we are now in a better position to understand just what the wisdom was that the hot, fat, bibulous, bestial preceptor taught his charge. Dionysos, it is well known, was a god who came to Greece – rather late, they say; in fact, in the seventh or sixth century B.C. – in the form of a bull or snake or hunter of animals, to promote the growth of the soil and revive the worship of ancient gods in a period when the two had declined together because of the appearance of a cold, rationalising spirit among Greeks who were looking, as we might say nowadays, for a scientific road to unalloyed material security. The remedy proposed by the so-called Seven Sages for poor crops and the uncertainty, perplexity, toil, and tragedy of life was law and more law, a movement that found literal expression in improved constitutions for the city states of Greece, such as Lykurgos' code in Sparta and Solon's in Athens. States were reorganised on the principles of a more detailed jurisprudence and a more efficient civic economy. Apollo, it seems, was the patron of this new civic religion, and the Seven Sages repaired to his shrine at Delphi with a garland of new saws to be engraved in gold on the façade of the temple: "Know thyself", "Know the proper time", "Nothing too much", "Misery is the consequence of debt and discord". Solon of Athens was the poet–politician of this make-everything-fruitful-through-law movement. With his new code he aimed to reform irrational human nature, for he held that it was disdain for law that had filled Greek life with sedition, inverted the seasons, and blasted the crops. But all this Solonic multiplication of laws does not seem to have brought in an age of peace and plenty. Great Pan, great Silenos, had been driven to forest fastnesses and their worship, their kind of wisdom, neglected and ridiculed in the name of a repressive legalism, conventional worship, which brought only additional aridity to the soil and spirit of Greece.

It was at this point, the myth tells us, that Dionysos, still a young god but tutored in an ancient wisdom by a revoltingly obese and horse-tailed old teacher who had brought him up from birth, came to lead the rebellion against political ambition, racial jingoism, and excessive common sense codified in interminable laws. Simple-minded people saw his bull horns shining on the mountain tops, whence he descended from bleak Thrace into Greece as the deliverer, Dionysos Eleutherios. He came to save men from a prudence that had turned to cold calculation, from a rationalised security-hunt that had opened the way to a monstrous scramble for honour and power. The vine was sacred to this young saviour, and its juice became the blood he shed for men's deliverance from their own and others' self-seeking. In a delirium of intoxication his devotees periodically demolished the web of laws imposed upon them by their philosophic but perhaps not really wise governors. Shouting, reeling, and brandishing torches and spears of pine tipped with living cones, they mocked the police, flouted sexual decency, derided the wisdom of calculated security, and even, it is said, tore a bull – the image of their god – to pieces with their hands and ate the warm sun-flesh in divine frenzy. Prominent in these rites were representatives of the mountainous, horsy Silenos and also, it would seem, of goatish Pan, for many of the revellers were disguised, we are told, in goatskins. In these revels Silenos, an ancient deity of the pre-Aryan or Pelasgian peoples of Greece, seems to have regained lost status and firmly enthroned a young prince of the gods by instructing him in a sagacity very unlike that of his elder brother Apollo, who had been very imperfectly educated in the ancient love-wisdom of the Greek peninsula by the satyr Marsyas. Now, indeed, law as a protector of tyrannical power, honour, ambition, and cruelty was shown for what it really was, and ancient secrets of fertility for man, beast, and nature disclosed and practised.

Later the orgiastic rites performed in imitation and honour of Silenos and Dionysos were turned into ritualistic plays called, because the original participants in them were dressed as goats, *tragedoi* or goat-songs – that is, tragedies. This is no place to embark on a discussion of Greek tragedy, but it is impossible not to note that the famous trilogy of Aeschylus on the legend of Prometheus was a dramatic parable on the presumption of human foresight (Prometheus) which, to the glory of the patron of the play Dionysos, is tortured, humbled, and allowed to remain on Olympus only after recanting and consenting to wear forever about his brows the wreath of *agnus castus* symbolic of repentance for a sin committed directly against divine wisdom. Not to labour this point, we may say that Greek tragedy indicates that true being, heroic being, charismatic being, is not to be found in the strict observance of man-made law or the self-preservative avoidance of pain and passion through a form of foresight which fosters selfishness in the name of law and religion. It is rather to follow, in the spirit of Antigone, a law more ancient, the changeless law of love which keeps nature fruitful even at the expense of life, which strengthens the soul even by the daring of death. The whole matter is summed up in the famous song of the holy women of Dionysos in Euripides' *Bacchae* and brilliantly rendered in English by Gilbert Murray:

> A strait pitiless mind
>   Is death unto godliness;
> And to feel in human kind
>   Life, and a pain the less.
> Knowledge, we are not foes!
>   I seek thee diligently;
> But the world with a great wind blows,
>   Shining, and not from thee;
> Blowing to beautiful things,
>   On, amid dark and light,
> Till Life, through the trammellings
>   Of Laws that are not the Right,
> Breaks, clean and pure, and sings
>   Glorying to God in the height![24]

In lieu of evidence to the contrary, I must suppose this song to be a fine statement of the wisdom that Silenos taught his pupil. In rough language Falstaff's philosophy of "sherris" adds up to the same point: only the wine of Dionysos can warm into humanity and courage the upright yet naturally cold, pitiless, treacherous blood inherited from Henry IV by Prince John of Lancaster and Hal himself. In many of the Greek tragedies King Kreon, a kind of stock tyrant, seeks to enforce what he calls law and justice at the expense of what Heaven calls righteousness and love. But only these latter qualities can (when practised on the level of the senses) make the earth bloom or (when practised on the level of the spirit) make social life flower in works of art and statesmanship. Thus Kreon must be crushed repeatedly in honour of Dionysos while the chorus sings wonderful songs filled with the wisdom of the half-animal, half-divine creature who was Dionysos' nurse, friend, and teacher.

The events in the story of King David's son Absalom, as related in the

Hebrew Old Testament, may be referred more directly to the seasonal ceremony in which a long-haired creature was, for a week or more, dressed in a real king's robes, set on his throne, and allowed – perhaps even compelled – to overeat, drink, and lie with the royal concubines. At the end of the period of revelry through which the Mock King led a populace joyously released from work and legal restraint – a period which was sometimes brought to an end by a sham battle in which he and his ragamuffin rout drove off the powers of darkness – the hairy man was, you recall, stripped of his royal robes and hanged or impaled.

Now the role which Absalom plays in 2 Samuel 15–18 bears a striking resemblance to the pattern of the Babylonian festival known as the Sacaea, described in Chapter V (p. 65). The only detail in which the Absalom story departs from that of the Sacaea is the fact – shocking, to be sure – that the Substitute King is not a so-called criminal but the real king's son. There is, however, a great deal of evidence pointing to the ritual killing among many of the early Semites of the eldest son (the first fruit) for the purpose of strengthening either an ageing father or a weakening God – a rite happily abandoned by the Hebrews of later times in favour of the lesser bloodshed of circumcision. We read in the Bible and on a famous victory-stele, astonishingly preserved, that a king of Moab once won a great victory over the Hebrews by sacrificing his first-born to his sun-god Chemosh. When we keep these practices in mind, and remember that Absalom may have been, in some sense, a criminal, his ritual death for the good of his father and country in the period of David's old age is not necessarily surprising.

The Biblical account sounds something like history but, read in the light of the Sacaea pattern, it sounds still more like ritual drama. For the period of Absalom's mock kingship, David with his court and priests passed over the brook Kidron "toward the way of the wilderness", much as the king of Babylon deserted his city at the Sacaea. There David ascended Mount Olivet weeping, his head covered and his feet bare, "and all the people that was with him covered every man his head and they went up, weeping as they went up". There is some evidence that the true king of Babylon underwent a period of mourning in which he lamented his decline in vigour and perhaps the moral faults which had endangered his land. It is said that at one of the Babylonian seasonal festivals – this was the true New Year festival, the Akitu celebration, not the Sacaea[25] – a priest slapped the face of the king until he cried, while in the Bible Shimei with impunity cast stones at David and his followers and cursed them for the bloody deeds by which they had supplanted the house of Saul. While David was undergoing this rough ritual handling, back in Jerusalem Absalom was saving him from still worse treatment and probably death by using the short period of his rule to upset the laws in favour of "the people" and to revel with David's concubines. At last Absalom was having, if only for a little while, his wish "that I were made judge in the land, that every man which hath any suit or cause might come unto me, and I would do him justice!" Shrewdly, the ageing David had left behind him "ten women, which were concubines, to keep the house", and now "they spread Absalom a tent upon the top of the house; and Absalom went in unto his father's concubines in the sight of all Israel". The "house" here referred to was probably a sacred edifice of the ziggurat-mountain shape, on top of which the sacred *connubium* was sometimes performed in the countries surrounding Palestine in the sight of the population. After this, Absalom having carried out the most important of his Mock King's duties, David was overtaken "a little past the top of the hill" of Olivet (he was slipping into a decline indeed) and summoned back to Jerusalem by a servant leading animals and objects which symbolised his regal restoration and a miraculous rejuvenation of the sun and soil: to wit, "a couple of asses saddled, and upon them two hundred loaves of bread, and an hundred bunches of raisins, and an hundred of summer fruits, and a bottle of wine". For the reinvigoration of David and the land not only did Absalom in Jerusalem play his part; a certain Jonathan, perhaps representing the deposed house of Saul, also helped the king by going down into a well presided over by a "wench" who was also anxious to help, "and the woman took and spread a covering over the well's mouth and spread ground corn thereon; and the thing [some fertilising ceremony?] was not known".

With all this magic assistance, David was able at last to leave the wilderness and fight successfully against the powers of darkness, here represented by twenty thousand Israelites smitten to death in the wood of Ephraim. After this (probably sham) battle in which he had led the losing "blacks", Absalom was ready for the ritual death. Like Mock Kings in many times and places, he was allowed to flee a certain distance before his executioners set out to overtake him. He escaped on a mule, held perhaps to be a debased and humorous form of the royal onager, but his long streaming hair, we are told, caught in the thick boughs of a great oak, leaving him "taken up between the heaven and the earth; and the mule that was under him went away".

There was no particular Ishtar or Delilah to point to as the cause of Absalom's downfall, but it is impossible at this point to avoid remembering that the oak was, of all trees, especially sacred in most countries to the earth goddess and her priestesses. Frazer tells us that the Substitute King of Babylon was hanged or impaled, and in this episode we see Absalom self-hanged, as it were, upon the holy rood. Contrary to the king's order that none should harm him, David's general Joab, hearing that Absalom was hanged, immediately hurried off to impale him by thrusting three javelins or darts "through the heart ... while he was yet alive in the midst of the oak. And ten young men that bare Joab's armour compassed about and smote Absalom and slew him." This last detail, which is perhaps out of place, may refer to a ritual scourging of the hung-up Mock King preparatory to his death. Then "Joab blew the trumpet", and Absalom was cast into "a great pit in the wood" with a "very great heap of stones upon him" (a mock form of the pyramidal tomb under which real kings were buried?). Perhaps the very last act of the rite was that in which David "went up to the chamber over the gate and wept", wailing that he would have liked to die for the man who had died for him – a scene which, as we shall see, closely parallels that in which Gilgamesh mourned the death of Enkidu.

It is impossible finally to leave Silenos and Dionysos without recalling another tutor–pupil pair based on them, this time among the Greeks. Their story is told by Plato in the *Symposium*, the scene of which is a classic and dignified Boar's Head, but a tavern just the same. As in Shakespeare's Falstaff plays, the attuned ear cannot help hearing in certain passages of the *Symposium* echoes of the seasonal dramas performed in honour of Dionysos and probably dominated, in the first place, by dialogues between the burgeoning deity and his tutor. I refer, of course, to the speeches exchanged by Socrates and Alcibiades, who may be supposed, in this philosophical satyr-play devoted to the elucidation of the true nature of love and honour, to take the roles of Silenos and Dionysos respectively.

In fact, Plato's comparison of Socrates to Silenos is almost over-emphasised. Small icons of the ugly fat god seem to have been popularly used in Athens, whether in bust or full-length form, to hold tiny figures of the other gods, presumably made of gold and jewels. This custom may have been symbolic of an apparent fact: that Silenos was an old Pelasgian Kronos who in some sense gave birth to the gods of Aryan Greece, or at least helped them to succeed himself. Or the custom may simply mean that Silenos figurines were used as jewel cases – a use which could, of course, have itself been symbolic, commemorating the days before the coming of the Achaean and Dorian invaders when Silenos presided over the Golden Age, for the Falstaffian deity frequently appears, as we shall see when we come to consider figures from India, China, and Celtic Gaul, as a god of wealth. Alcibiades makes much of the symbolic possibilities of the treasures concealed in the bosom of the gross Silenos-figure when he says of Socrates:

> I say that he is exactly like the busts of Silenos which are set up in the statuaries' shops holding pipes and flutes in their mouths; and they are made to open in the middle and have images of gods inside them. I will also say that he is like Marsyas the Satyr. You yourself will not deny, Socrates, that your faith is like that of a satyr ... and are you not a flute-player? That you are, and a performer far more wonderful than Marsyas. He, indeed, with instruments used to charm the souls of men. ... But you produce the same effect with your words only ... this Marsyas [Socrates] has often brought me to such a pass that I have felt as if I could hardly endure the life which I am leading ... he is the only person who ever made me ashamed, which you might think to be not in my nature, and there is no one else who does the same. ... And therefore I run away and fly from him. ... Many a time have I wished that he were dead and yet I know that I should be much more sorry than glad if he were to die: so I am at my wits' end.

> And this is what I and many others have suffered from the flute-playing of this satyr. ... Is he not like a Silenos in this? To be sure he is: this outer mask is the carved head of the Silenos; but O my companions in drink, when he is opened, what temperance there is residing within! Know you that luxury and wealth and *honour,* at which the many wonder, are of no account with him and are utterly despised by him. ... All his life is spent at mocking and flouting at those who pursue them. But when I opened him, and looked within at his serious purposes, I saw in him divine and golden images of such fascinating beauty that I did in a moment whatever Socrates commanded.[26]

How often have we all seen so-called portrait busts of Socrates with a broad satyr's face, flat, upturned nose and horse-like ears! How often have we read that the wisdom he taught (not necessarily parallel at all points to that attributed to him in the dialogues of Plato) was essentially pre- or non-Greek! Now here in the *Symposium* we seem to see him as the deposed king of an ancient royal line, ousted from his heritage but willing, for the love of his country and mankind – luxury, wealth, and honour mean nothing to him – to teach his conquerors wisdom; that is, to teach them how to break up winter's darkness and the ice-cake of ambition, how to live in such a way as to make the earth, the body, and the soul blossom and flourish together.

The way Alcibiades tells the story of himself and Socrates in the campaign of Potidaea makes the reader think of the historical battle as a symbol of seasonal conflict, much as Shakespeare's accounts of Shrewsbury and Agincourt must have made his audience think of the seasonal Mummers' Play. Socrates, as far as we can make out from Alcibiades' words, practically lived on wine yet was never drunk, the emptying of a two-quart vessel simply serving to sharpen his insight into truth, in the contemplation of which he would often stand abstracted from midnight to daybreak without moving a muscle. We are told that his boisterous young companions "brought out their mats and slept in the open air that they might watch him and see whether he would stand all night. There he stood until the following morning; and with the return of light he offered up a prayer to the sun and went his way."[27]

In battle Socrates aided and protected his pupil and once saved his life. In this story the roles of Hal and Falstaff at Shrewsbury are somewhat reversed, for in Shakespeare Hal gives his old tutor credit for repulsing that fiend of darkness, the Hot-spurred Turkish Knight, while here Socrates, after saving Alcibiades' life and repelling the enemy, insists that his Greek St George-cum-Hal be given the prize. Since episodes like this, told one way or the other, occur in so many of the tutor–pupil stories we are about to recount, it is likely that it is modelled on an episode common to seasonal mystery plays or rites all over the world which, if only imperfectly preserved in the English Mummers' Play and some of its worldwide variants, lives on in a comparatively complete if sophisticated form in Plato's story. "I will also tell, if you please – and indeed I am bound to tell –," says Alcibiades,

> of his courage in battle; for who but he saved my life? Now this was the engagement in which I received the prize of valour: for I was wounded and he would not leave me, but rescued me and my arms; and he ought to have received the prize of valour which the generals wanted to confer on me partly on account of my rank, and I told them so ... but he was more eager than the generals that I and not he should have the prize.[26]

Alcibiades conceived of Socrates, with his scorn of conventional warriors' values, as "the sort of man who is never touched in war" and who guarantees, as if by a magic of inner warmth and endurance, victory for the side on which he fights. Alcibiades observed of Socrates at Potidaea that, though (should he not have said, because?) he could drink all his followers under the table,

> his fortitude in enduring cold was ... surprising. There was a severe frost, for the winter in that region was really tremendous, and everybody else remained indoors, or if they went out had on an amazing quantity of clothes, and were well shod and had their feet swathed in felt and fleeces: in the midst of this Socrates with his bare feet on the ice and in his ordinary dress marched better than the other soldiers who had shoes ...[26]

Falstaff did not manage his forced marches as easily, but we can hardly help imagining that under the feet of both these theriomorphic characters, as under those of good King Wenceslas, the snow itself melted, leaving a track of warm footprints in which their young companions or pupils could follow them safely to a victory over winter's sadness.

It is of interest that the *Symposium* ends with the picture of Socrates compelling Agathon and Aristophanes, respectively great tragic and comic poets, "to acknowledge that the genius of comedy is the same as that of tragedy and that the true artist in tragedy is an artist in comedy also", a proposition to which "they, being drowsy and not quite following the argument, were constrained to assent".[26] I think we can see what he meant if we recall that for Alcibiades, for his pupil, saved from destruction during the battle and now trained successfully to wield sun-power and wisdom on his own, the battle had ended in comedy, but for the tutor, for Socrates himself, it had ended in something like tragedy. He had imparted his love-wisdom, his sun-bright magic, and was now to be dispensed with by the pupil who had often, as we know from his own confession, wished the old man dead. According to the pattern of the seasonal Mystery, it was necessary for him to die in order that his pupil might give the *coup de grâce* to winter darkness and spiritual dreariness – to make the sacrifice by which alone he could transmit the last full measure of his own love-energy to his favourite pupil and entourage of revellers. Additionally, it was inevitable that Old Father Antic should hound a half-feral creature whose wisdom ran counter to the Greeks' cold-blooded love of pelf, their frosty cultivation of honour, and their mechanical administration of a legal *quid pro quo* in the name of justice, to his death on the charge of corrupting youth. In the end, though his friends offered him many means of escape, Socrates simply insisted upon dying, as if he were the leading actor in a divine drama the lines and acts of which could not possibly be changed. As we know, Socrates was possessed of a *daimon*, which spoke to him in his all-night trances or in sleep; worked, he thought, by love; and comprised "all that intercourse and converse which is conceded by the gods to men".[27]

The life of man is continually threatened by adverse weather from without and by wintry hate and ambition from within, beggarly and embeggaring passions which, if men are to survive at all, compel Poverty to desire a child by Plenty. From the urgent embraces of Poverty and Plenty is born Love, said Socrates, which is at once the voice of God and the counsel of man's direst necessity. Accordingly the old tutor, or corrupter, of youth insisted on dying in order to enrich Athens and the world by showing them the essence of golden love, true justice, as contrasted with the letter of man-made law. To have consented to live when the message of love could be best clarified by death would have been to betray the *daimon* or divine voice surging within. The shouts of the roisterers in the alehouse, the intoxicated conversation in the Athenian Boar's Head, evocative of fertility on every level of body and spirit, must not be allowed to fade and die on the wintry air. The words of the *daimon* urging him to his love-death were the voice of God enforcing the Divine Order of the universe. Had Socrates failed to follow them, the sun that was hovering on the morning hilltops as he drank the hemlock might, both literally and metaphorically, never have risen to warm and preserve mankind.

> *Soc.:* Crito, my dear friend Crito, that, believe me, that [love lore] is what I seem to hear as the corybantes hear flutes in the air, and the sound of those words rings and echoes in my ears and I can listen to nothing else. Believe me, ... if you speak against them you will speak in vain. Still, if you think you can do any good, say on.
>
> *Cr.:* No, Socrates, I have nothing I can say.
>
> *Soc.:* Then let us leave it so, Crito; and let things go as I have said, for this is the way God has pointed out.[28]

Plain Jack Falstaff of course rose to no such philosophical heights on his death-bed, yet he did play with flowers and babble happily of green fields while his motley followers roistered in the tap room below and Hal, now Henry V, who under the hand (and thumb) of Old Father Antic had rejected and in one way or another killed him, was at last enabled – perhaps by his mysterious tutor's mysterious death – to sail for France and give the *coup de grâce* to a still wobbling Turkish Knight. And thereby he turned the pleasaunce which Richard and his murderer had allowed to become choked with weeds back into a place of peace and plenty, to which he added "the world's best garden",[29] France.

So much for the Falstaff-persona as an animal incarnation of the benevolent sun, a "bolting-hutch of beastliness" who nevertheless seeks to save the world by preaching and practising solar generosity and dispensing world-wide warmth in the noblest sense of the word.

IV
Bes of Egypt
Who was "Born with a White Head and Something a Round Belly"

Artistic representations of the Falstaffian figure I intend to consider in this chapter show him as perhaps the most repulsively bestial of all the avatars of the hot, friendly, nurturing, tutorial sun. I refer to the god Bes (Besa, Basu, etc.) of Egypt. He was most popular in that country and in the Roman Empire in the millenium between 400 B.C. and A.D.400, though the Egyptians had a strong tradition to the effect that he was indeed the first and greatest of all the gods of the sacred land watered by the Nile. Thousands of figurines and representations of him have come down to us because he was a household deity in the strict sense of the word, his effigy serving to ward the home against misfortune and the nursery against dangers arising from the noxious insects and wild animals over which he, as a kind of composite animal himself, was lord. He also brought sound rest and good dreams to both children and parents. Usually he is represented in the form of a baby-bodied dwarf with a huge, bearded, monkey-like face, a great flattened nose, shaggy eyebrows fashioned to suggest horns, projecting animal ears, long thick arms, a pot belly, and bow legs. Around his body he sometimes wears the skin of a panther whose tail hangs down to the ground behind, while on his head he wears a crown of feathers or of feathery spikes of grain. Like other Falstaff figures he is a master of dance and ritual capering and is often, like many a Greek satyr or Indian *vidyadhara*, represented as playing a musical instrument, usually the harp. In this role he

Bes of Egypt

was the god of the pleasures of life so conscientiously cultivated by the Egyptians and the master of ceremonies at the drinking parties and merry-making festivities depicted with such infectious warmth on a thousand Egyptian temple and tomb paintings. More particularly, he seems to have presided over domestic fun, notably over the play of children, of whom he was the special protector against accidents and reptiles.

This role of child-guardian Bes came to play in virtue of the famous story in which he had a royal pupil whom he had protected in infancy and educated against the dark day when he would have to meet and fight the power of evil, Set or Setekh, who had maimed and slain the child's father Osiris. The pupil's name was Horus. In Egypt the fact that the Falstaff-persona prepared his pupil to fight sometimes led to his being represented in art as a god of war, though it is possible that the weapon he brandishes over his head or bangs against his shield is a toy, something like the sword of lath carried by the Vice in the Moral Interludes and so congenial to the imagination of Falstaff. Had there been firearms in Bes's heyday, I suspect that in the seasonal battle he would have been found carrying a bottle rather than a revolver in his holster. The Roman soldiers who had served in Egypt, along with many who had not, loved amulets of the fat, dancing dwarf flourishing a knife or short sword, but this does not necessarily mean that they thought of him as a patron of slaughter; rather, it is believed, they wished with his help to think of war as softened by those other qualities that he stood for: laughter, the dance, zest, fruitfulness, family life. Perhaps they recognised in Bes's sword-brandishing capers a sword-dance of the ceremonial kind once popular, apparently, from China to the British Isles.

More often than not, the figure of Bes was carved not on chariot wheel-hubs but on bedsteads, especially those in which the wife of a Pharaoh expected to give birth to a royal child. According to Sir Wallace Budge and Professor Wiedemann,

> One of the oldest representations of Bes is found in a relief in the famous temple of Hatshepset at Der Al-Bahari where he appears [by the side of the couch] in the chamber where the birth of the great queen is supposed to be taking place.[1]

In ladies' boudoirs his simian face was all the rage, being carved on the handles of mirrors, vessels containing rouge and eye make-up, and the wooden pillows on which Egyptian women rested their dainty heads. Scenes on the walls of temples depicting chambers where royal children were born, suckled, and brought up almost always show his ugly face. Heads and full-length bas-reliefs of him were the most common of nursery objects, and suggest that he not only protected children from mishap and scorpions but devoted himself to devising new games and amusements for the playroom. From Taanach in Palestine comes a green porcelain representation of the god which must have been used as a child's toy or doll and shows that his worship was adopted wherever Egyptian culture penetrated. Representations of him were worn on rings and necklaces by both children and anxious parents, a custom which may be revived in our time by those who care to purchase what is said to be a fast-selling replica of a gangsterish Bes head obtainable in certain American museums.

As we have seen, not only ape-like Bes but also Ta-urt (Trau-urt, Thoueris, etc.), the hippopotamus-shaped Goddess of the Marshlands, presided over childbirth in ancient Egypt. We do not know exactly how Bes came first to be associated with the child Horus, but it is clear that Ta-urt, whose weird and rotund figure is clearly allied to that of Bes, acted as midwife when Isis gave birth to Horus in the marshes, and immediately afterward protected the baby from the murderous attacks of his father's enemy Set. This story is represented on many a bas-relief and amulet. Ta-urt is just as fascinating a grotesque as Bes and, when you get to know her, the most lovable member of his motley rout. She has a hippopotamus head and a crocodile spine and tail, pendulous breasts and a great belly that seem human, and human arms and legs terminating in the paws of a lion. This was her first and always her most popular form though later, as Apt or Apet, she became more human, acquiring a woman's head and losing her crocodile tail if not her feline extremities. Ta-urt may, indeed, have been the Mother Goddess of the pre- or proto-Egyptian peoples but, unlike Bes, she never recovered a high place in the Egyptian pantheon. She remained at best a gross and jolly Hat-Hor, bearing about the same resemblance to this love-goddess as that which Doll Tearsheet bore to Helen of Troy. We are interested in her precisely because of her grossness, precisely because she played a perfect Doll to Bes's Falstaff, matching him in body as well as spirit. In this respect she contrasts strongly with the beautiful paramours of most Falstaff-personae from Silenos to Merlin, but recalls Shakespeare's creation not a little.

That Bes protected and cared for Horus throughout his childhood and young manhood, initiating him into the mysteries of sun-wisdom, especially by teaching him to play and dance, is clear from evidence both written and iconographical. One of the dances he taught him may have been a sword-dance which helped prepare him for the seasonal contest with Set. Then, his duty done, his pupil prepared, it seems (from the icons) that Bes lost his head, or rather his body. The sun-face was left, aureoled in flaming hair and smiling benevolently through thick animal lips. This head then shrank, like the Cheshire cat's, into a smile without a face (or so we may think), at which time Bes's spirit passed into his charge and one could say of him, as one can perhaps say of many of these Falstaff-personae, that he was reborn in his pupil. On the famous Metternich stele, a wonderfully rich iconographical document found in Alexandria in 1828 and dating from about 370 B.C., we find Bes described as "the Old Man who renews his youth, the Aged One who maketh himself again a boy". On this stele, as on hundreds of so-called "*cippi* of Horus", the ancient god, represented by his head only, hovers over a plump naked figure of young Horus, who stands on crocodiles and grips scorpions and reptiles in his hands. This transformation of the old man into the boy, this rebirth of the tutor in the pupil, is perhaps an attempt to represent symbolically the phenomena of the winter solstice when the sun, which has been steadily losing heat and power for months, turning every day more dangerously sick and pallid, suddenly begins slowly to regain force and brilliance. It is the same sun, everyone recognises, but just as it reaches the frightening nadir of senescence, it is miraculously reborn, as a New Year's babe, as if from its final spasms of pain. It dies into life – a phrase used in many countries to describe this Old-Sun-into-New-Sun transformation.

Our far-off ancestors could think of no more appropriate way to account for this phenomenon than to picture the sun in its decline as a dying old man who carried his baby self in his womb, giving birth to this infant – his bearded self in child shape – at the solstice. Before passing away entirely during the unsettled and unpredictable weather before springtime proper, Old–Young Bes raised Young–Old Horus into a plump deity well-tutored in every form of solar activity. When this annual drama of a fading–reviving sun-god was visualised as enacted, there were almost bound to be two avatars, one characteristically old – a Bes surrogate – the other young – the crown prince Horus himself who on the Pharaoh's death would accede to power as a full-fledged solar god. On the purely human (if this is the right word) level we have, then, two avatars of the sun-god: a top-heavy, dwarfish representative of the pre-Egyptian possessors of the land, now driven into the land of Punt or Ghosts with their solar secrets, and a lovely little heir-apparent of their supplanters in search of a freakish teacher. The dwarf, both as dwarf and as sun-king of his displaced people, would often be more round-bellied, more child-bodied, than his charge – and it is thus he is most often shown in icons, the great paunch surmounted by the bearded face of a wise old man or monkey. Having trained his pupil by drinking, dancing, lovemaking, etc. to conquer evil Set, he slowly faded into the Cheshire-cat head I spoke of and found immortality on the curious *cippi*.

Something of this primitive mythmaking, this ancient imagery, clings to nearly every one of the tutor–pupil pairs we are going to consider – softening to some extent the cruelty and even death which the pupil is sometimes represented as inflicting upon the master. Characteristically, Silenos was an old–young god while Dionysos was characteristically a young-old one. And what of our friend Falstaff, who loved to refer to "us youth" and robbed the travellers at Gad's Hill shouting, "What, ye knaves! Young men must live"?[2] When, later, the Chief Justice sought to reprove him for this escapade, Falstaff immediately took the offensive.

Fal.: You that are old do not consider the capacities of us that are young; you do measure the heat of our livers by the bitterness of your galls; and we that are in the vaward of youth, I must confess, are wags too.

Ch. Just.: Do you set down your name in the roll of youth that are written down with all the characters of age? Have you not a moist eye, a dry hand, a yellow cheek, a white beard, a decreasing leg, an increasing belly? Is not your voice broken, your wind short, your chin double, your wit single, and every part about you blasted with antiquity, and will you call yourself young? Fie, fie, fie, Sir John!

> *Fal.*:   My Lord, I was born about three o'clock in the afternoon with a white head and something a round belly. ... To approve my youth further I will not. The truth is, I am only old in judgment and under-standing; and he that will caper with me for a thousand marks, let him lend me the money, and have at him![3]

In this connection it is pertinent to remember that at his death Falstaff "went away as it had been any christom child",[4] playing with flowers and babbling of green fields. Here it is impossible not to think of a famous picture of Bes with the bewhiskered face of an old man but the rotund body of a baby, holding papyrus flowers in either hand while the well-known spikes of grain sprout from his head. Sir Wallace Budge explains this union of young and old, this coalescing of teacher and pupil, in a rather ponderous way and with some aid, or so I should suppose, from his imagination:

> At some period under the New Empire the original attributes of Bes were modified, and he assumed the character of a solar god and became identified with Horus the Child, or Harpocrates; little by little he was merged in other forms of the Sun-god until at length he absorbed the characteristics of Horus, Ra, and Temu. As Horus, or Harpocrates, he wore the lock of hair, which is symbolic of youth, on the right side of his head, and as Ra-Temu he was given the withered cheeks and attributes of an old man. On the Metternich stele we see the head of the "Old Man who renews his youth, the Aged One who maketh himself once again a boy" placed above that of Horus, the god of renewed life and of the rising sun, to show that the two heads represent, after all, only phases of one and the same god.[5]

Egyptology since Budge's day allows us to adopt the simpler explanation of the *cippi* of Horus which I have suggested above.

If the Bes–Horus story (much of it is lost) was, like so many versions of the tutor–pupil myth, founded on human as well as solar events, it probably came about somewhat as follows. The Egyptians had a very long written history, but their unwritten one was undoubtedly much longer. It may be that the Egyptians of history, who were some kind of Mediterranean people, conquered the valley of the Nile in prehistoric times from Negro tribes such as those who still inhabit equatorial Africa. Possibly the supreme god of these people, who may themselves have had pygmy characteristics, was a dwarfish figure characterised by a bulging stomach and certain animal traits – perhaps those of the cynocephalus or dog-faced ape – such as we have come to expect in a sun-god or his avatars.

It is further possible that groups of the conquering Egyptians often quarrelled among themselves, as we know the people of the so-called Upper and Lower Kingdoms did for several centuries. In one of these quarrels the losing side, that headed by a famous king called Osiris, who was treacherously slain by his enemy Set, was forced to call to its aid the ancient deities of the land, simian sun-god Bes and the hippopotamus-shaped Mother or Earth Goddess Ta-urt. Myth tells us that Isis, wife of Osiris, in order to give safe birth to Osiris' son, fled in this time of trouble to the marshes. There the earthly representatives of the old deities with their irrepressibly lively, though conquered, followers were themselves perhaps hiding, and there these aborigines consented to save, protect, and restore the dynasty of Osiris. Both Ta-urt and Bes presided over the birth of Horus, an event commemorated in after times by the statues of them placed on either side of many an Egyptian queen's birth-bed; Ta-urt saved the baby from malignant Set in a fierce fight, and Bes brought him up, teaching him the secret craft (military or magical) needed to overcome his father's enemy. This Set may have been a real-life foe or simply a mythic demon of darkness with whom a real king had become identified. Why displaced and persecuted sun-kings agree to save and educate their conquerors, especially their children, I cannot say, but this is a turn the old-tutor myth often takes and it is safe, I think, to suppose it embalms some kind of prehistoric occurrence. Silenos, the monstrous deity of the Pelasgians, consented (as we have seen) to bring up and die for a son of Zeus when blight had attacked the garden of Greece, while uncouth Jack Falstaff, perhaps looking on himself as the true king, appeared from the woods, as it were, during the days of Henry IV's sickness to teach the king's son how to become an effective sun-king. The assumption underlying all such stories seems to be that these monstrous old fellows, outlawed representatives on earth of outlawed deities, constitute the true sun-lineage and that they alone know the secrets, formulas, rites, dances, and actions necessary to persuade the sun to operate with maximum efficiency, save him in crises and renew his beneficent life at the cost of their own.

There is evidence from all parts of the world to show that conquering peoples have sought in every way to placate the gods of the dispossessed and in crises to lure back from the forests, marshes, and jungles, whither they have fled, representatives of the old ruling families either to serve as interim kings or to import fertility secrets to the unprospering usurper's heir or both – frequently both. Thus we may assume that Ta-urt and more especially Bes, that is, their earthly representatives, were sought out by the Egyptians when plagued by civil strife or fertility troubles, and brought back from marshland hiding or even from equatorial Africa, whither perhaps they had been driven, to play the roles I have indicated, restoring order to society and abundance to the earth. At least, Sir Wallace Budge believes that

> The knowledge of the god [Bes], and perhaps figures of him, were brought from this region [equatorial Africa], which the Egyptians called "the Land of Spirits", to Egypt in the early dynastic period, when kings of Egypt loved to keep a pygmy at their courts. The early kinsmen of the god who lived to the south of Egypt were, no doubt, well known even to

the pre-dynastic Egyptians, and as the dynastic Egyptians were at all times familiar with the figure of Bes, those of the late period may be forgiven for connecting him with the "Land of the God", or Punt,[6]

which could not have been the country of his origin. Budge records, as pointing to the ancient domination of Egypt by black men, that all the Egyptian gods were endowed with animal tails and plaited beards such as were traditional ornaments in historical times with the people of Punt.

Budge's reference to the early Pharaohs' love of keeping pygmies at their courts immediately makes us think of the story of certain Dangas (the name seems to have been tribal, not personal) who were brought from Punt (Puanit, etc.) to the court of Dadkeri-Assi, a Pharaoh of the Fifth Dynasty, and his successors, Papi I and Papi II. In her book *The Fool: His Social and Literary History* Enid Wellsford considers that a Danga

> was probably valued as a curiosity; the entertainment afforded by his wild appearance and extravagant posturing being much enhanced by the fact that he had been purchased in Puanit, and therefore hailed from those mysterious lands to the south of the country, which the Egyptians regarded as "ten leagues beyond man's life", shadowy regions inhabited by ghosts and talking serpents.[7]

She thinks he was the earliest form of royal jester and diverted the court by shouting and dancing. It is easy, however, to adduce much stronger reasons why these ugly Dangas or pygmies from the south were prized. Henri Frankfort has clearly demonstrated that every Pharaoh throughout his royal life was identified by himself and his subjects with the god Horus (sun-hawk son of Isis and Osiris) and considered to be his avatar or living incarnation. What could be more appropriate and in every way auspicious than that the living Horus should be united in visible fact to a living embodiment of the original Horus' protector, tutor, entertainer, friend, and companion in arms, who at last died, in one sense or another, in order to endow his foster-child with all his remaining strength for the final contest with Set?

Though the *cippi* of Horus cannot indicate it, this strength of the tutor seems to have been imparted to the pupil in the course of the magical dance we have spoken of, much as the remaining energy of Silenos was transferred to Dionysos when he danced himself into a river of perspiration before the great battle with the Indian king. For the Pharaoh the great thing about the Danga was that he "could dance the God", and Miss Wellsford notes, appropriately, that

> Apparently to "dance the God" means that he was able to imitate the dance of Bisu [Bes], the foreign God from Puanit, who was represented as a hideous, big-headed dwarf clothed in a leopard-skin, "at once jovial and martial, the friend of the dance and of battle".[8]

She does not realise, it seems, the symbolical importance of this dance. In it the lost sun-secrets of life and growth, the strength to conquer famine and darkness, were in all probability imparted by the tutor to the prince or king. She does note, however, that in a formula that occurs for the first time in the Pyramid of Papi I – a king who came to the throne about forty years after the death of the first Danga-owner, Dadkeri-Assi – the justification for King Papi's ghost being piloted safely across the sky-ocean to the Blessed Isles of Osiris is that Osiris and the inhabitants of the Other World will, naturally, be glad to see him because he, Papi, is now "the Danga who dances the God [Bisu], and who rejoices the heart of the God [Osiris] in front of his great royal palace".[9] "Of all the bizarre stories of fools this is perhaps the strangest and most pathetic", says Miss Wellsford, emphasising the absurdity of the notion that a powerful Pharaoh should expect safe conduct to the palace of Osiris because he had so thoroughly identified himself with a dwarfish jester and so perfectly mastered certain dance-steps that he was qualified to become a celestial court-buffoon. She does not seem to realise that the dance she so slightingly refers to was the dance of life itself. Mastered by the living Pharaoh, it was perhaps the "step" or "dance" which enabled the king periodically to renew his own vigour and re-establish his title to the Kingdoms of Upper and Lower Egypt by rekindling the energies of the soil at the Sed Festival, described in Frankfort's *Kingship and the Gods*.[10] Perhaps "to dance the God" meant to make motions forcing the sun from decline to rejuvenation.

At the Sed celebration, rejuvenating for man and soil, the king (the incarnate Horus) ran or danced over a field or, perhaps, "an area ... marked out in the temple court to symbolise Egypt as a whole, brandishing the deed to Egypt bequeathed him by his father". The text describing the version of this rite performed at Edfu says, "The Good God [the King] ... runs round fast holding the Will" and, we may assume, larding the lean earth with his divine sweat. Now this dancing or running brings renewal, it seems, not only to the soil but to the whole universe of men, animals, and departed souls: "He runs crossing the ocean and the four sides of Heaven going as far as the rays of the sun disc, passing over the earth"[11]. Obviously such a dance, even if performed by the mere ghost of the Pharaoh, would revive precious intimations of immortality in the shades who thronged the halls of the King of Death. Perhaps it was even supposed that, as Bes had dance-died to give his pupil a decisive victory over Set, every Pharaoh could die-dance the inhabitants of the Other World into a renewed victory over death.

The profound importance for both life and death of bringing together with the living Horus a living incarnation of Bes is indicated in a letter of the son of Papi I, Papi II, engraved four thousand years ago on the façade of the tomb of Harkhuf, Lord of Elephantine, Ritual Priest and Caravan Conductor to the Pharaoh at Aswan. This letter was written to Harkhuf by his eight-year-old monarch after the priest had sent word that he was bringing his king a bandy-legged dancing dwarf from the deep south. Harkhuf was so proud of this letter that he defied convention by having it chiselled at the end of his own mortuary document. Justly famous, the letter from the boy-king runs, in part, as follows:

> I have noted the matter of this thy letter which thou hast sent to the king [me]. ... Thou hast said in this thy letter that thou hast brought a dancing dwarf of the God from the Land of Spirits like the dwarf which the Treasurer of the God, Burded, brought from the Land of Punt in the time of Isesi [Dadkeri-Assi]. Thou hast said to my majesty: "Never before has one like him been brought by one who has visited Yam."
>
> Come northward to the court immediately; thou shalt bring this dwarf with thee ... living, prosperous, and healthy from the Land of Spirits in order that the dances of the God may rejoice and gladden the heart of the King of Upper and Lower Egypt, Neferkeri [me] who lives forever. When he goes down with thee into the vessel, appoint excellent people who shall be beside him on each side of the vessel; take care lest he fall into the water. When he sleeps at night, appoint excellent people who shall sleep beside him in his tent; inspect ten times a night. My majesty desires to see this dwarf more than the gifts of Sinai and of Punt. If thou arrivest at court, this dwarf being with thee alive, prosperous, and healthy, my majesty will do for thee a greater thing than that which was done for the Treasurer of the God, Burded, in the time of Isesi, according to the heart's desire of my majesty to see this dwarf.
>
> Commands have been sent to the Chief of the New Towns, the Companion, and the Superior Prophet to command that sustenance for the dwarf be taken from every store-city and from every temple, without any stinting thereof.[12]

Clearly Papi II realised how desirable it was for the crops of Egypt and for the souls of all Egyptians, living and dead, that this incarnation of Bes, protector, tutor, dancer, warrior, saviour, railer, jester, should arrive not only in good shape but in the right Falstaffian shape!

Sometimes the old Egyptian god who dance-died into youth – or into *a* youth – was represented as a single head with two faces looking in opposite directions. One face is that of the thick-lipped, flat-nosed, animal-eared, and heavily whiskered demi-ape we know so well by now while the other face is that of a plump-cheeked, smiling child or young man. The amulets on which they are so shown perfectly symbolise the gravamen of the Bes–Horus myth. Like the figurines of Bes himself, such icons seem to have spread from Egypt over the whole Mediterranean world and have been found all around the circuit stretching from Palestine through Greece to Rome and by way of North Africa back to Egypt. The most famous amulet of this kind, dating apparently from the seventh century B.C., was found in Aegina in Greece.

Such figures make us think immediately of the two-faced Janus so popular in Roman, especially late-Roman, times, when Bes himself was one of the favourite mascots of the empire's soldiery. In those days Janus was often called the most ancient of all the Italo-Roman deities, as Bes was acknowledged the oldest god of Egypt. He seems to have been almost certainly a god of the sun, conceived of as opening the gates of heaven as he rose fresh-faced in the morning and as closing them when he went into bearded retirement at night. Or it may be that the whole symbolism of Janus refers to a certain day in his life: the day of the winter solstice when, a spent old man, he endowed a younger, self-produced, well-tutored double of himself with all his remaining potency. The worship of Janus was conducted by a college of singing and dancing priests in whose hymns he was hailed as "the good creator" and "god of gods". Like Bes, he presided over happy home life, though he was not as intimately connected with the nursery as was Bes. He was a lord of fruitfulness, and on his festival day he was honoured with meal cakes called *ianuae* while people exchanged gifts of sweets and fruits and white cattle were sacrificed on the Capitol. After 153 B.C., this festival day was identified with the beginning of the solar year and was called the first day of January, the whole opening month of the new year being named after Janus and consecrated to him. On his holiday he was invoked as the god of good beginnings or re-beginnings,. and it would seem that the Romans walked ritually through a fane founded for him (so it was said) by Numa, entering by way of a door surmounted or surrounded by Janus' old and heavily bearded aspect (it is possible that the whole façade of the building was a great face, with the door as its mouth) and leaving by an opposite door symbolising his reborn aspect. Like all fertility gods, he was associated with both peace and war: as we have so often seen, the chill battle front of winter must be broken with the help of symbolical wars before the planting can begin, yet there can be no plenty without peace. For this reason even the tiniest quarrel was avoided on the first day of the year, and the Italians of old went out of their way to be kind and cheerful. So long as Rome was at war Janus' temple was never closed, in token perhaps of the Roman view that every war constituted a symbolic quarrel with the powers of infertility. It may even be that soldiers leaving for the front marched through the fane, in at the old face and out at the young, and that perambulation of the temple by those who stayed behind was thought to help in bringing any war in which Rome was engaged to a successful end. It is interesting that Ganeśa, the elephant-headed god of India, pot-bellied and Falstaffian, is still invoked in his country, as Janus was in Rome, as a god of good beginnings, whether the enterprise be business or art or war; sometimes he is represented as double faced, one face being whiskered, the other baby-elephantine.

Other traditions about Janus held him to be the most ancient king of Rome raised to the status of a god, and he was said to have invited Saturn, the Kronos of Greek myth, to take refuge in Italy when overthrown by his son Zeus. In Greece Kronos was held to have been justly deposed and banished, but he was identified by the Romans, perhaps as a Hellenising gesture, with an old god of sowing and husbandry who was held to have presided over a now lost golden age of eternal summer, which the Romans sought to recover, at least symbolically, during the midwinter festival that preceded the celebration of Janus' opening of the new year. This, of course, was the famous Saturnalia, which lasted from 17 to 23 December, during which time there was an attempt to recreate conditions that were thought to have obtained when the joyous life in all men had its fullest and richest play.

On the first day of the Saturnalia, Saturn's own festival day, there was an outdoor banquet attended by senators and equites or knights – that is to say, the gentry of Rome – who laid aside their togas, if not for the animal skins believed to have been worn by Saturn and his frolicsome followers, at least for a loose-fitting and fringed gown called *synthesis*. After drinking and feasting they separated with the famous cry, "Io Saturnalia!" and then for a week school children had holidays, the law courts were closed, all work was stopped, war was suspended unless the enemy insisted on attacking, and no criminals were killed or punished.

This was clearly a celebration meant to stimulate by sympathetic magic the declining powers of the sun, now in his most pallid and decrepit phase, and to encourage the barren winter fields, along with wombs both human and animal, to ready themselves for the fructifying power soon to return as baby-faced Janus. Everybody was encouraged to drink and dance and grow hot with happiness, while celebrants gave each other presents of wax candles (*cerei*), lamps richly wrought, sometimes even in gold, dolls (*sigillaria*), and branches of evergreen, and gambled for nuts, considered a symbol of fruitfulness. Slaves were given all kinds of liberties if not liberty itself, and were entertained at feasts and served by their masters in remembrance of the absence of any differences of class or rank in the days of Saturn. Everyone, the heights and depths of society now being socially equated, was encouraged to shout and sing, eat and drink, dance and be happy, while slaves and children (groups customarily seen and not heard) had their day, and the whole community revelled in a great "dance of the god" calculated to rejuvenate everything that had grown grey, settled, fixed, rigid, sclerotic, conventional, chilly. Unfortunately Ovid, whose *Fasti* describes nearly all the major Roman feasts and customs, has not left us an account of the Saturnalia, while Lucian's is perhaps too highlighted for lifelikeness; we may nevertheless presume that from household to household the celebration was presided over by slaves

> who gave their orders and laid down the law as if they were invested
> with all the dignity of the consulship, the praetorship, and the bench.
> Like the pale reflection of power thus accorded to bondsmen at the
> Saturnalia was the mock-kingship for which free men cast lots at the
> same season. The person on whom the lot fell enjoyed the title of king
> and issued commands of a playful and ludicrous nature to his temporary
> subjects. One of them he might order to mix the wine, another to drink,
> another to sing, another to dance, another to speak in his own dispraise,
> another to carry a flute-girl on his back round the house.[13]

Sir James Frazer, from whom I have been quoting, was "tempted to surmise" that the Mock King who presided over the revels may have originally represented Saturn himself. It is just as conceivable that he represented

Janus, the reputed sponsor of Saturn in Italy, and that the whole celebration was symbolic of the process by which the ageing sun with the help of the whole population, conveyed by homoeopathy or sympathetic magic, danced his way from old age back to childhood. For the Old Sun, of course, this capering was a death-dance, and Frazer suggests that in ancient Rome, as well as in many other civilisations, the Mock King – identified with the Old Sun – may at one time have been actually slain in order that the remains of his strength should pass into the living representative of the New Sun. The latter figure need not necessarily have been a youngster, he points out, but simply the rightful king seeking to avoid death himself.

My concern in this chapter has been to throw whatever light I can on the possible meaning of Falstaff's deep conviction that he is both old and young at once, having been born with "a white head and something a round belly". This icon combines the Old Sun with the New in an immemorial image. This material of the chapter should throw some light, too, on the death-bed scene described by Dame Quickly. The stricken Old Sun merely fools with flowers and babbles of the green fields of his prime, but all the while he is giving birth – "the Old Man who renews his youth" – to a "christom child", a newborn baby whose look in its christening clothes is suggested as he dies by his great paunch heaving to stillness under the snow-white sheet. Quickly's description of Falstaff's death has always constituted something of a critics' mystery, and I am here suggesting that it can be explained, if magic can be explained at all, only in terms of a seasonal rite, a dramatic performance which is also a clerical mystery. Perhaps Falstaff is, across millenia in time and hundreds of miles in space, actual kin to the lovable Egyptian monster known as "the Old Man who renews his youth, the Aged One who maketh himself again a boy". Psychologists tell us that the human mind wherever found on the face of our planet shows an almost tiresome uniformity in formulating symbols or figures to illustrate the nature and value of the great human experiences, of which rebirth, whether of the body or the spirit, is perhaps the most fascinating.

I do not claim, of course, to know what *actually* lay behind and beneath Shakespeare's great creation; that, no one will ever know. I have merely tried to elucidate as well as I could the age-old folklore of the Young–Old god. That the clearest clue to Falstaff in this role lies in ancient Egyptian myth points to a homogeneity in the human spirit, an unperishable content in the human psyche, so remarkable that we are almost tempted to believe in what certain psychologists have called, referring of course to mankind, "the racial unconscious".

In the next chapter we shall continue to be concerned with this old–young, solar–feral, fighting–dancing tutor–friend of critically embarrassed young would-be sun-kings, stressing a facet of his prowess which was perhaps more highly developed in the religion and art of the Ancient Near East than in those of any other culture-complex.

V

Enkidu,

"the Town Bull" of Mesopotamia

In almost the very first words of the first scene in which we meet Shakespeare's Falstaff, we hear of his sexual prowess.

> *Fal.:*   Now, Hal, what time of day is it, lad?
> *Prince:*   ... What a devil hast thou to do with the time of day? Unless hours were cups of sack and minutes capons and clocks the tongues of bawds and dials the signs of leaping-houses and the blessed sun itself a fair hot wench in flame-coloured taffeta, I see no reason why thou should'st be so superfluous to demand the time of the day.

In other parts of the Henry plays, chiefly *1 Henry IV*, III, iii, as well as in *The Merry Wives of Windsor*, Falstaff admits to having some little capacity in the sexual line, as where he says to Bardolph, "Come sing me a bawdy song; make me merry. [In my better days] I was as virtuously given as a gentleman need be ... swore little, dic'd not above seven times a week, went to a bawdy-house not above once in a quarter – of an hour ...". Though Silenos and Bes, the two Falstaffian figures we have considered so far, were Great Lovers and frequently appear in art with bulging phalli and surrounded by wild ithyphallic followers, I have found it desirable to attach our discussion of this aspect of the Falstaff-persona to the Mesopotamian figure of Enkidu, best known to us in the epic of *Gilgamesh*.

Gilgamesh seems to have been compiled from already ancient stories and ballads of Sumer about 2000 B.C. and translated into Babylonian about 1700 B.C. We know it chiefly from the last of a long series of redactions in a New

Babylonian text dating from about 700 B.C., supplemented by such odds and ends of the Old Babylonian and Sumerian versions as have survived. Two or three good translations of the conflated pieces exist, the most quotable being perhaps that by William E. Leonard, made from Hermann Ranke's German version as *Gilgamesh: Epic of Old Babylonia*. I shall use it in the following discussion.*

Enkidu varies a little from Silenos and Bes insofar as his relation to Gilgamesh is almost solely that of a protector and self-sacrificing friend, though the tutorial note can be detected too. Also, Gilgamesh is represented as an anointed monarch rather than simply as a would-be sun-king; but when the epic begins his subjects, like those of the typical stricken father of the prince-with-a-wild-tutor, are being oppressed in typical fashion while the land itself has become barren. It is clear that Gilgamesh cannot without help bring peace and plenty to his city of Uruk (the Biblical Ur of the Chaldees). Gigantic, mighty, and handsome as he was – two-thirds of him, it is said, was divine, but one-third, which seems to have been too much for everyone's good, was merely human – he needs to be helped and taught and even died for by a creature whose:

> Whole body was shaggy with hair,
> Hair he bore on his head like a woman,
> The plenty of his hair sprouted like grain.
> He knew naught of [town?] life and people,
> He was clothed like the god of the herds.
> With the gazelles he eats the plants,
> With the wild beasts he drinks at the watering-place,
> With the throng at the water he makes glad his heart.[1]

This weaponless monster is for all his uncouthness called "a hero, a glorious scion" by Aruru, "she the great goddess" who moulded Enkidu for this crisis by pinching up some clay and spitting on it.

---

*The interested reader should not overlook:

(1) W.E. Leonard, *Gilgamesh* (New York, 1934); Leonard gives the wild creature's name as "Engidu".

(2) M. Jastrow and A.T. Clay, *An Old Babylonian Version of the Gilgamesh Epic* (New Haven, 1920);

(3) S.N. Kramer, *Sumerian Mythology: a Study of Spiritual and Literary Achievement in the Third Millenium B.C.* (Philadelphia, 1944), which contains a partial translation with interpretation;

(4) A. Heidel, *The Gilgamesh Epic, an Old Testament Parallel* (Chicago, 1946);

(5) S. Langdon, *Babylonian Wisdom* (London, 1923) and *Semitic Mythology* (Boston, 1931);

(6) T. Jacobsen, "Mesopotamia", *The Intellectual Adventure of Ancient Man* (Chicago, 1946).

All interpretations advanced so far seem to me inadequate to account for the genesis, acts, and fascination of the figure of Enkidu.

We are not told that Enkidu was particularly fat, but with his animal traits, his hair like grain, and his hirsute figure we seem clearly to be in the presence of a Near Eastern Silenos or Bes. Like them he may be assumed to have come from an oppressed and conquered people and to be the representative of a deposed royal line descending straight from a hairy totemic father who was himself an avatar of the sun. Only Enkidu can teach Gilgamesh the secrets of the life more abundant and help him to fight the internal dissension, cold, and flood that rack his kingdom. In the usual seasonal battle he receives, while protecting his pupil–friend, an injury from which he later dies. From this point on the Gilgamesh story, which if it followed the usual pattern would show the now instructed and strengthened king winning a second great battle entirely on his own, takes a turn practically unknown in any other version of the pupil–teacher myth. Heartbroken and frightened by the death of his friend, Gilgamesh seeks to achieve immortality only to learn that even a ferally initiated sun-king must himself suffer a decline and undergo in age a death necessary for the good of his land and people. Perhaps, however, we can look on this unusual part of the Gilgamesh story as a direct continuation of the fertility-education into which Enkidu had initiated his friend:

> All things he [Gilgamesh] saw, even to the ends of the earth,
> He underwent all, learned to know all;
> He peered through all secrets,
> Through wisdom's mantle that veileth all.[2]

Had Enkidu taught him to foresee his inevitable collapse and the need to find additional monster-victims to help his dynasty battle against the always encroaching waste?

Perhaps we do not really possess icons of Enkidu, but there is in Mesopotamian art a figure, occurring again and again, which has been widely identified by students of Near Eastern archaeology and literature with our Lord of Beasts. The Gilgamesh story does not tell us specifically that Enkidu had, like this figure, bull's legs, a bull's tail, and what Falstaff would have hailed as a "bull's pizzle", or that he had a round belly and a smiling face, bearded and topped with curly hair and bull's horns. Mesopotamian art has, however, convinced us that he had. Of all the Falstaffian figures, his is perhaps the most consistently ithyphallic and the episode of his loves with Ishtar or her priestess holds a place of great importance near the beginning of the poem.

Gilgamesh first hears of Enkidu when a hunter reports to him that a strange, bestial creature is protecting animals by filling up the pits dug by the hunter and destroying the traps he has laid. At the advice, apparently, of his divine mother Ninsun, who is looking for a protector for her son, Gilgamesh sends a sacred prostitute, a priestess or avatar of Ishtar, to lure the monster away from his wild companions and bring him to the city. This luring is a seduction, and this seduction more like a ceremonial testing of Enkidu's sexual prowess than a mere device for enticing him from the hills and forests.

It appears that peace and abundance for the land depend, in the first place, on the Falstaffian figure's potency. Accordingly, when the priestess saw him, "the great strong one, /The wild fellow, the man of the steppes", she

> loosened her buckle,
> Unveiled her delight, for him to take his fill of her.
> She hung not back, she took up his lust,
> She opened her robe that he rest upon her.
> She aroused in him rapture, the work of woman.
> His bosom pressed against her.
> Enkidu forgot where he was born.
> For six days and seven nights
> Was Enkidu given over to love with the priestess.[3]

After this apparently lost week, Enkidu, now estranged from his animal followers of the Boar's Head pond, was easily persuaded by the priestess, who kept exclaiming, "Enkidu, how beautiful thou, how like a god!"[4] to return with her to Gilgamesh at ramparted Uruk. There the people, adorned with fillets, were keeping a great feast for the proper celebration of which Enkidu was desperately needed. During the days of Enkidu's orgy with the priestess, Gilgamesh seems to have been dreaming of the arrival of help in the form of a divine statue from heaven or a shining axe, both of which in dreams he had gathered close, like a woman, in his arms. These dreams his goddess mother, "the lady Ninsun, who knows all", had interpreted to mean the imminent arrival of a strong man,

> Who was born in the steppes, and whom the hills reared. ...
> A comrade who rescues his friend.
> His power will be strong in the land,
> And mighty as an axe will be his strength.[5]

Having conducted Enkidu safely to Uruk, the priestess

> stripped off the one of her robes,
> And clothed him therewith;
> In the other robe she herself remained clad.
> She took him by the hand
> And led him like a bridegroom
> To a festal meal at a pinfold ...[6]

Now Enkidu ruled the roast like a Substitute King. When bread was set before him and wine, the bestial one, accustomed to eat plants with the gazelles and suck the milk of wild creatures, was bewildered but soon learned to take the advice of the sacred Tearsheet:

> Then Enkidu ate bread till he was full,
> Then he drank wine seven beakers.
> His spirit loosed itself,
> He grew merry,

His heart rejoiced and his face glowed ...
He anointed himself with oil, and became like a noble,
He put on a robe and was then as a bridegroom.
He took his weapon, he attacked lions,
So that the great shepherds found rest at night,
For Enkidu was their safeguard ...[7]

No wonder the people loved him. In addition, though this is not said in so many words, the farmers of the fields about Uruk now began to sleep better too, safe in the knowledge that this extraordinary creature's bountiful love passages with the priestess of Ishtar were just the thing to guarantee rising rivers and the growth of the soil.

It seems to me that we can hardly fail to recognise (though it has not, so far as I know, been recognised hitherto) that the feasting of Enkidu corresponds to a Babylonian–Persian festival called the Sacaea. We do not know much about this festival, but it resembled in spirit and in certain details the Roman Saturnalia. Unlike the Saturnalia, however, it was not so much a New Year's celebration as a festival held yearly to forestall or neutralise all yearly fertility crises. Sir James Frazer describes and comments on it as follows:

> it would appear that in remote times, though not within the historical period, the kings of Babylon or their barbarous predecessors forfeited not merely their crown but their life at the end of a year's tenure of office. At least this is the conclusion to which the following evidence seems to point. According to the historian Berosus, who as a Babylonian priest spoke with ample knowledge, there was annually celebrated in Babylon a festival called the Sacaea. It began on the sixteenth day of the month Louis, and lasted for five days during which masters and servants changed places, the servants giving orders and the masters obeying them. A prisoner condemned to death was dressed in the king's robes, seated on the king's throne, allowed to issue whatever commands he pleased, to eat, drink, and enjoy himself, and to lie with the king's concubines. But at the end of the five days he was stripped of his royal robes, scourged, and hanged or impaled. ... Considering the jealous seclusion of an oriental despot's harem, we may be quite certain that permission to invade it would never have been granted by the despot, least of all to a condemned criminal, except for the very gravest cause. This cause could hardly be other than that the condemned man was about to die in the king's stead, and that to make the substitution perfect it was necessary he should enjoy the full rights of royalty during his brief reign. There is nothing surprising in this substitution. The rule that the king [i.e., the so-called Divine King whose sexual potence encouraged by homeopathy the fertility-efforts of the soil] must be put to death either on the appearance of any symptom of bodily decay or at the end of a fixed period is certainly one which, sooner or later, the kings would seek to abolish or modify.[8]

No more than Gilgamesh, of course, could such a king prolong his life for ever. However, we are not concerned here with Gilgamesh's frantic quest for immortality after the death of his friendly substitute, but with Enkidu's death itself. This took place in our story not through hanging or impaling but according to the later (earlier?) pattern of this festival in which the criminal–tutor helped his pupil–friend to win a battle against an atrocious incarnation of bad weather called Khumbaba (Sumerian: Kuwawa), the mere vision of whom in dreams so frightened Gilgamesh that he would have abandoned the attempt to kill him had he not been cheered on by Enkidu. When this fright opened its mouth,

> The heavens shrieked,
> The earth bellowed,
> Storms gathered,
> Darkness came forth,
> A flash flamed,
> A fire shot up,
> The clouds thickened,
> It rained death.[9]

The fight with Khumbaba is clearly a seasonal-crisis conflict which the brutish teacher helps his charge to bring to a successful conclusion. Sometimes the tutor saves the pupil's life at the expense of his own, as seems to have happened here, for after the battle Enkidu's strength wanes until, with his death, his last energies pass into Gilgamesh. As I have said, this old epic differs from other forms of the myth in adding material about the pupil's quest for immortal life, but we are not here concerned with anything but the miraculous lovemaking of the friendly teacher.

That by sympathetic or homeopathic magic the lovemaking of people should be held able to stimulate the growth of the soil illustrates a form of primitive thinking which is not entirely incomprehensible to those who pondered for centuries the concepts of microcosm, macrocosm, and their intimate relations. Such difficulties as arise are made easy when we remember that the passionate couple were usually considered divine; were, that is to say, a Divine or Substitute King, held to be a descendant of the sun through a line deriving from an avatar or incarnation on earth of that hot luminary in animal form, and a Divine Queen or priestess, considered a descendant of the earth goddess through a lineage deriving from a woman born straight from a furrow. In the mating of the Divine King with his Queen or, at a later period, in that of the brutish Substitute King, recalled by a conquering monarch from forest hiding to play this part, with the true king's wife or concubine, or with a priestess in whom the earth goddess was thought to be incarnate, religious faith is called into play and poetic symbolism appears at its most powerful.

Enkidu's iconographic relation to the sun is shown in many ways but foremost, of course, in his bull traits. Everyone has heard of the Apis bull of Egypt in whose relations with his naked female caretakers the fertilising sun-power was strikingly if obscurely symbolised, of Zeus who in bull form abducted Europa, of the Cretan bull-god who coupled with Queen Pasiphaë, and of the bullish representative of Dionysos who made love to the Athenian archon's wife in the *bukolion*. Traditionally, there are three ways in which an animal avatar of the sun like Enkidu (if the bull–man of Near Eastern seals is really he) can be represented in art: either as the animal itself, in which case semi-human features and a very handsome beard are often added unto him; as a man with a bull's head, a form of the Mesopotamian hero which approximates the figure of the Minotaur found on Cretan coins; and, finally, as a more thorough combination of man and beast, that is to say, as a bull-horned man with the animal's legs and sexual member, the form in which Enkidu is most commonly represented on the cylinder seals of the Near East.*

Sometimes we see this figure in his half-man, half-bull shape standing before the goddess, who is lifting her dress to attract him, as the priestess unrobed before Enkidu in the poem. On one cylinder seal we see the bull–man, doubled for heraldic effect – that is, split into twins, one on either side of the goddess – helping her lift her dress. Another shows the bull–man (here his bearded profile seems much more animal than human) making overtures to the goddess, who is at this point of the story still fully clothed; she seems to be amusing herself by juggling with the seven stars so character-istic of Ishtar in what may be called a diversionary action. On this entertaining seal, dating from about 2000 B.C., the figures are all done in an elongated style which diminishes our hero's usually prominent stomach. This same seal shows a proper bull, perhaps Enkidu in another form, who seems to be carrying on his back an elongated object which Frankfort calls a shrine, but which could very well pass for a gate or door, and might just as easily be the Gate of Heaven as the gate of a temple. Thus the bull-figure may stand for the sun itself, it seems to me, for the Gate or Gates of Heaven were often equated with clouds through which the sun had to break – which it had to carry off – before it could begin its daily shining. On two other cylinders a similar portal borne on the back of a bull seems clearly to

---

*Dozens of fine reproductions of bas-relief and cylinder-seal figures of all these kinds may be found in:

(1) H. Gressmann, *Alt Orientalische Texte und Bilde zum Alten Testament*, v. ii (Berlin and Leipzig, 1927);
(2) H. Frankfort, *Cylinder Seals: A Documentary Essay on the Art and Religion of the Ancient Near East* (London, 1939);
(3) E. Porada, *Mesopotamian Art in Cylinder Seals of the Pierpoint Morgan Library* (New York, 1947); and
(4) H.T. Bossert, *Altsyrien: Kunst und Handwerk* (Tubingen, 1951).

Most of these books contain illustrations by the hundred, and the last one contains 1,417 figures of ancient Near Eastern art, many of which have never appeared in a book before. Most of these books are invaluable not only for figures of the bull-man but also for several of Bes as he came to be known and loved in the Near East.

represent clouds, for rays flame out on either side of it, once in the form of wings. On these seals (reproduced by Frankfort) the great bull, bearing the Gates of Heaven on his back, kneels captive at the goddess's feet. On one she is represented holding him by one horn and binding him with a leafy vine suggestive of green withes. On the other she is holding the bull at her knees by a rope passed through his nose while a priest, standing behind the bull, is about to plunge a dagger into its back. Both these seal pictures indicate that the mating of the bull or bull–man with the goddess or priestess is over and that the time has come for his ritual slaughter.

It is no wonder, perhaps, that Enkidu, having enjoyed his day or week ("six days and seven nights") as much-fêted Substitute King and overfed lover of the goddess-surrogate, came in the old epic to the point of cursing Ishtar. He attributed to her, it seems, rather than to Gilgamesh the fate which came upon him as Mock Monarch destined not merely to maul the priestess but also, at the height of the crisis, to force the portals of darkness or vanquish bellowing Khumbaba. Perhaps he performed both these tasks at the same time – and by the same superhuman effort. In tablet seven of the Gilgamesh story, he seems to attribute his death to a gate or door,

> "Two and seventy ells is thy height,
> Four and twenty ells is thy breadth,"[10]

set in the palisade-like fortress in which the storm-black monster was hiding. The text is imperfect, and we are not told that he lifted the gate from before the sun, bearing it off on his back, but only that he handled it in some way which left him mysteriously weak unto death:

> "Had I known, thou door,
> That this would come to pass,
> And that beauty would bring this disaster,
> I had lifted the axe and shattered all of you!"[11]

Dying, he curses the priestess who had entrapped him, praying that the outcast and unmanned may smite her on the cheeks because she lured him from his fields and forests. Hearing this blasphemy, Shamash, the sun-god – perhaps the very deity whose life-force has been renewed by Enkidu's sacrifice – calls to him from heaven:

> "Why, O Enkidu, beshrewest thou the priestess?
> She who gave thee dishes to eat
> Such as beseem a god only?
> She who gave thee wine to drink
> Such as beseems a king only?
> She who clothed thee in a gorgeous robe,
> And gave thee the glorious Gilgamesh for friend? ...
> He maketh thee to dwell on a bed well-prepared,
> To dwell in a quiet dwelling-place ...
> The princes of the earth kiss thy feet.

He maketh for thee
The people of ramparted Uruk to weep,
To sorrow for thee.
Much people he maketh to serve thee.
Himself after thy death will put on mourning ..."[12]

A passage like this seems to suggest that the Substitute King could be almost as honoured in his ritual death as in his days of ritual splendour if he had a Gilgamesh rather than Hal for his friend.

Enkidu, however, cannot perfectly reconcile himself to having been tricked into playing this tragic role by the merry priestess who tweaked his horns in the spring and taught him to "piss his tallow" beneath the trees. Broken by contact with the gate and the strenuous victory over Khumbaba,

Enkidu lies stricken;
For one day,
For a second day,
Enkidu suffers pain in his bed.
For a third day,
And a fourth,
Enkidu lies stricken.
For a fifth, a sixth, and a seventh,
For an eighth, a ninth, and a tenth day,
Enkidu lies in his bed ...
He calls Gilgamesh and speaks:
"A god hath cursed me, my friend."[13]

Such a passage makes one wonder whether the Mock King of the Sacaea died a prolonged death in order to save the real king, or whether we have here merely a symbolic description of the slow demise of the Old Sun during the twelve days following the winter battle – the twelve-day period which witnesses the New Sun slowly taking a firm hold on his kingdom as the dying tutor's strength (such is the mythologem) passes into him. Is this scene to be understood as an early form of the post-solstice celebration, on the last night of which (Twelfth Night), the darkness-danger having been definitely overcome, the young or rejuvenated king can grasp back his full power and prerogatives while his friend dies "at midnight, just at the turning of the tide"? Is this ancient death-bed scene to be compared with that of Falstaff on the "bed well-prepared" of the tavern?

Echoes of the Near Eastern seasonal festival adumbrated in the Gilgamesh story can be found, it seems to me, in half a dozen Biblical tales of plump, "ruddy", "hairy" figures such as Esau but most notably, perhaps, in the story of Samson. For centuries the mythical nature of the Samson story has been recognised, but the first serious attempt to treat the various legendary and symbolic problems involved was that of H. Steinthal.[14] The Hebrew form of Samson's name, Shimshon, had long been derived from Shimsh or Shemesh, meaning sun, and On, meaning god – just as Dag, meaning fish, was combined with On to make the name of the merman god of the Philistines. If Samson was not the sun-god himself, he was at least a solar hero, that is to say, a lineal descendant who, though fallen on evil days, could play the role of Substitute King in seasonal crises. It has often been pointed out that Samson's adventures set him quite apart from other judges such as Barak, Gideon, and Jephthah. In fact, he does not seem to belong in a Hebrew setting and his continual running away to Philistia suggests that he too felt the incongruity of his position. His story may, in fact, represent an awkward Hebrew attempt to understand and appropriate for patriotic purposes a series of popular Philistine icons telling an Enkidu story of heroism and sacrifice.

The first thing one notes is that Samson acts always with clearly supernatural force, his achievements being miraculous from beginning to end.

> In spite of this, Samson's action is not only destitute of any proper result, but also – what is more significant and far worse – devoid of even the consciousness of any aim, devoid of plan or idea. He – Samson the Nazarite consecrated to God! – looks for wives and mistresses among his own and his people's enemies. He teases, irritates, injures his enemies, and kills many of them. But there appears nowhere the consciousness of any mission which he had to fulfil for the good of his native land against his enemies. He is inspired by no idea of Jahveh, driven forward by no impatience of a shameful yoke. He is roused only by pleasures of the senses and the caprice of insolence. Samson is utterly immoral. He is exactly an old heathen god ...[15]

I would go so far as to suppose that Samson in the beginning was not a Hebrew hero at all, but rather the chief figure in a Philistine seasonal rite, resembling Enkidu or the Substitute king of Mesopotamian festivals. Probably some kind of Sacaea was common throughout most of the Near East, and Samson may be the double of a Philistine Enkidu. Inasmuch as most of Samson's story takes place in Philistia, the Biblical account may be simply the sketchy libretto of a Philistine festival which the Hebrews adopted for seasonal-crisis performance in their own country. The powers of darkness would in that case be identified, somewhat ironically, with their Philistine enemies. Here, as in the Enkidu story, Samson with his long, uncut hair flaring around him (did it, like Enkidu's, reach to his waist?) killed a lion with his bare hands in order to give the shepherds rest at night and sought to help the farmers to better crops by sun ceremonies and ritual lovemaking with a Goddess-persona, variously represented by his wife from Timnath, a harlot of Gaza, and the wondrous Delilah. Delilah must have been, at the very least, a priestess of Ashtaroth, the Philistine Ishtar, and as such corresponds perfectly to the priestess who captured Enkidu.

In Judges 14:20 it is said that Samson's Philistine wife was taken from him and given to a mysterious person mentioned only at this point in the story: "his companion, whom he had used as his friend". This is the only evidence still remaining in the tale that Samson had a friend or pupil whom by his tremendous feats he was both teaching and defending. It is unnecessary to dwell on his ritual lovemaking and on the great seasonal battle in which, probably protecting his mysterious friend, he slew a thousand enemies with the jawbone of an ass. The nature of Samson's weapon suggests that his animal associations were not so much with the bull as with, perhaps, the ass, i.e., the dangerous onager or wild ass that seems clearly to have been the divine sun-animal of the Moabites and which, tamed, was the royal creature on which at a later date the kings of Israel rode to and from their coronations. If we had Hebrew cylinder seals, we would probably find an onager rather than a bull flirting with the goddess and bearing on its back that great gate of Gaza "with its two posts" which Samson carried on his shoulders. Only Samson, the sun-hero, rescuing his heavenly relative from behind the cloud gates, can account for the stress laid on this distinctly peculiar incident. Or so I think.

And now, the priestesses being thoroughly loved, the children of darkness slaughtered en masse, and the great sun released from its prison, Samson himself was for the dark. Delilah's role in "betraying" him to his sacrificers helps a little, I think, to explain Enkidu's resentment of Ishtar and her priestess. In this cognate story the priestess not only enticed the powerful wild man into his back-breaking exploit but periodically tested his declining strength by binding him, as he slept on her knees, with ropes and "green withes that were never dried" (Judges 16:7), as on the cylinder seals I have described. Finally, his magic halo of hair having shrunk (?), Delilah delivered him to the prison-house, followed him for the last rites and let him die embracing her sacred asherah. It may be that in Philistia, or even Mesopotamia, the Substitute King, having successfully helped the real sun and the real king through the seasonal ordeal, was sometimes blinded, shorn of his flaming hair, and made to grind a little symbolical corn in the dark prison-house, into which he descended for the good of the land. Shades of Falstaff's incarceration in the Fleet!

The populace may even have made sport of him when he was brought from the prison to re-enact his most fabulous feat – the stealing of the gates. And it is even possible that a priest plunged a dagger into the Mock King as, covered in the divine-animal skin, he bowed his back for the last time to bear away the double hinge-posts – "they set him between [below?] the pillars". If this is what happened, we must assume the icon that recorded his end was fancifully interpreted by the Hebrews to bolster their national pride. There was no slaughter of Philistines but Samson's mysterious "companion", endowed with the reversion of his vigour and his wife, harlot, or sacerdotal concubine (I suppose all three Philistine women to have been forms of the same ceremonial figure) may, like Hal at Agincourt, have slain more enemies of light after his death than Samson slew in his lifetime.

It must be admitted that these Near Eastern Falstaffs hardly seem, from the fragments of their stories which have come down to us, to have been exactly jovial, but Samson does display a wild and overweening sense of humour in the riddles he propounds and the vengeful practical jokes he plays, as when he ties pairs of foxes together by their tails with "a firebrand in the midst" to burn up the corn (a typical prank of a sun-surrogate gone berserk?). He is a great boaster and, we must suppose, an enormous eater and drinker, though as a Nazarite he would have been forbidden wine. It is supposed by many Biblical scholars that Samson's Nazaritism is a late addition to the story, introduced to account for the fact that he enjoyed a great halo of hair and beard. When we remember that Nazarites were vowed to abstinence not only from wine but also from women, this supposition seems highly likely. The very scribe who sought to account for Samson's uncut hair by declaring that he had been brought up "a Nazarite to God from the womb" recognised the impossibility of squaring his acts with the ascetic rules of that elite, and made the angel to whom Samson's father prayed for clear advice on the boy's upbringing refuse to prescribe for this hero any rules of self-control. This angelic advice practically left Samson where he must have begun – a Philistine mock-king figure not a little resembling Enkidu.

In the light of what we have been able to puzzle out about the sexual ceremonies of the Near Eastern Sacaea or renewal celebration, the scenes between Falstaff and Doll Tearsheet in the Boar's Head Tavern may surely now be allowed a new dimension of significance. Here too we have a form of public lovemaking carried on between two creatures who are actually compared to a Lord of Misrule and to the prostitute–priestess of a pagan goddess. Falstaff's page calls the roisterers at the Boar's Head "Ephesians ... of the old church," a phrase of some obscurity which seems to make Hal think of the multiple-breasted Diana of Ephesus, for he immediately says:

> *Prince:* Sup any women with him?
>
> *Page:* None, my lord, but old Mistress Quickly and Mistress Doll Tearsheet.
>
> *Prince:* What pagan may that be?
>
> *Page:* A proper gentlewoman, sir, and a kinswoman of my master's.
>
> *Prince:* Even such kin as the parish heifers are to the town bull. ... From a God to a bull? A heavy descension! It was Jove's case.[16]

During the revel at the Boar's Head, accompanied by music and dancing, Mistress Doll, as we know, compares her meaty old lover to a boar more often than to a bull, but the import of both comparisons was much the same: from the ancient Near East to India and China and back to Europe the fat boar was popular as a sun symbol, as we have seen in the *varaha* avatar of Visnu and shall see in certain Falstaff-personae to come. For all her rough ignorance, Doll has a certain glibness in comparing Falstaff to mighty mythic characters, some of whom carried either the boar or bull as cognisance.

> *Doll:* ... Come on, you whoreson chops. Ah, rogue! I' faith, I love thee. Thou art as valorous as Hector of Troy, worth five of Agamemnon and ten times better than the Nine Worthies. Ah [referring to Pistol, whom Falstaff has just driven from the inn] villain!
>
> *Fal.:* A rascally slave! I will toss the rogue in a blanket.
>
> *Doll:* Do, an thou dar'st for thy heart. An thou dost, I'll canvass thee between a pair of sheets. (*Enter music.*)
>
> *Page:* The music is come, sir.
>
> *Fal.:* Let them play. Play, sirs. Sit on my knee, Doll. A rascal, bragging slave! The rogue fled me like quicksilver.
>
> *Doll:* I' faith, and thou follow'dst him like a church. Thou whoreson little tidy Bartholomew boar-pig, when wilt thou leave fighting o' days and foining o'nights, and begin to patch up thine old body for heaven? (*Enter, behind, Prince Henry and Poins disguised as drawers.*)
>
> *Fal.:* Peace, good Doll! Do not speak like a death's head. Do not bid me remember mine end. ...
>
> *Poins:* Let's beat him before his whore.
>
> *Prince:* Look whe'er the wither'd elder hath not his poll claw'd like a parrot. ...
>
> *Fal.:* Kiss me, Doll.
>
> *Prince:* Saturn and Venus this year in conjunction! ...
>
> *Fal.:* Thou dost give me flattering busses.
>
> *Doll:* By my troth, I kiss thee with a most constant heart. ...
>
> *Fal.:* I am sad, I am old.
>
> *Doll:* I love thee better than ever I love e'er a scurvy young boy of them all.
>
> *Fal.:* A merry song, come! It grows late; we'll to bed ...
>
> *Prince:* Why, thou globe of sinful continents, what a life dost thou lead![17]

In the absence of actual libretti describing the love-play of the Near Eastern Mysteries, perhaps we may be allowed to imagine them as not very different from those scenes at the Boar's Head in which a fat, bearded creature, comparable to nothing so much as the lord of the Saturnalia himself, sports in the face of imminent death with a brutalised Venus or Ishtar, while his pupil, the prince for whose benefit this performance is being staged, looks on. Falstaff realises only too clearly that he is playing the part of a victim, whether he is being compared to a bull, a boar, or, as in *The*

Merry Wives of Windsor, a stag representative of the sun, whose immeasurable heat and unencompassable shape he so nearly embodies. Perhaps we may even be allowed to transfer to the Boar's Head setting a few lines from *The Merry Wives*:

> *Fal.:*   Now the hot-blooded gods assist me!
> Remember, Jove, thou wast a bull for thy Europa; love set on thy horns. Oh, powerful love! That in some respects, makes a beast a man, in some other, a man a beast. ... For me I am here a Windsor stag ... Send me a cool rut time, Jove, or who can blame me to piss my tallow? (*Enter Mistress Ford and Mistress Page.*)
>
> *Mrs. Ford:*   Sir John! Art thou there, my deer? My male deer? ...
>
> *Fal.:*   Divide me like a brib'd buck, each a haunch.[18]

No one but Falstaff seems to understand that in his lovemaking he is rendering his country an indispensable service in the form of a sacrifice almost mystic. Sometimes he complains a little, but never fails to embrace his fate: "As I am a true spirit, welcome!" That is, a true fertility spirit, a lord of love and father of increase, bound to woo "both high and low, both rich and poor, / Both young and old, one with another"[19]. At least, this is the view taken by one of those with whom his name is scandalously connected, Dame Quickly, mistress of the Boar's Head in the *Henry* plays but in *The Merry Wives* a mysterious servant who can most beautifully preside as the Fairy Queen, the English descendant of the earth goddess, over Falstaff's sun-stag persecution beneath the great oak.

That the murderous and impotent "singing man of Windsor", Henry IV, fails to appreciate him, Falstaff takes for granted, and perhaps he even foresees that his pupil, having grown with Falstaff's help into a potent solar prince, will himself soon reject him, cast him into prison, and indeed bring about his death.

But this is the very prospect which it is the Mock King's duty to laugh off, and we must pass on, now, to another side of his activity – to Gargantuan laughter itself, especially as it is directed against Old Father Antic the law in witty tirades which furnish a cascading accompaniment to cruel tricks and ritual robbery.

VI

Abu Zayd of Islam,

Who Thumbed His Nose at "Old Father Antic the Law"

In the very first scene in which we meet Falstaff, he is planning a robbery and begging Hal, when the latter will have become king, to tear down all gallows and no longer permit "resolution" to be "fobb'd as it is with the rusty curb of old father antic the law. Do not thou, when thou art king, hang a thief."[1] When the prince adroitly refuses to commit himself on this point, Falstaff recalls that in order to get Hal properly educated, he has had to put up with a good deal in the way of scorn and rebuke from certain self-styled pillars of the state, who are as slippery as Hal himself in making what is essentially right and necessary appear corrupt and wrong.

> *Fal.:* An old lord of the council rated me the other day in the street about you, sir, but I mark'd him not; and yet he talk'd very wisely, but I regarded him not; and yet he talk'd wisely, and in the street too.

> *Prince:* Thou didst well; for wisdom cries out in the streets and no man regards it.

> *Fal.:* O, thou hast damnable iteration and art indeed able to corrupt a saint. Thou hast done much harm upon me, Hal; God forgive thee for it! Before I knew thee, Hal, I knew nothing; and now am I, if a man should speak truly, little better than one of the wicked. I must give over this life, and I will give it over. By the Lord, an I do not, I am a villain. I'll be damned for never a king's son in Christendom.

> *Prince:* Where shall we take a purse to-morrow, Jack?

Fal.: 'Zounds, where thou wilt, lad; I'll make one. An I do not, call me villain. ...

Prince: I see a good amendment of life in thee; from praying to purse-taking.

Fal.: Why, Hal, 'tis my vocation, Hal. 'Tis no sin for a man to labour at his vocation.[2]

This exchange between the prince and his tutor makes clear that Falstaff's wisdom, if such it be, is not the wisdom of this world. As this world goes, the old lord of the council had indeed talked wisely, and Falstaff pretends to have been more than half-convinced that it is foolish of him, if not wicked, to persevere in dangerous acts which go unappreciated. Even the "most comparative, rascallious, sweet young prince" seemed for a moment to be going to try to discourage him from the performance of his favourite evening rite, his midnight voluntary. Now for Falstaff to have given over cadging and stealing would have been a real corruption of the duties of the office to which he had been called. It would have been to admit that the topsy-turvy values of the world do not need to be set upright by being themselves subverted. A conversion to this world's conventions is the mortal danger in which Falstaff's vocation, and with it his country's good, is put through his constant association with an apparently inept pupil. Like any serious teacher who is making no headway, he seriously thinks of giving up the student! Just at this point, however, the prince changes his tune, begging his old friend to carry out the purse-lifting.

To controvert a country's laws in the name of real justice for the people, as in the story of Absalom, seems to have been a sacred duty for the Mock King of the Sacaea, for his fellow of the Saturnalia, and for the Lords of Misrule, the fool-Kings of the Middle Ages, as well as for Father Christmas in the Mummers' Play. Stealing was simply a striking way in which the Mock King laboured at his calling, dramatising the essential injustice of the world's values and sacrosanct judges by thumbing his nose at law codes and converting the tenets of the so-called wise. On looking over the Falstaff-personae I have collected to see which exemplifies this "calling" of the Mock King most interestingly, I find none better qualified to demonstrate its practice and explain its true inwardness than another Near Eastern figure, widely separated in time from Enkidu but perhaps not entirely unrelated in spirit and religious lineage. I have in mind Abu Zayd, ostensibly the creation of the eleventh- and twelfth-century Muslim poet al-Hariri of Basra, but actually a figure with roots deep in Near Eastern folklore and myth. Why this aspect of the Falstaff-persona should have been rather more highly stressed in the medieval Near East than elsewhere I do not know, unless it was because the Semitic tendency to multiply laws was bound to stimulate a strong Islamic reaction (the Ten Commandments were elaborated into 655 offences punishable both here and in the hereafter, while the legalists of

Abu Zaid of Islam (Ms. Marsh 458, fol. 88v).

Islam often threatened to balloon simple directives of Muhammad into an equally heartbreaking burden of prohibitions).

This reaction was not only strong but deep, and al-Hariri's Abu Zayd has such a copious genealogy that certain of his forebears must be mentioned. One of the most famous of these is a mysterious figure immortalised in the eighteenth Sura of the Koran which is called "The Cave". Khadir (Khazir, Khidr, Khizr, Chidher, etc., meaning the Evergreen Man) is reputed to have been the vizier and friend of Dhoul Karnain (the Two-horned One), the name by which Muslims know Alexander the Great. The ram's horns with which the head of Alexander is decorated on certain coins and busts commemorate putative descent from Zeus-Ammon of Thebes in Egypt, and when we recall that Nonnos identified Dionysos, followed by his goatskinned army, with Alexander as the conqueror of a dark king of India, it is not hard, perhaps, to see in this Khadir a descendant of Silenos himself. In the Koran we are told nothing, of course, of his wine-bibbing, but he is nevertheless a great drinker, partaking so liberally of the Fountain of Life that the desert blossoms with flowers wherever he goes. And wander he will, for he is immortal and immortally bent on reproving in the light of his ancient wisdom lawmakers, lawgivers, lawyers, judges, policemen, censors, and all their tribe for their literal and envy-inspired interpretation, application, and multiplication of all statutes of limitation.

In the Koran it is told that Moses, searching for enlightenment, found Khadir by the Fountain of Life, an odd yet majestic figure known to God as "one of Our servants, whom We have clothed with Our grace and wisdom". Moses asked to be allowed to follow him through the world in order to gain insight. "Verily," said Khadir, "thou canst not have patience with me, for how can a man be patient in matters whose meaning he comprehendest not?" But Moses insisted, "Thou shalt find me patient if thou please, nor will I disobey thy bidding." Then said Khadir, "Ask me not of aught that may happen until I choose to give thee an account thereof." Hereupon they set out on a mysterious journey through the puzzling press of a myriad-faceted world. But Moses, who was after all a professional lawgiver himself, and of God's law at that, simply could not refrain from questioning and reproving Khadir's every act. True, Khadir did strange things such as staving in the side of a boat in which he and Moses were travelling, and setting upright a tottering wall without demanding pay for it. To Moses these acts seemed like attempted murder of the boat's crew and wilful self-robbery, for he and Khadir were in need of cash. After bearing several of Moses' reproofs, all inspired by a hopelessly literal interpretation of law, Khadir explained his acts: the vessel, he said, had "belonged to poor men who toiled upon the sea, and I was minded to damage it, for in their rear was a king who seized every sound ship by force", while "as to the wall, it belonged to two orphan youths in the city, and beneath it was their treasure: and their father was a righteous man: and thy Lord desired that they should reach the age of strength and take forth their treasure through the mercy of thy Lord. And not of mine own will have I done this. This is the interpretation of that which thou couldst not bear with patience."[3] Having made clear that the will of God is frequently frustrated rather than furthered by a strict adherence to what are called His commands, Khadir dismisses Moses as a stiff-necked and unteachable person to whom he cannot play the role of friend and tutor.

This episode in the Koran has given rise in Islam to a whole literature in which Moses is taken to task by Khadir or God himself for an unimaginative attempt to codify His will, whether in the primary commandments or the six hundred-odd laws of Deuteronomy. Actually, civil–religious law suffered from considerable hypertrophy among the Muslims themselves, which is perhaps the reason why these anti-Mosaic stories had such a vogue in Islam. Several are to be found in the poems of Rumi, and it was, ultimately, from a Muslim source that Benjamin Franklin derived his famous "Parable Against Persecution". In this, of course, the legalist appears as Abraham rather than Moses and the Teacher as God Himself, who condemns Abraham's seed to be afflicted in a strange land because the patriarch drives into the wilderness an idolatrous stranger who ignores the letter of the law.

In Muslim lore and literature, the deathless Khadir appears in various incarnations to reprove the legalism of Old Father Antic in the light of that true righteousness which alone can make body and soul, earth and heaven, flourish and put forth ever more lovely growths. The exact relation between Khadir and the figures I am about to mention is uncertain, but it is impossible not to recognise in them the unconventional blood of the mythical prime minister of Alexander the Great. To a man, they are advisers, entertainers, and reprovers of kings and sultans, and seem to have ancient Persia or Babylonia as their point of provenience. Sometimes the spirit of Khadir appears in a gross, hairy peasant who belittles the wisdom and decisions of Solomon himself; again, in a professional court jester who challenges the judgment and the judgments of the Khalif; or yet again, in an irrepressible beggar and thief who tempers his apparently outrageous conduct with sermons on love, Allah, and the purpose of life so moving that the lay genre to which his story – both for matter and manner – is assigned now ranks second only to the Koran. I refer, of course, to the *Maqamat* of al-Hariri, one of the most fascinating books in the world, whose scoundrelly hero Abu Zayd can stand as the *pièce de resistance* of this chapter. First, however, we must have some *hors d'oeuvres* in the persons of Marcolf, who plagued King Solomon; Buhlul-al-Madjnun, the jester-poet of the famous Harun-al-Rashid; and Nasr-ed-din Hodja, the popular buffoon-hero of all Islam.

Marcolf, a folk figure, seems to go far back before the time traditionally assigned to Khadir, but is in his scorn of Solomon's judgments a blood-relative of the Evergreen Man. A portrait of him which occurs in a Latin dialogue translated into English about 1492 begins:

> Upon a season heretofore as King Solomon, full of wisdom and riches, sat upon the king's seat or stool that was his father David's, he saw coming a man out of the east that was named Marcolphus, of visage greatly mis-shapen and foul; nevertheless, he was right talkative, eloquent, and wise.[4]

A possible original for the oafish yet wizardly wise Marcolf is perhaps to be found in Josephus' story of King Solomon and King Hiram of Tyre, who built the Temple. Between these two, says Josephus, sprang up a friendship based on their love of exchanging problems and enigmas for elucidation. In these wit encounters King Hiram was aided by a strange companion or familiar called Abdemon, "a very youth in age, who always conquered the difficult problems which Solomon, King of Jerusalem, commanded him to explain". Now Solomon, we know from Talmudic stories, needed for the building of the Temple not merely the help of Hiram but also that of the Prince of Demons Asmodeus, who may perhaps be identified with Hiram's wise young familiar Abdemon, especially when we recall that, according to the Talmud, Solomon, after binding Asmodeus with a chain bearing the name of God, was more interested in making the captive answer questions than in making him complete the Temple. When, in an unwary moment,

Solomon set Asmodeus free and gave him his magic ring, the prankster took the great King's place on the throne, dealt unconventional justice to his people, and revelled in his fabulous harem. This story contains echoes of the Sacaea festival and suggests perhaps that Solomon, in a lost legend, had shielded himself from divine-king death by providing himself with a witty substitute king. If there was a lost story of this kind, it would seem to have been the first one from the Near East in which the Mock King or Enkidu-character was identified with a fiend – actually the Devil himself.

Nobody knows how Marcolf's tale travelled into Europe, but in the fifth century Pope Gelasius excised from the Canon a certain *Contradictio Salomonis*, and in Anglo-Saxon literature of the tenth or eleventh century appeared *Solomon and Saturnus*, a dialogue between two wise men on Biblical and cosmological subjects. Here Solomon asks most of the questions and Saturnus gives the answers. In this there is nothing surprising because Saturn, one-time lord of the Golden Age, is here identified with a King of Chaldea, "earl of a [sky?] country where no man may step with feet", who has gained knowledge and wisdom from travelling throughout the Orient, and has even pitted his strength and wisdom against the Biblical Jehovah's. In other words, the Anglo-Saxon Saturnus seems to be no other than the Near Eastern Asmodeus, and this kingly philosopher-devil, while not identified with Marcolf, is said to have visited the "land of Markolf, which is between the treasure hall of the Medes and the realm of Saul". At any rate, William, Bishop of Tyre, thought that Josephus' Abdemon, who solved Solomon's riddles while in chains (here the bishop has clearly identified Hiram's familiar with Asmodeus, Prince of Demons) was Marcolf. "This, perhaps, is he that the fabulous story of the vulgar [i.e., the folk] names Marcolf, of whom it is told that he solved Solomon's riddles, and replied, propounding in like manner riddles to be solved in their turn." E.G. Duff suggests that the dispute between Solomon and Saturnus–Asmodeus–Marcolf was originally a contention "between inspired and infernal wisdom" though in medieval Europe the hellish King of Chaldea degenerated into something of a boor and perpetrator of practical jokes. Nevertheless,

> It is not forgotten that Marcolf, though frankly a buffoon, was also a sage in his own peculiar way and even in some respects a greater sage than Solomon; for he represents practical sense as against theoretical idealism, the dispute being no longer between Heaven and Hell, but between the upper and lower classes of this world.[5]

The Latin dialogue, translated about 1492, with its record of coarse pranks played by Marcolf on Solomon is a kind of Saturnalia in Topsy-turveydom. Solomon is anxious to keep Marcolf out of the court and away from his wives but has little success. Finally he banishes him with the words, "Out of my sight, and let me never look you between the eyes again", whereupon Marcolf hides himself in an old oven, lying there in such a posture that when the king finds him, he sees a face with fat cheeks but, indeed, no eyes. This insult being more than Solomon can bear, the king orders his servants to hang the incorrigible creature, allowing the condemned no more mercy than the choice of the tree on which he is to hang. But hereupon this Mock King, we read, travelled with his servants "through the valley of Josaffat, and over the hill of Olivet, and from thence to Jericho, and over the river Jordan, and through all Arabia and over the Grand Desert to the Red Sea, but they never found a tree on which Marcolf chose to be hanged".

At one point in the story Solomon wonders how it is that Marcolf can answer all his riddles while he, the most famous wise man in the world, is hopelessly puzzled by many of his servant's. Marcolf says that this is probably because both of them once ate of the heart of a wise vulture or owl-like creature. It had been cooked by Bathsheba for Solomon only, but some of its blood had moistened a crust of bread which Bathsheba threw in anger at the head of Marcolf because he was making a nuisance of himself in the kitchen. Solomon is shocked at this explanation of his own and Marcolf's wisdom, so much greater than his, because it smells of witchcraft. Instantly he asserts that it is God, no vulture's heart, that gives him his wondrous insights; as usual, however, Marcolf has the last word, retorting in the spirit of Socrates on the Bible's celebrated wise man, "He is holden wise who reputeth himself a fool." Generally, Marcolf's vulgar pranks may be thought of as a Germanic addition to the story of a deposed and degraded Near Eastern sun-king, who may have been Solomon's demonic tutor, and it is not too fantastic to connect Till Eulenspiegel's favourite icons, the mirror and the owl from which he got his name (in English, Howle-glass) with the sun- and bird-lore in the various tales of Marcolf.

That actual monarchs in Islam kept near their thrones inspired fools who were much more than mere court buffoons can be seen in the story of Harun-al-Rashid (ninth century) and Buhlul-al-Madjnun (meaning Buhlul the Djinn-inspired), whose fame lasted for centuries. The Arabs, like many other Semites, believed in supernatural beings called *djinn*, perhaps to be identified with deities of the days before Muhammad, who in the time of Islam lived in the wilderness or on solitary mountains yet frequently took possession of human beings, endowing them with a form of supernatural insight which looked to their fellow human beings like madness. These possessed men, especially those known as *sha'iar*, were poet–prophets who cast spells or induced hypnosis by a peculiar kind of rhymed prose called *saj*, which later developed into regular verse. A *sha'iar's* presence, even if he did not fight, was considered indispensable on the battlefield, and he seems at one time to have acted as a judge and dispenser of justice, though perhaps he played this role only periodically on Sacaea-like occasions. It is interesting to recall that Falstaff seems to have fancied himself as a judge:

> *Fal.:*   Do not thou, when thou art king, hang a thief.
>
> *Prince:*   No, thou shalt.
>
> *Fal.:*   Shall I? O rare! By the Lord, I'll be a brave judge.
>
> *Prince:*   Thou judgest false already.[6]

It is said that Buhlul-al-Madjnun, a *sha'iar* who flourished in the days, and perhaps at the court, of Harun-al-Rashid, was included by a certain Jasei among some saints of whom this writer composed biographies. Chiefly he figures in a tenth-century collection of stories about wise fools, the anonymous author of which regarded him as

> a madman who lingers by wells and tombs, gets kicked and mocked by the youths of the city, and yet possesses considerable power of repartee, can deliver traditions [that is, sayings of Muhammad supposed to have been delivered to or overheard by his companions] and show himself to be a shrewd judge of character. He has frequent encounters with Haroun-al-Rashid whom he treats with much candour and asperity, on one occasion even reducing him to tears by showing up his ignorance. ... On another occasion when Haroun-al-Rashid came to Kufa on a pilgrimage, he ordered that Buhlul should be dressed in a black garment and a long cap and be brought to a certain place where he was to pray for the Caliph. Buhlul obeyed, but his prayer was both comical and uncomplimentary, for it implied that the Caliph cared for nothing but money. The governor of Kufa beat the fool for his impertinence, but the Caliph only laughed.[7]

From this it is clear, I think, that the relation between the Caliph and the sainted fool had something ceremonial about it. Buhlul thought that the courtiers had by flattery ruined the judgment and judgments of the Caliph, a condition which he was determined, for the good of king and country, to correct. He seems not merely to have reproved the monarch but to have made fun of his acts and pronouncements by great bursts of laughter. At any rate, the proper name Buhlul came, soon after his death, to signify both "saintly idiot" and "great laughter". True idiots, according to the historian Ibn Khaldun, are incapable of sanctity because they have lost their thinking souls and become like animals, whereas a *buhlul* has lost merely his reason. Some Muslims have even suggested that one cannot become a real saint or truly wise man, cannot see beyond the letter of the law, without in some sense losing one's reason. The *Encyclopedia of Islam* says that the jester, especially the saintly fool, enjoyed the liberty of being above the Islamic laws and might also make them the butt of his insolent mockery. Among *buhluls* occur, says Ibn Khaldun,

> wonderful stories of the Unseen, for they are not limited by anything and can give their speech full course therein. The canon lawyers sometimes deny that they are saints at all on account of that dropping of the external ritual of the law which is seen in them, and because it is held that sainthood comes only through devotional exercises. But that is an error, for the grace of God comes to whomsoever God wills. ... You will find in these idiots a distinct turn for religious meditation and devotion, although not according to legal conditions, because they are not under the law.[8]

This putting the jester outside of or above the law provided Islam with perpetual Lords of Misrule who could treat a ruler to supra-legal guidance, insolence, or cheer whenever the good of the land was threatened by his succumbing to legalism, pride, or the doldrums.

At the court of Harun we have a poet–fool much more substantial than the rather nebulous Buhlul. This is Abu Nuwas, a historical figure remembered as the boon companion and court jester of the monarch. He is not as obviously a saint–fool as is Buhlul, though I am not at all sure that, after his fashion and in a way we are coming to understand in this study, he wasn't a kind of saint. Though clearly a historical character, he is just as clearly a Falstaff-persona. His name, meaning "father of the lock of hair", was given him in honour, they say, of the two great locks that hung over his shoulders. Also, though he is said to have been born of humble parents, he was strangely proud of the (royal?) Persian blood he had inherited from his mother: "the Arabs in God's sight," he said, "are nobody."[9] In the *Arabian Nights* he appears as a tremendous drinker, an adviser and pandar to Harun-al-Rashid, and an open scoffer at Muslim Law. Since in Islam law is equated, in theory at least, with divine commands or God's will, many of his poems amount to blasphemy. In them he openly urges men to sin against Muslim legal regulations, assuring them that God (not necessarily the Muslim Allah) is too merciful to punish people for transgressing what is commonly called His will:

> Accumulate as many sins as thou canst:
> The Lord is ready to relax his ire.
> When the day comes, forgiveness thou wilt find
> Before a mighty king and gracious Sire,
> Nor gnaw thy fingers, all that joy regretting,
> Which thou didst leave for fear of Fire![10]

R. A. Nicholson does not seem to find anything mythic about this great poet, but the stories told of him and even the events of his life suggest the presence of something more than meets the eye. When Nicholson writes that Abu Nuwas was "a man of the most abandoned character, which he took no pains to conceal", and that "by his flagrant immorality, drunkenness, and blasphemy, [he] excited the Caliph's anger [we must remember that al-Rashid means 'the Orthodox'] to such a pitch that he often threatened the culprit with death and actually imprisoned him on several occasions",[11] we seem to sense the outlines of a story with which we have become quite familiar.

The *Arabian Nights* contains (Nights 289 and 290) an adventure of Abu Nuwas and the Caliph in which the monarch, finding himself in an evil humour about a love affair, sends for his poet-companion, jester, and tutor in love- and wine-lore to distract him. As usual, Abu Nuwas is to be found in a tavern (his drinking songs, even when compared with those of Hafiz, are called incomparable):

> Ho! a cup, then fill it up and tell me it is wine,
> For I will never drink in shade if I can drink in shine!

Curst and poor is every hour that I must sober go,
But rich am I whene'er well drunk I stagger to and fro.[12]

From the tavern he is brought back to the palace so intoxicated that he improvises a poem making improper advances to a girl whom the Caliph has chosen for himself. This may be the preconcerted first act of a rite, for what immediately follows seems to describe a ceremony used by Arun the Orthodox to banish sadness.

> The young woman gave wine to the Kalifah, who invited the [already intoxicated] poet to empty the great cup himself. Abu Nuwas took it off at a single draught and soon felt the effects of the heavy vintage. As he reeled where he stood, the Kalifah rose in jest and fell upon him sword in hand, making as if to cut off his head. The poet ran hither and thither around the hall with great cries of terror and Harun-al-Rashid pursued him into all the corners pricking him with the blade. [Because of the circumstances of this episode, it is probably not *à propos* to recall at this point Hal pricking Falstaff at the battle of Gad's Hill, but it is also hard not to remember Falstaff roaring like a bull-calf as we listen to Abu Nuwas!] At last the Kalifah cried: "Enough! Return and drink another cup." At the same time he signed to the girl to hide the vessel. She immediately concealed it beneath her robe, but Abu Nuwas saw the movement in spite of his drunkenness and sang:

> > Even as I desire the cup
> > The cup desires
> > Lips secret and more pleasant,
> > And has gone up
> > Within her garments hollow;
> > Whither the cup aspires
> > Nuwas would follow,
> > If only Harun were not present.

> The Kalifah laughed consumedly and, as a further jest, said to the poet: "As Allah lives, I must raise you to some high employment. From this time forth, I appoint you accredited chief of all the pimps in Bagdad." "In that case, O Commander of the Faithful," retorted Abu Nuwas with a grin, "what may I have the pleasure of doing for you tonight?"
>
> Harun-al-Rashid flew into a rage and commanded the eunuch to call for Masrur the sword-bearer, his executioner of justice, ordering him to strip Abu Nuwas of all his clothes, to saddle him with an ass's pack-saddle, to pass an ass's halter around his neck, and thrust a spur up his fundament. When this had been done, the unfortunate poet was led up and down before all the pavilions of the King's favourites that they might laugh at him; and Masrur had instructions, when this exhibition had been completed, to take Abu Nuwas to the gate of the city, to cut off his head in the presence of the people, and to bring it back upon a dish.
>
> The despairing poet was paraded before each of the three hundred and sixty-five palaces, and, when their inhabitants heard of the death he was about to die, they grieved for him because they loved his wit, and as a sign of their sympathy threw gold and jewels before his path.[13]

A memory of the Ancient Sacaea of Babylon? Finally, after the poet had been reduced to tears, the Caliph, who had been enjoying this spectacle from a hiding place, burst into a hearty laugh and brought the little play to an end by pardoning the jester for his so-called offence against law and order in drinking and insulting his king.

Shahrazad, who told this tale, was fond of stories of Abu Nuwas, but after hearing three, King Shahryar, shocked by conduct which violated the Islamic legal code in minute detail, forbade her to speak further of "this crapulous poet, who had no respect for Kalifas or laws".[14]

Just the same, Abu Nuwas, in the very depths of his apparent foolishness, lawlessness, depravity, and blasphemy, always spoke with the self-confidence and authority of a man who knew exactly what he was doing. Though the coarse and ignorant misunderstood and sought to punish him for deeds done for the common good, it is hard for us not to feel in him the surviving spirit of a prince or priest, perhaps Persian or even Arabic, of the days before Muhammad – the priest perhaps of a goddess rather than a god, one resembling Dubayyah, one-time custodian of the shrine of Al-'Uzza, who was killed by Khalid in the early days of the New Dispensation, and lamented by al-Hudhali as follows:

> What is wrong with Dubayyah? For days I have not seen him
> Amid the winebibbers; he draws not nigh, does not appear.
> If he were living he would have come with a cup
> Of the banu-Hatif make, filled with Bacchus' oil.
> Generous and noble is he; no sooner his wine cups
> Are filled than they become empty, like an old tank full of holes in the
> midst of winter.[15]

Elsewhere we are given to understand that Dubayyah was, like Abu Nuwas, a short man with a red complexion and an enormous stomach. We might have known!

By now we have heard a good deal of the sexual and drinking habits of the Muslim Falstaff-persona and something of his love of horseplay, but so far nothing of his thievery, which is the particular aspect of his lawbreaking which I wish to stress in this chapter. This side of the sacred fool is more noticeable in the stories told of Nasar-ed-Din or Si-djoha (Khoja, Hodja, Goha, etc.) who in the Turkish version of his adventures is represented as having been court jester to the conqueror Timurleng (Tamerlane, Tamburlaine, etc.) of the fourteenth century. This figure was the hero of a tenth-century Arab book entitled *The Jests of Si-djoha*, and his fame, either in connection with or divorced from the name of Timur-leng, survives to this day in the Near East. His so-called tomb at Aqshehir is the centre of a cult whose members invoke the sacred jester's blessing or tell his ghost their wishes, which are then supposed to come true. It is recorded that Timur attached Si-djoha to his court as buffoon only after he had successfully answered a whole series of questions during an interrogation where one single failure would have meant the loss of his life. Many of these questions were of cosmological import, and it is pretty certain that Timur-leng was in search of the wisdom which helps a conqueror to stimulate crops and happiness in a land with which he is unfamiliar. It is said that he often asked Si-djoha to pray as well as to caper for him, and in some stories the jester is represented as a man learned in the lore of psychic health with a great reputation for sanctity and an entourage of eager pupils.

Sir Harry Luke, who has written at some length about this character,[16] holds that he was a sort of Imam or country parson famous for his ability to give moving sermons but still more famous for the many tricks by which he evaded, or seemed to evade, his ecclesiastical duties. This trait connects him with Khadir of old and looks forward to the wondrous Abu Zayd of al-Hariri's *Maqamat* or *Assemblies*, discussed below. His likeness to Abu Zayd is further emphasised by anecdotes in which he appears as a poor tradesman, even a beggar, who seeks to get food and money by sly trickery or brazen theft. A typical tale tells that, when starving, Si-djoha asked certain fellow-students of the scriptures (shall we assume that they were, more particularly, sacred law books?) to dine with him. In order to pay for food for them and himself, he collected the shoes which they had ceremoniously left outside on entering his house and pawned them, compelling each student later on to redeem his own property. Like Khadir, he sometimes committed acts of apparent cruelty, going far beyond the sacred fool's licence to disregard the law. It is said that once, for a good fee, he helped ten blind men to cross a river, but let one of them be drowned. Folklore initiates may imagine that he had a good reason for this act, but he did not divulge it to the nine survivors, who complained bitterly. "Just pay me one piece of money less," he said, "that will put matters right."[17] By hook and crook, he laid his hands on a good many silver shekels and was reputed to possess magical instruments and animals which could produce gold.

A story, quite weird unless taken in some mythic sense, is told of how he increased his wealth by tricking four friends into paying enormous sums for a knife with which they could stab their wives repeatedly without really killing them. When all the wives were dead Si-djoha, fearing reprisals, pretended to be dead too. He concealed himself in a tomb in which he had made a hole near which he stood with a red-hot branding iron, tipped with his father's seal, in his hand. When the friends came to peer into the burial place, he branded them on the forehead by thrusting the iron through the hole. Finally, however, they were able to drag him before the judge and accuse him of murdering their wives. The fool retorted that his accusers were merely escaped slaves branded with his father's seal, and the judge, guided by circumstantial evidence, condemned them to serve Si-djoha for the rest of their lives.

This is undoubtedly some kind of sun-myth having to do with fierce manifestations of heat in a season when the female earth is scorched to death and the sun-branded farmers robbed of their savings and reduced to perpetual bondage. It is at this very mausoleum, or rather at one constructed in honour of this tale, that the cult I have referred to above is carried on. In this tomb is a round hole through which the spirit of the sacred fool is supposed to continue to look out at the world, warming and enlightening it, while inside, over the coffin, hangs another sun symbol, a ball with which he is reported to have played during life, amusing and medicining Timur-leng and other notables. Need we be told that Si-djoha was killed by the machinations of a close friend, the one man in all the world whom he trusted and for whom he had spent his best energies? Perhaps, though this is not recorded, the notoriously ungrateful companion was Timur-leng himself.

The most famous of these sacred fools of Islam, the one who practically made a religious ritual of irreligious lawbreaking and especially of thievery, was Abu Zayd, the disreputable old rascal who is the hero of a book, the *Maqamat* or *Assemblies* of al-Hariri of Basra (1054–1122), which Professor Nicholson says is "next to the Koran, the most celebrated book in Arabic literature".[18] This work, written in rhymed prose and verse, consists of fifty *maqamas* or adventures supposed to be related by one al-Harith who is a great admirer, and speaks of himself as a pupil, of the scoundrelly hero. Usually Abu Zayd is represented as an ugly old man, often muffled in a ragged cloak, but he has a lovely young son to whom he is teaching his beautifully worded wisdom of life and death and, more especially, his tricks for extracting gold from the rich and hoodwinking those puffed-up guardians of the law, the *kadis* or judges, who try to lord it over the unfortunate throughout the cities of Islam. On the other hand, Abu Zayd sometimes appears as a youth himself, being able – like Bes, Janus, and others – to pass from an aged to a boyish shape overnight after the manner of the sun which sets, old and pallid, on the shortest day only to rise the next morning with the flush of babyhood on its face.

Very little is made of Abu Zayd's animal associations, but we read of him appearing now and again, like Bes, in the skin of a leopard, an image that probably points to totemic drapery now lost, for there is too much folklore in al-Hariri's work to permit us to believe that this fascinating rogue is an entirely original creation.

To set Abu Zayd clearly in the tradition of the Falstaffian figures we have met so far, the twelfth *maqama* or "Assembly of Damascus" is useful. In this, al-Harith, the imaginary narrator of al-Hariri's poems – remember that he has not encountered his old friend and tutor for a long time – joins for the purpose of crossing the desert between Syria and the Euphrates a caravan whose departure is delayed by its inability to find an escort to protect it from robbers. A pious hermit or dervish promises the men of the caravan that he can conduct them safely from east to west with the help of a magic form of words known to him alone. When the men prove incredulous, he swears "by heaven and its starry train, and by the earth with its highways plain, and by the streaming rain and by the blazing lamp of the Inane, and by the sounding main" that his power to give protection and guidance through the waste will prove efficacious – and so it does. But he conceals from the men of the caravan the means by which he nourishes his magic strength. They think it is due to his rosary, his talk of vigils, and his constant muttering of prayers, but they are wrong. The moral of this "assembly", duly assimilated by al-Harith, seems to be that forbidden wine, women, and dancing are the stuff on which old sky-birds, old sun-guides through the Waste-land (like Abu Zayd), nourish their powers. After having collected a full bag of gold from the travellers, the mysterious dervish secretly leaves them, short of their destination but in sight of it –

off he skipped as the cutpurse skips, and away he slipped as quicksilver slips. We were distressed by his defaulting and amazed at his bolting, and we sought everywhere for a clue ... till we heard that since foot in 'Ana he set he had never quitted the cabaret. The foulness of this rumour egged me on to test the ore of its mine and meddle with what is not in my line. Long before sunrise I repaired to the tavern in disguise, and lo, amidst jars and vats, there was the old varlet in a robe of scarlet, and around him cup-bearers beaming and candles gleaming and myrtle and jessamine and pipe and mandolin: now he would be broaching the jars, now waking the music of guitars, now inhaling sweet flower-smells, now sporting with the gazelles. When I struck upon his guileful way and the difference of his to-day from his yesterday, I said, "Woe to thee, O accursed one! So soon hast thou forgotten the day of Jairun?" But he guffawed with a will and began merrily to trill:

"I ride and I ride through the waste far and wide, and I fling away pride to be gay as the swallow;
Stem the torrent's fierce speed, tame the mettlesome steed, that wherever I lead Youth and Pleasure may follow.
I bid gravity pack and I strip bare my back lest liquor I lack when the goblet is lifted:
Did I never incline to the quaffing of wine, I had ne'er been with fine wit and eloquence gifted.
Is it wonderful, pray, that an old man should stay in well-stored seray by a cask overflowing?
Wine strengthens the knees, physics every disease, and from sorrow it frees, the oblivion-bestowing!
Oh the purest of joys is to live sans disguise, unconstrained by the ties of a grave reputation,
And the sweetest of love that the lover can prove is when fear and hope move him to utter his passion. ...
While to hand thee the bowl damsels wait who cajole and enravish the soul with eyes tenderly glancing,
And singers whose throats pour such high-mounting notes, when the melody floats, from rocks would be dancing!
Obey not the fool who forbids thee to pull beauty's rose when in full bloom thou'rt free to possess it ..."

> I said to him, "Bravo, bravo for thy recitation, but fie and shame on
> thy reprobation! By God, whence springeth thy stock? Methinks thy
> riddle is right hard to unlock."
> He answered,

> > "I do not wish to explicate but I will indicate:
> > I am the age's rarity, the wonder of mankind,
> > I play my tricks among them all, and many a dupe I find.
> > But then I am a needy wretch whom Fortune broke and beat ..."

> Said the narrator [al-Harith]: Then I knew he was Abu Zayd, the
> rogue of his race, he that blackens the face of hoariness with disgrace;
> and I was shocked by the greatness of his iniquity and the abomination
> of his obliquity. "Old man," I said, "is it not time that thou draw back
> from thy course of crime?" He growled and scowled and fumed and
> pondered a moment and resumed, " 'Tis a night for exulting, and not for
> insulting, and an occasion for wine-quaffing, not for mutual scoffing.
> Away with sorrow till we meet to-morrow!"[19]

Needless to say, al-Harith learns the lesson that this Near Eastern Boar's
Head has to teach, though the next day he promises God perfunctorily never
to visit a wine shop again, and leaves his old tutor in peace to enjoy the
company of *his* old tutor, Iblis or Satan, among the gazelle-girls and wine
vats.

When Abu Zayd referred to himself as a wretch broken by fortune, he was
thinking of a great rather than a little fall in status, "for at one time he
claimed to be of the race of Sasan and at another he made himself kin to the
princes of Ghasan; and now he sallied forth in the vesture of poets; and anon
he put on the pride of nobles."[20] The point that this old beggar is a direct
descendant of the Sassanid kings of Persia, dethroned by the Muslims, is
made again and again, and we are given to understand that he heads a group
of jolly beggars, true to the old faith in sun and wine associated with the
teachings of Zoroaster, a ragged crew who constitute a sort of politico-
religious underground movement in Islam. The movement is not intended,
to be sure, to overthrow the conquerors but simply to make sure that the
growth of the soil and the joy of the people continue to flourish under
whatever monarchs. It is not clear that al-Harith, the pupil of Zayd, is of the
ruling family of the conquerors, but there is a possibility that he communi-
cates what he learns from this aged scoundrel to the great houses of Islam.

Meanwhile, Abu Zayd uses every kind of device and trick to lay hands on
other men's money, which he treats as if it belonged as of right to himself.
Sometimes he goes almost incredibly far, as when, in the "Assembly of
Wasit", he arranges to marry al-Harith to the daughter of very wealthy
people who are staying in an expensive hostelry or khan. He himself invites
all the guests of the khan to an elaborate wedding feast and, after having
delivered a marvellously beautiful and pious sermon, performs the marriage
ceremony himself. After this he produces sweetmeats which al-Harith finds

no time to partake of because he is so busy handing them around to the guests. When suddenly all the company fall senseless to the ground, al-Harith is terrified, thinking them poisoned, but Abu Zayd informs him that they are merely drugged, and proceeds to rob his guests and steal everything of value from every room in the great hotel. Al-Harith calls him bitter names, but he justifies his act and similar enormities previously committed by insisting that the injured people are far more sinful than he and asserting that if all were known, he is merely plucking back his rightful property.

> "Thou comprehendest me not in what I have done, but as for them, I
>   know them full well:
> Heretofore I sought their hospitality, and I saw them unheedful of their
>   guests.
> I probed them, and when I tested them, I found them to be base coins.
> Amongst them is none but who strikes terror when he can ...
> None sincere in friendship, none trustworthy, none benevolent, none
>   kindly disposed.
> So I sprang upon them the spring of the tearing wolf upon the sheep,
> And left them prostrate as if they had been made to drink the cup of
>   death.
> And my hand possessed itself of what they had hoarded, for they were
>   the abhorrence of men's nostrils. ...
> Just how often have I despoiled owners of the state-chairs and carpets
>   and curtains. ...
> How often have I shed blood ... and desecrated the sanctuary of the
>   high-minded;
> How many a pernicious course have I taken into sin, how many a
>   headlong rush,
> But withal I have laid in a goodly opinion with my God, my Lord, the
>   Compassionate."[20]

After Abu Zayd, weeping tears of contrition, has admitted (Falstaff-like) that perhaps it is time for him to stop breaking what the world calls law, al-Harith, hoping "for him that which is hoped for the guilty who confesses his guilt", forgives him – whereupon the old villain and his young son make off safely with the booty!

Frequently Zayd is summoned before this or that *kadi* for his crimes and misdemeanours, but he usually manages to trick Old Father Antic into letting him off while in "Assemblies" like that "of Rayy" he actually reproves, humiliates, and, we are given to understand, reforms a tyrannical, false-dealing governor-judge by a speech on true justice. After this, the reformer approached al-Harith and said:

> "I am he whom thou knowest, Harith,
> The talker with kings, the wit, the intimate.
> I charm as charm not the triple-twisted strings,
> At times a brother of earnest, at times a jester.

Events have not changed me since I met thee,
Nor has vexing calamity peeled my branch;
Nor has any splitting edge cloven my tooth;
But my claw is fixed in every prey:
On each herd that roams my wolf is ravaging ..."

Then I [al-Harith] said, "By Allah, now thou art surely Abu Zayd, yet thou hast been godly [i.e., in the lecture on justice which he has just given the Governor] beyond 'Amr Ibn 'Obayd!" – Then was he cheerful with the cheerfulness of the hospitable when he is visited, and said, "Listen, my brother:

Keep to the truth, although it scorch thee with the fire of threatening;
And seek to please God, for the most foolish of mankind is he who
angers the master and pleases the slave."[21]

This passage reproduces authentically the authoritative, almost hieratic, tone in which Falstaff lectures two princes of the royal house and the Chief Justice of England in such lines as those where he insists:

"Never call a true piece of gold a counterfeit.
Thou art essentially mad, without seeming so."[22]

On other occasions Abu Zayd uses his wit and poverty to practise upon the pride and gullibility of a *kadi* in such a way as to cause him to part with great sums of money, to rob himself, as it were, in order to give alms. Falstaff, we recall, sought to borrow a thousand pounds of the Chief Justice, but at cadging he cannot be compared to his Islamic counterpart. On one occasion the hoary Zayd is haled before a judge for living off a woman by cheating her, borrowing money, and finally taking away her clothes and her furniture piece by piece in order to revel in idleness. The circumstances strongly resemble those in which Dame Quickly seeks to have Falstaff arrested by the officers Fang and Snare for having stuffed all her "substance into that fat belly of his"[23] and borrowing so much money under the pretence of marrying her that she will have to pawn her plate to pay her debts. The Chief Justice, appearing upon the scene, will not credit Falstaff's denunciation of Dame Quickly, and demands that he right the villainy he has wreaked upon the good mistress of the inn:

Ch. Just.: Sir John, Sir John, I am well acquainted with your manner of wrenching the true cause the false way. It is not a confident brow nor the throng of words that come with such more than impudent sauciness from you that can thrust me from a level consideration. You have, as it appears to me, practis'd upon the easy-yielding spirit of this woman and made her serve your uses both in purse and in person. ...

Fal.: My Lord, I will not undergo this sneap [i.e. reproof] without reply. You call honourable boldness impudent sauciness; if a man will make curtsy and say nothing, he is virtuous. No, my lord, my humble duty rememb'red, I will not be your suitor. I say to you, I do desire deliverance from these officers, being upon hasty employment in the king's affairs.

Ch. Just.:   You speak as one having power to do wrong ...[24]

Circumstances rather than cunning help Falstaff to escape the Chief Justice here, while it is Abu Zayd's mellifluous throng of well-chosen words that saves him under the same circumstances – not merely saves him but enables him to wheedle out of the judge a substantial contribution to the support of the Oriental Quickly, a prostitute with whom, it turns out, he had made an arrangement to accuse him of sponging and theft! Once again, however, in both scenes the accused adopt effectively a tone not merely of injured innocence but of piously hieratic authority.

In a poem which he improvises in the "Assembly of Sa'dah", Abu Zayd mentions Khadir and elsewhere compares himself to the mysteriously potent power that laughs in the sun and burgeons in the earth. In winter by crouching naked on the ground and croaking a song about his imminent demise, he is able to trick a dozen rich men out of their furs and cloaks and thus regain the strength, heat, and size appropriate to an Old Sun arranging his own rebirth. Finally, in the "Assembly of Sur", Abu Zayd reveals himself to al-Harith as the descendant of Sasan al Akbar, son of Bahman, son of Isfendiyar, son of Kushtasif, once prince of the true sun-line of western Persia and later, his family having fallen on evil days, the famous chief of all beggars. True descendant of this "grand-master of matters", Zayd is found by al-Harith presiding over a strange group of mendicants in "a mansion high of structure, wide of area, which testified to the builder's wealth and exalted state". On entering the building, however, he found the vestibules covered with tattered garments and littered with begging baskets, by the evil augury of which he was so frightened and depressed that he almost, but not quite, forgot to ask to whom the mansion belonged. An aged man sitting on a handsome rug answered, "It has no distinct owner and no manifest master; it is but the inn of the importune beggars and low artisans and the den of ballad singers and the rehearsers of the traditions [that is, of the sayings traditionally attributed to Muhammad]."[25] Al-Harith would have liked to run away, but his unfailing curiosity led him into this lowest depth where, lo! the inner rooms were adorned with state-chairs carved and gilded, deep-piled carpets, cushions in rows, and swaying curtains, while a wedding ceremony was being performed by a grey-bearded old man who talked impressively about the duties of the rich toward the poor before uniting in marriage two young people who resembled nothing so much as a King and Queen of the May. Following the marriage came a great feast, served on a table beautifully dressed with every conceivable kind of food. Then at last, al-Harith, as usual, recognised in the master of ceremonies his old friend Abu Zayd, who spoke to him of the many pains he had undergone for ungrateful mankind since having been driven from the land and power to which he was born. In this passage we feel that more is left unsaid than is said by the young–old scoundrel, but we can guess that this was the height of al-Harith's enlightenment, for "I continued the time of my stay in Cairo to resort nightly to his guest-fire, and to fill both my shells with the pearls of his utterances, until the raven of separation broke between us and I parted with him as the lid would part with the eye."[26]

Though only al-Hariri's book, of all those written in Arabic, is ranked near the Koran, it is in many ways a kind of counter-scripture and its author, whom after-generations have insisted on identifying with Abu Zayd's pupil al-Harith, has often been reproved both inside Islam and without for his transparent love of the old villain. Chenery, one of the English translators, himself writes:

> But undoubtedly the spirit of the whole composition might have offended the more scrupulous. Abu Zayd, with his dishonesty and dissoluteness, is made too attractive, and it is plain that in the mind of the author his genius more than compensates for all his faults. Hariri depicts too favourably the witty and cynical improviser. ... Then the appending of discourses, filled with the most lofty devotion, to the adventures of a profligate, the mingling of the sermon with jest, of the psalm with the bacchanalian song, will find objectors at all times. ... [Hariri] mingled sacred things with something like ribaldry in a manner that must have given deep offense to strict professors.[27]

Chenery shows himself so shocked by al-Hariri's adding to passages of audacious attack on Muslim law passages of "a licence still more audacious" that we can only conclude that by the word "professors" used above he meant, not the *mullahs* of Islam, but university teachers of the Dover Wilson school.

The story of Abu Zayd, master of beggars and thieves, brings into focus an aspect of the Falstaff-persona which is perhaps central to the interpretation of all these mythical figures. Here they emerge with absolute clarity as the descendants of the Divine Kings of peoples who have suffered conquest. Nevertheless, reduced to poverty, clad in the rags of wretches, they retain a certain odd majesty and self-possessed *savoir-faire* based, perhaps, on their conviction that they alone have the secrets, they alone know how to lead the lives, that can make nature and society flourish. Broken royalty, they are nevertheless true to their ancient duties to sun and soil and seek to enact their indispensable calling either from hidden lairs, with only the dispossessed and *déclassés* in their train, or from the dangerous thrones of Mock Monarchs. As Mock Kings perhaps their most important act, next to their copious lovemaking, was to turn the laws of the conqueror upside down, administering old-fashioned justice – even if for only a week – to the now depressed, enslaved, and expropriated possessors of the land in the hope of averting seasonal calamity from the whole country. To them the laws, the justice administered by the conquerors, were travesties that threatened the life of nature itself. It is no wonder that they fought these both secretly and openly in behalf of mankind, and considered it not a sin but a duty to try to recover, by whatever means, the land, the sun-treasure, and the talismanic emblems of royalty. Let justice be done, or the heavens would fall on their beloved country.

That fruitfulness and fertility in men, animals, and nature go hand in hand with the goodness and justice of rulers was an ancient idea believed well into modern times. In 1491 Savonarola, the pious reformer of Florence, said in a famous sermon:

> I must tell you, then, that all the evil and all the good of the city depend upon the conduct of its head, and therefore great is his responsibility even for small sins, since if he followed the right path, the whole city would be sanctified.[28]

It is therefore not surprising that the deposed monarchs considered robbery a ritual act or that their bad-conscienced monarchs of Mesopotamia or ancient Rome should have consented to, perhaps insisted on, having their new law codes and social conventions temporarily overturned whenever the fruitful functioning of nature was in danger. Perhaps it was decreed that the Mock Monarch and his rabble should actually steal from the present owners in order to right, if only for the period of the Mock King's sway, an ancient wrong. Perhaps the land could not be blessed on any condition except that of at least temporary ownership. Perhaps the Mock King's princely pupil was encouraged to rob his father or himself in order to feel himself into the role of the satanic figure whose *mana* and fertility wisdom he was desperately anxious to acquire. This is just about what Hal does at the battle of Gad's Hill. Of course, any robbery perpetrated by a prince on himself or his father may be readily set right when the days of danger have passed.

In many lands, as we shall soon see, a famous sun-avatar or his Divine King representative carried a sack or purse filled with grain or symbolic gold in his hand or under his arm, and the Substitute King playing the role of this ancient deity would have been incompletely equipped without this symbolic appurtenance. However, neither the impotent king on whose behalf he was acting nor the prince he was educating to be a kind of wealth-god himself could have been expected to supply the Interrex with gold which he intended to take back. Nothing could have been more appropriate, therefore, than that the Mock King be allowed or compelled to steal this emblematic commodity from the conquerors during and for the period of his so-called misrule. Customarily the Mock King seems to have stolen chiefly gold and jewels, symbolic perhaps on one hand of the brilliance and colour of the sun and on the other of the fruits of the earth, which he was supposed to animate.

In the light of these considerations it is not surprising that Falstaff felt he had been dishonestly deprived by Hal of the gold he stole at Gad's Hill (though the episode made it obvious that the prince had learned this fertility lesson) or that he tried to recoup his loss by borrowing the like amount or more from the Chief Justice (unsuccessfully) and from Master Shallow (successfully). Like any good Mock King, Falstaff is stung to aggressive attack by the presence or even the mention of judge, justices, or officers of the law. He cannot bear to see Silence and Shallow glorying in the title of Justice and the possession of great estates. They have not the right temperaments, not the right shapes, not the right rites to promote increase and felicity.

> *Fal.:*   As I return I will fetch off these justices. I do see the bottom of Justice Shallow. ... I do remember him at Clement's Inn like a man made after supper of a cheeseparing. When a' was naked, he was, for all the world, like a fork'd radish with a head fantastically carv'd upon it with a knife. A' was so forlorn, that his dimensions to any thick sight were invincible. ... And now is this Vice's dagger become a squire and talks as familiarly of John of Gaunt as if he had been sworn brother to him ... you might have thrust him and all his apparel into an eel-skin. The case of a treble hautboy was a mansion for him, a court; and now he has land and beeves. ... If the young dace be a bait for the old pike I see no reason in the law of nature but I may snap at him.[29]

There is matter for humour, unintended by Falstaff, in the fact that these lines are sometimes quoted by critics to show that Falstaff is "impervious to ridicule, moral imperatives, demands of honour, truth, social position, or personal sensitiveness".[30]

We may bring this chapter to an end by noting that large numbers of Jews, themselves members of a people historically associated with the love of multiplying laws and commandments, legal commentaries and juridical interpretations, ended by identifying their expected Messiah with a shining figure, not infrequently compared to the sun, who would deliver them from the burden of rabbinic legalism. In *The Messian Idea in Jewish History* Greenstone says that "The Arabian Jews were the first to question the supreme authority of the rabbinic law ... It was probably their intercourse with the cultured Arabs that produced an intellectual independence unknown to their co-religionists living in less favoured circumstances."[31] When, about A.D. 720, Serene of Syria proclaimed himself the Messiah, he won a great following throughout Jewry by setting about, as the first work of redemption, "abolishing Talmudic ordinances, changing the ritual, disregarding the dietary laws ..., permitting the use of wine that had been touched by a non-Jew, neglecting the details of the preparation of marriage contracts, ... and even allowing intermarriage within the forbidden degrees of consanguinity and affinity".[32]

. Many of the self-declared Messiahs who flourished from the eighth to the eighteenth century have strikingly Falstaffian characteristics. In the *Book of Zerubbabel*, compiled probably by an Italian Jew in the tenth or eleventh century, the angel Metatron tells Zerubbabel, scion of the house of David, that the Messiah has been living in Rome since the days of Nebuchadnezzar in the disguise of a dwarfed and hideous Bes-creature but that he will be transformed 990 years after the destruction of the Temple (that is, about 1058 or 1060) into a beautiful youth who will inaugurate and preside over the Millenium. In *Man and Temple in Ancient Jewish Myth and Ritual* R. Patai, one-time director of the Palestine Institute of Folklore and Ethnology, points out that the messianic kingdom is always envisaged as filled with precisely that kind of prosperity which ancient Near Eastern texts attribute to the powers of a divine sun-king or his substitutes, that is, an unlimited productivity in the earth and its dumb creatures capable of furnishing forth an endless feast upon which the righteous will banquet at the end of days. Items in this feast will be

> a tremendous ox "lying on a thousand mountains and fed on the produce of a thousand mountains," and ... wine kept in the grapes since the creation of the world. ... The rabbinic pictures of the Messianic age were taken literally by many generations of Jews, who even believed in the poetic conception of the Rabban Gamaliel, that the Palestinian soil would produce cakes and silk dresses, the trees of Palestine would bear fruit continuously, and Jewish women would give birth to children every day.[33]

Certain of the false Messiahs, especially Sabbatai Zvi and Yankiev Frank, seem to have held great feasts either in order to prove that the Millenium had already arrived or to coerce its arrival by creating in advance the fabulous conditions proper to it. These included the abolition of rabbinic law and even an attempt to abrogate the written law. Greenstone tells us that

> When some of the Rabbis of Amsterdam tried to oppose the new enactments of Sabbatai that had the avowed purpose of abolishing ancient laws and institutions, they were almost stoned by the enraged populace. It is related, that when Sabbatai Zebi offered the paschal lamb in Constantinople, he had the disciples eat of the forbidden fat and pronounced the blessing "Blessed art Thou ... who looseneth the bond," meaning thereby the loosening of the bonds of traditional Judaism. It is a marvellous phenomenon, this tremendous influence exerted over a whole nation by one man – an influence so great that the few sober-minded Jews, mostly Talmudic scholars, had to conceal their resentment for fear of incurring the fury of the mob.[34]

Certain Jews justified such "orgies of lawlessness" as among the "messianic woes" necessary to usher in the Millenium because it was thought that social and political abuses would have to reach an awesome climax of depravity before the saviour would or could come, but it is pretty clear that for most of the false Messiahs and their followers anarchy or the breaking of the law was an indispensable condition of the return of Adam into Eden. Tender-minded rabbis prayed that the Messiah might never appear in their days because, prelusive to his coming, judges and officers of the law will lose authority, the study of the law be abandoned, law-abiding citizens despised, and the Temple turned into a house of harlots, but the false Messiahs gloried in a new dispensation of love, a new covenant with a god older than Jehovah, and the renewed practise of a dimly remembered, ancient justice. They were, it seems, almost the last of the Substitute Kings to reign on earth, heroes of a Sacaea or Saturnalia which was intended to last for ever but which involved them, as usual, in sacrificial death – which does not necessarily prove that the world's wise are in the long run truly wise, but simply that they know how to make good use of a saviour–victim for a short-run purpose.

VII
From Kuvera to Ganeśa:
Indian Falstaffs Who "Forgot What the Inside of a Church Is Made Of"[1]

To attack and break a country's laws is indirectly to misprise and deny that country's current god or gods, for the legal, social, and political institutions are generally held to embody the divine will. The whole preceding chapter has dwelt indirectly on the Falstaff-persona's rejection of the regnant deity, but we have also seen that fools may be exempted from, perhaps because they are in some sense above, religiously commanded law. We have repeatedly heard the buffoon referred to as sacred, and we know that the Substitute King was believed to be in touch with transcendent secrets and holy powers not enjoyed by the deity or deities of the ruling group. As we have so often seen, early peoples worshipped the fructifying forces of nature, more particularly the sun, who was believed to incarnate himself from time to time in the form of prepotent animals and come to earth to relieve seasonal crises and father one or another of the totem tribes of men. It was more particularly, then, in the form of an ancestral animal or animal–man or Divine King avatar that early people usually worshipped the life force which brought health, haematinia, happiness, and fruitfulness to the earth. After the original people of a given country had been conquered and their royal family driven into exile, this worship often continued in an underground form, whether in forests, swamps, or the beggarly lower depths of cities. When, on critical occasions, a scion of the old royalty was lured from the jungle or cellar to play the Mock King, it was in the skin and horns of his original family deity that he, in token of a *bona fide* apostolic succession, arrayed himself. In this dress he made magnificent love, overturned the law in favour of temporary justice to the oppressed and dispossessed, and, it appears, made fun of the god or gods of his people's supplanters. It is with the Mock King's scorn for the new gods, a vituperation which clearly became an important part of the ritual libretto of his interregnum, that I wish to deal in the present chapter.

I have chosen India for my discussion of the ritual irreverence of the Mock King, not merely because it yields fine examples but because we find there an interesting phenomenon: a displaced deity, resurrected from time to time in the form of a Substitute Monarch, who finally won back a good deal of his ancient status. It may well be that the very oldest deity known to India – at least, he is often said to be – is at the present time the most beloved figure in the Indian pantheon. Something like this happened to Bes of Egypt, but he cannot be classed with Ganeśa as a living deity who may have been worshipped in substantially his modern form for three or four thousand years. This jolly elephant-headed god has, of course, an enormous stomach and is usually shown in art eating, drinking, dancing, or sitting with his Tearsheet (his Sakti) on his knee. When painted, his face and body are red and he is associated in a dozen other ways with sun-worship. He is also linked to linga or phallus worship. Sometimes he is represented as Janus-faced, his Old Sun countenance being human while the New Sun one is that of a baby elephant. One of the epithets by which he is known is "Ganeśa the Thief", and there is artistic evidence to point to a tradition that he has from time to time been martyred. In a word, no single Falstaff trait that we have yet considered is lacking in this beloved Indian figure. Some Indian and French *pandits* identify him with Siva, who is his putative father, and it is true that both are known by the epithet *Gana-pati* or "Leader of the Ganas", *Ganas* itself being best translated, perhaps, as an uncouth rabble or rout. Also, "Ganeśa" is the elided form of Gana-iśa, which means "supreme Lord of the Ganas". Nevertheless Ganeśa's obvious ties are not with the ascetic Siva but with an ancient and more than half-forgotten God of Wealth called Kuvera, whose form in art, apart from the head, is indistinguishable from the elephant-god's.

We have no very ancient images of Kuvera, nor for any of the gods of India. It was necessary for the Indians to abandon woodcarving for metal- and stone-work before their icons could last. Our first statues of Kuvera date, therefore, from around the first or second century B.C. and are found on Buddhist monuments. Kuvera is not himself an elephant-headed god – at least the few early elephant-headed statues that survive cannot be definitely identified with him – but he and his followers, who consist on one hand of beautiful, narrow-waisted, deep-breasted women called Yaksis and on the other of short, fat, ugly, hairy dwarfs called Guhyas, are closely associated with the elephant. Both Yaksis and Guhyas may be more or less correctly called tree spirits, and Kuvera's train included also plump male tree spirits called Yaksas. In Buddhist art, as at the great stupa at Sānci, all these followers of Kuvera are found standing or riding on elephants. Sometimes the Guhyas, especially those who sport along the rail-copings of the old temple of Bodhgaya (about 100 B.C.) have elephant ears and genitals of elephantine proportions. When the followers of Kuvera are not riding elephants, they are usually mounted on an elephant-headed, fish-tailed creature called a *makara*. As for Kuvera himself, there is good reason to suppose that he may have appeared in the lost woodcarving of India as an elephant or a man with elephant ears or, perhaps, like Ganeśa himself, with an elephant head. There are dozens of icons of Sri (Siri, Sir mi Devata, etc.) or Lakśmi, supposed to be one of the oldest incarnations of the Earth Mother and identifiable as the goddess of abundance and good fortune, which show her standing on an elephant or flanked by elephants which conceivably represent Kuvera, doubled for heraldic effect. One version of this icon of Sri, dating from about the eighth century, shows her with Kuvera to her proper left and elephant-headed Ganeśa to her right. Their pudgy bodies are indistinguishable, and one can only suppose that the statue is a very late and sophisticated form of an early icon representing Mother India with her aboriginal husband.

When we encounter him in Buddhist art Kuvera, though sometimes lacking a beard, is a perfect Falstaff-persona. Frequently he is found drinking from a great wine cup, served him in his jungle inn by a beautiful Tearsheet–Yaksi. His belly is often so heavy that it rests on the earth, his legs seeming, as in certain representations of Bes, to be mere dangling appurtenances quite incapable of supporting the god should he try to stand. If he succeeded in getting up, his guts would surely "fall about his knees" unless

Kuvera with mother and brother — wooden carving (Hindu)

Collection of Roderick Marshall, Oxford

girdled in, as we are told Falstaff's were. In one Indian statue we see Kuvera actually wearing a belly-support called a *patta*. His round, happy, thick-lipped face is surmounted by a wealth of curly hair which streams down his back and is not infrequently encircled by a great sun-halo. In his left hand, that which does not hold the wine cup, is a long purse stored with golden coins, indicating that he is the lord of abundance. From Sri Lanka or Tibet, centres of Buddhism where the memory of Kuvera flourished after it had been practically lost in India, we see the god resting his right foot on an overturned urn from which streams grain or gold, while the purse that he traditionally holds in his left hand has turned into a stylised mongoose which is vomiting a torrent of jewels. Kuvera (named Jambhala in Sri Lanka, and in some parts of northern India, Pancika) is frequently shown standing or sitting beside his Sakti (that is, his creative energy personified in the form of a lover or wife) called variously Laksmi, Bhādrā or Haritī. Not less frequently she is found sitting on his knee and bussing him with most sincere Tearsheetian kisses.

Like Falstaff, Kuvera can spring from lovemaking to warlike activity against the demons of cold and darkness, in token of which he sometimes carries, especially in Tibetan art, a pike surmounted by a war banner. In many of his Indian representations he is shown standing against or sitting under the sacred fig or banyan, whose long slender leaves twine about his body or stream above his shoulders like tongues of flame suggesting the prime symbol of the generous growth of the soil. As I said above, Kuvera is followed by a great host (his Ganas) of Yaksas or tree spirits, collectively designated Vaiśrāvana-kayka-devas, meaning deities who make up the rout of Vaiśravana, a Buddhist name for Kuvera, under which name he acts as the power – the Lokapala or guardian of the North – which repels invasions of cold and darkness.

On the southern side of a mythical northern mountain called Kailása he presides over an earthly paradise filled with beautiful palaces and ever-blooming groves and gardens. His favourite grove, called Caitraratha, is full of trees whose leaves are jewels and whose fruits are the beautiful girls called Yaksis. When A.K. Coomaraswamy sought to analyse the provenance and nature of Kuvera and his followers, he came to the following conclusions:

> Kuvera and other Yaksas are indigenous, non-Aryan deities or genii, usually beneficent powers of wealth and fertility. ... The designation Yaksa was originally practically synonymous with Deva or Devata [god or goddess], and no essential distinction can be made between Yaksas and Devas; every Hindu deity, and even the Buddha, is spoken of, upon occasion, as a Yaksa. "Yaksa" may have been a non-Aryan, at any rate a popular, designation equivalent to Deva, and only at a later date restricted to genii of lower rank than that of the greater gods.[2]

Coomaraswamy believes that the use in Buddhist worship of rosaries, incense, bells, and lights – practices which many scholars think came into Christianity from Buddhism – has its ultimate source in non- and pre-Aryan Indian forms of worship. It is also likely that this early worship was characterised by a good deal of overeating, overdrinking, and overcoupling on the part of Kuvera's beautiful but rowdy followers, the Yaksas and Yaksis, with the grotesque Guhyas carrying on in the background. The law book of Manu says disapprovingly that meat and strong drink are specifically the food of Yaksas, while in the *Meghaduta (Cloud-Messenger)* of the poet Kalidasa, Yaksas are described as drinking wine, produced from *kalpa* trees, in the company of beautiful girls. In the art of Gandhara, which flourished from the first to the fifth century, we find many bacchanalian scenes traceable on the formal side to Greek influence but surely representing in spirit and content the revels on Mount Kailása which defended prehistoric India against the winds and snow of the Northland and guaranteed great crops of grain, kalpas of calves, and crores of babies for India.

In the absence of historical documents it is difficult for us to make out what the early India of Kuvera was like, but it is clear that it must have been a land filled with millet and rice, great trees that furnished men with shadel fruits, silk-cotton from which to spin clothes, sites for whole tree-cities, incredibly strong and handsome animals, and human beings so in love with life that they welcomed a future composed of an endless round of reincarnations here on earth, whether as men, animals, or plants. Finding life so wondrous, so pervaded by a divine spirit of growth which was ever seeking to achieve new forms of beauty and abundance, they did not care to escape to a heaven beyond the sky. Of course, we know that this idyllic period, this Indian Eden or Golden Age (it was perhaps called that because lighted by the use of much gold in personal adornment) came to a sorry end.

It was succeeded by a period as miserable and unhappy as the former had been blissful, a period in which many Indians seem to have spent much of their time devising and trying to put into effect ways of escaping forever in the round of reincarnations in which they had once rejoiced. In India, as elsewhere, the Golden Age seems to have been destroyed by invaders, these being a white-skinned people calling themselves Aryans or "noblemen", who sought to reduce the dark-skinned people of that earlier blissful Indian – we call them, very loosely, Dravidians – to the status of slaves. These conquering Aryans seem to have been about as unscrupulous and self-conscious a "master race" as the world has ever seen. On the coffee-coloured people of India they loosed a torrent of those ugly passions with which we are only too familiar in certain types of white man to this very day: power madness, race madness, colour madness, eventuating in large-scale cruelty, destruction, and enslavement, and in the petrifaction by studied guile of injustice created by studied violence.

The creation of the caste system, especially as it affected the Sudras (the servant or non-Aryan caste, those who work with their hands) and outcastes, was not, I think, an example of the evil which men unwittingly do. It was rather, perhaps, the world's foremost glass-case exhibit of the misery that a handful of race-proud, power-intoxicated soldiers can wilfully inflict on their fellow-creatures, not for a few decades or centuries but for millenia, provided their aggression is successful and their claims equated with God's will by a clever propaganda machine like the old Aryan priesthood. The invading Aryans, who seem to have arrived in India in successive waves at various times during the second millenium B.C. provided with war horses and armour, had little difficulty conquering the Dravidians, especially since their armies were composed to a large extent of half-clothed women archers – their civilisation seems to have been, like that of so many Golden Ages, still matriarchal or characterised by matrilineal societal and political institutions. The Eden–Kailása of Kuvera was shattered, and Kuvera's elephant (could this have been Kuvera himself?) became the *vahana* or vehicle on which Indra, the war god of the invaders, rode over a good part of northern India. Kuvera was now reduced to the status of a demon, a horrible example of depravity, a forest-dwelling bogey man with stories of whom mothers frightened their children.

The caste system, only in 1950 abolished by law though by no means in fact, was an attempt on the part of the Aryan conquerors, who seem to have brought few or no white wives with them to India, to prevent themselves from being entirely absorbed by the dark Dravidians. Their fetishistic adoration of whiteness led, after a good deal of miscegenation had taken place, to the creation of an almost unique example of a cruel and divisive social system.

The Sanskrit word for caste, *varna*, means complexion or skin colour, nothing else, and the caste system was intended to prevent the further darkening of the Aryans at the same time that it froze the by then multi-coloured people of India into social strata on the basis of comparative whiteness. At the apex of this system were set the Brahmins, whose supposedly undiluted whiteness was held to prove their intelligence and nearness to God; they were priests, teachers, and scribes. Next came the Ksatriyas, the warrior or ruling caste, whose "red" complexion would seem to indicate a certain dilution of Aryan purity. The Vaisyas, the landowning, trading, and banking caste, are variously described as yellow, green, or brown in colour, indicating a still larger admixture of native blood. At the bottom of the scale were the black men, the Sudras, who were theoretically unfitted by the hue of their skin for anything but menial hand work. People who would not submit to this classification or who attacked it openly or who violated its rules against inter-caste marriage and dining were declared outcastes, and for hundreds of years were subject to be killed on sight. Later they were allowed to return from jungle hiding to the towns in order to be bearers of night soil or tanners of the skin of the tabooed cow, but they had to carry bells with them and continually announce their presence when they walked abroad in order that caste-Indians might avoid the religious impurity incurred by brushing against them or even by falling within the contaminating blackness of their shadows.

I have no room here to go on describing the blight which the conquerors brought upon the abundant, loving, carefree life that seems to have characterised the early Dravidians by equating caste duty with the Divine Will and punishing its violation with unspeakable degradation in this life and throughout endless incarnations. In fact, observance of caste duty, doing one's *dharma* or caste work, was made the very heart of Hindu religion, both practice and theory, for one could believe in any of the mutually contradictory notions of God or Ultimate Reality presented by six different philosophical systems, two of which were, essentially, atheistic!

Here we see in sharp focus how religion can be made to serve the worldly purposes of a relatively small group who have relatively large battalions, and why those whose wisdom is not the wisdom of this world may find themselves pitted against prevailing rites, dogmas, and theology. Perhaps the Aryans were no worse than any other conquerors, but the racial problem, the question of skin colour, led in India to fiercer and more ingenious forms of oppression, to a more violent rejection of the native gods, and to more reluctance to bring the exiled descendants of Divine Kings out of forest hiding for the purpose of presiding over an Indian Saturnalia, than any that we have encountered elsewhere. Nevertheless, ancient powers of life and love and beauty insisted, at least, on reasserting themselves in protestant movements such as Jainism or Buddhism, which gained such influence among the Indian masses that Hinduism might have been entirely supplanted had it not admitted to its pantheon Kuvera or Kuvera-like fertility deities from the ancient past, and absorbed liberal amounts of the morality, art, and culture of the submerged Dravidians.*

Buddhism, a movement which took form early in the fifth century B.C., nourished by roots sunk deep in the soil of India's pre-Aryan past, protested against caste distinctions and sought to make an end of the violence to which India seemed to be eternally condemned by the inviolable divine obligation laid on each rajah, with his warriors, to prey on his neighbours and die fighting in boots filled with his streaming blood. Siddhartha Gautama, later known as the Buddha or Enlightened One, was a crown prince, that is, by Hindu standards, a Ksatriya born not only to rule but to inflict and suffer

---

*The nature and extent of Dravidian influence on Indian culture may be glimpsed, if rather fitfully, in:

(1)   L.D. Barnett, *Antiquities of India* (London, 1913);
(2)   T.C. Hodson, *The Primitive Culture of India* (London, 1922);
(3)   G. Slater, *The Dravidian Element in Indian Culture* (London, 1924);
(4)   P. Mitra, *Prehistoric India: its Place in the World's Culture* (Bombay, 1925);
(5)   S.V. Viswanatha, *Racial Synthesis in Hindu Culture* (London, 1929).

violent death; not a few of the many stories told of his life indicate that it was this obligatory violence more than any other single thing which led him to seek to upset caste and devise a way of life softened by compassionate insight and rounded by deeds of affectionate self-sacrifice. Of course, I do not mean to suggest for a moment that the Buddha, with his attack on caste and cruelty, was a humorous religious genius or more than remotely reminiscent of Falstaff. Nevertheless, he must have called his way of righteousness the Eight-Fold Aryan Path in irony because it was the opposite, in almost every respect, of the literally Aryan way. Right belief, right resolve, right speech, right behaviour, right occupation, right effort, right contemplation, and right concentration cannot be twisted to include even a shade of fighting or violence, and the Buddha would have been readier than Falstaff to detect something essentially wrong in Hotspur's contention that any man who will not quarrel at the drop of a hat is no Christian – "What a pagan rascal is this! An infidel!"[3] – or Henry IV's praise of the

> renowned Douglas! whose high deeds,
> Whose hot incursion and great name in arms,
> Holds from all soldiers chief majority
> And military title capital
> Through all the kingdoms that acknowledge Christ.[4]

Over the centuries Buddhism underwent many developments in both theology and morality which would probably have shocked the Buddha himself, but I am pretty sure he would not have objected to those achievements of Buddhist art which brought Kuvera and his Sakti back into India's consciousness and associated the pacific prince himself with the elephant in a hundred striking ways. In Buddhist legends the life force which later became the all-compassionate Buddha is represented as having descended from on high into his mother's womb in the form of a little white elephant. His mother, Maya, seems herself to have been a Yaski or Indian dryad and she bore him, as Yaksis bore their children, standing under a tree to the lower branches of which she clung in her birth-pain, while Indian art records that a Yaksa king, perhaps Kuvera himself, standing under a tree surrounded by the shrine at which he is accustomed to receive homage, was the first to worship the divine child. No stories connected with the Buddha are so common as those in which an elephant appears, whether in the various more or less synoptic lives of the Buddha, in the *Jatakas* or stories of Gautama's many former incarnations, or the *Dhammapad-Attha-Katha*, which undertakes to illustrate the precepts of the *Dhammapada* or book of keynote sermons by stories of what the Buddha saw and underwent during his life.[*]

---

[*]The best of the old lives and stories of the Buddha available in English are:

(1)   *The Lalitavistara*, tr. R. Mitra (Calcutta, 1881–96);
(2)   *Asvaghosa Buddhacarita*, tr. E.B. Cowell (Oxford, 1894);

Perhaps the most famous of the *Jatakas* is the story of the persecution and self-sacrifice of the Buddha as a great king of elephants with three tusks on either side of his great trunk. The *Dhammapada Commentary* or *Buddhist Legends* is full of stories of elephants who minister to the Buddha; who, when they could easily crush them, merely rebuke hunters for trying to kill them, who refuse to trample on the virtuous even when goaded to do so, and who die of a broken heart when forced to part from the Buddha. In Mahayana Buddhism the Bodhisattva, Samantabhadra, who represents the principle of particularity or compassionate love to all living things, is always represented as riding on an elephant, while a Japanese version of this deity, Fugen, is usually shown sitting on a lotus which is carried on the back of a handsome white elephant. Especially in China we find figures like Pu Tai, known as the laughing Buddha, who, while not elephants even in part, have heads, chests and stomachs which are perfect studies in pachydermous circles and rhomboids. There is hardly a Buddhist temple in China or Japan in which Pu Tai is not worshipped, and he is enthroned in the vestibules of monasteries as a monk who was especially friendly to babies and children. Sometimes he is shown with babies swarming up his arms and legs, and there is no doubt that he is in direct descent from the Buddha himself, who has usually come to be identified, in northern Asia at least, with the principle of love as it operates on both the physical and spiritual planes, producing abundance of rice, children, enlightenment, herds, and lovingkindness quite indiscriminately.

In the *Bhagavad-Gita* the warrior prince Arjuna, who is about to engage in a great battle with his near relatives, a battle in which thousands of men and animals are likely to die, hesitates to join the attack because he shrinks, Buddhist-like, from slaughter, though he rationalises his repugnance to war by telling his charioteer, Krishna, that slaughter weakens respect for law, and that disrespect for law will destroy the caste system. This gives Krishna, no ordinary charioteer, an opportunity to expound and defend the caste system, but what a two-edged or two-faced defence he makes! It is generally agreed that the *Bhagavad-Gita* saved Hinduism from the alarming inroads

---

(3) The *Abhiniskramana Sutra* of the *Vinaya Pitaka* of the Dharmagupta sect, translated from a Chinese version as *The Romantic Legend of Sakya Buddha* by S. Beal (London, 1875);

(4) Ksemendra, *The Avadana Kalpalata*, tr. N.C. Das as *Legends and Miracles of Buddha* (Calcutta, 1885);

(5) *Nidana-Katha*, a Pali life of Buddha affixed to the great collection of *Jatakas*, tr. T.W. Rhys-Davids as *The Story of the Lineage* (London, 1880);

(6) *The Jataka: or Stories of the Buddha's Former Births*, tr. in seven volumes by various people under the editorship of E.B. Cowell (Cambridge, 1895–1913);

(7) *Aryasura*, a Sanskrit version in poetic form of several of the Pali *Jataka*, tr. J.S. Speyer (London, 1895);

(8) *Dhammapad-Attha-Katha* or *Dhammapada Commentary*, tr. E.W. Burlingame as *Buddhist Legends*, 3 vols (Cambridge, Mass., 1921).

*Head of Kuvera being cut off by prince for whom he has obtained kingship
(Buddhist)*

Collection of Roderick Marshall, Oxford

of Buddhism and so thoroughly weakened the latter religion that by the eleventh century it had, with the help of Muslim invaders, practically disappeared from India. This statement is roughly true, I suppose, but Krishna saved Hinduism only by appropriating for it so much old Dravidian and Buddhist lore and precept that Hinduism thenceforth carried in its own breast forces bound to undermine and dissolve the injustices of caste and the astringency of religion-commanded injuriousness. Now just who was this strange charioteer, this enormous, handsome–ugly Krishna who, though a mere horse-driver, undertook to tutor a great Aryan prince in the deepest mysteries of religion?

Krishna's story has, on the face of it, much of the pattern which we have come to connect with the career of a Substitute or Mock King.* In time he came to be called an avatar of the Sun-God Visnu, Aryan husband of Lakśmi. Five young brothers called the Pandus or Pandavas – a band of self-appointed St Georges – are seeking to wrest power from their wicked relatives, the Kurus or Kuravas, because the latter by permitting and practising gross injustice have endangered the public welfare and the pro- ductivity of the land. These brothers, connected with the royal house which they seek to destroy, are clearly upstarts unpractised in bringing in an age of golden grain and crystalline happiness for all. Accordingly, they are forced to seek aid from the uncle of the wife whom they have married in common,

---

*The literature of Krishna can be read in English translation in the following books:

(1) *The Mahabharata*, tr. P.C. Roy, 18 vols (Calcutta, 1883–96);

(2) *The Haravasmśa*, an enormous tale tacked on to *The Mahabharata* and dealing with Krishna, tr. M.N. Dutt (Calcutta, 1897);

(3) *The Bhagavad-Gita*, the great but equivocal exposition of Hinduism by Krishna interpolated in *The Mahabharata* and translated upwards of three dozen times into English;

(4) *The Visnu Purana* (fourth century A.D.?), the fifth book of which, devoted to the story of Krishna, ranks next to the *Gita* in the theological interpretation of the avatar's impor- tance, tr. H.H. Wilson (London, 1840) and S.S. Aiyar (Madras, 1904);

(5) *The Bhagavata Purana* (tenth century A.D.?), a great work of semi-historical lore on the life, more particularly the love life, of Krishna, tr. M.H. Dutt as the *Shrimad Bhaga- batam* (Calcutta, 1895), by J.M. Sanyall, 5 vols (Calcutta, 1929), and in a condensed form by V. Raghavan (Madras, 1937);

(6) *The Prema-sagara*, a Hindi version by L. Lal of the tenth *skandha* or chapter of *The Bhagavata Purana*, tr. in full by F. Pincott (Westminster, 1897) and in part by A. Khan (Calcutta, 1879); a Kashmiri translation of the same *skandha* entitled *Sri-Krsnavatara- lila* was Englished by G.A. Grierson (Calcutta, 1928);

(7) Jayadeva, *Gita Govinda*, a great poem on the loves of Krishna and Radha composed in the twelfth century, tr. E. Arnold as *The Indian Song of Songs* (London, 1875) and adapted into English prose by Puran Singh in *The Spirit of Oriental Poetry* (London, 1926);

(8) Vidyapati, *Bangiya Padabali*, a series of poems on Krishna and Radha written in Braj Bhasa (an old form of Hindi) in the fifteenth century, tr. A. Coomaraswamy and A. Sen (London, 1915).

one Draupadi or Krisnā (the female form of a word meaning the Dark One). This polyandrous story would seem to indicate that the five Georges had married a Dravidian princess on her own more or less matriarchal terms, and it is she who persuades her beloved uncle, Krishna (the male form of the word meaning the Dark One) to save her husbands, who have overextended their battle line. It is probable that we should conceive of the great battle about to be fought on the field of Kuruksetra, described in the poem as a kind of Armageddon intended to inaugurate the new age of gold, as a glorified seasonal rite performed to redeem India from the forces of darkness. In dealing with this Indian material we must be careful not to attach any symbolical meaning to the dark skin of Krishna, the Sun champion and avatar; symbolically, he is a golden light shining throughout the poem in surrounding darkness. A report by special wire by Robert Trumbull to the *New York Times*, filed in Kuruksetra on 25 February 1952, will throw some light on the white-hot sun associations:

> While scientists in other parts of the world levelled expensive instruments at today's solar eclipse, more than half a million praying and chanting Hindus – men, women and children of all ages – gathered in this holiest place of India this afternoon to throw the weight of their religious devotion on the side of ... god in the struggle between the sun and the moon, which symbolises to them virtue in the grip of evil.
>
> While the shadow of the moon lay part way across the sun, thousands upon thousands ... jostled each other in the thick white dust and 90-degree heat to find a space in the seven sacred pools where, they believe, they can cleanse themselves of evil influence that falls upon the world as the sun is obscured. ... There were separate places for men and women, but to a great extent the separation of the sexes was disregarded under the impact of the need for prayer for all of beleaguered mankind in what the Hindus consider to be a time of great peril to the world and its rulers.
>
> In Hindu mythology the solar eclipse represents one of the repeated efforts of the bodiless demon Rahu ... to devour the sun. ... In their deep concern for the world's salvation as well as their own these teeming thousands ... last night, in tireless devotion, ... fought off sleep and chanted and prayed the night through to strengthen the sun for its coming struggle.

The prayers of these good Hindus are conceived of as doing for the kings and the good government of this world just about what Krishna did so long ago in the great battle which is supposed to have taken place on this very spot.

Like the other figures we have considered, Krishna is represented, at least in the *Gita*, as a helper, a tutor, and by moments a cosmically enormous being coextensive with the entire creation (elsewhere in the poem he is sometimes shown as uncouth and hugely intoxicated). He is ostensibly merely a dark-skinned chieftain whom the Kurus have invited to help them win the battle, during which he serves in the humble role of charioteer to

Prince Arjuna, of whom more especially he becomes the friend and tutor. He is possessed of a great stock of old Dravidian fertility lore. Though called, later, an avatar of Visnu, he seems to be the descendant of the sun through a totemic animal father. He has certain characteristics of a stag but is especially associated with the elephant by those myths which make him the father of Ganeśa. However, he is by no means such a feral creature as Silenos, Bes, or Enkidu. It is true that in his early life he was a refugee from the hatred of a usurping king who, at his birth, ordered a Herodian Slaughter of the Innocents. Hidden away on a farm, he grew up amongst cowherds and milkmaids, but before joining the Pandus he had won back his patrimony, and he seems to have united with them simply as the result of Draupadi's persuasion and his own voluntary action. In fact, by the time when he was introduced into the *Mahabharata* he was not so much a deposed and degraded king of the aborigines as a figure commanding, even from his enemies, a good deal of veneration. In a more dignified way than most of the Falstaff-personae he was famous for miracles of field and fold, for feats of superhuman strength, and for egregious and inexhaustible sexual prowess. Undoubtedly it was, in the first instance, the lore of fruitfulness which he taught to the Pandu Georges, thus furnishing them with the star-spangled sword by which they were able to cut their way to victory. It is related of him not merely that he helped the Pandus to power but that he released some twenty thousand kings from captivity to the forces of darkness and evil; not merely that he made ritual love for Arjuna's benefit to ten or twelve queens or concubines in addition to Radha and Rukmini, who were called his favourite wives, but that he rescued from captivity sixteen thousand and one hundred princesses, all of whom he married and by each separate one of whom he had ten lotus-eyed and yellow-frocked sons and a daughter as beautiful as Lakśmi, Goddess of Fortune. In spite of these tremendous feats, Krishna's power declined during the last days of the great battle-rite and, as the story goes, some thirty-six years (days?) after the victory at Kuruksetra, Krishna perished miserably and alone, while all his people (he had, of course, a rout or train of followers, the Vrisnis, who were in the beginning simply the uncouth cowherds and milkmaids of his boyhood days on the great farm at Braj) were destroyed. Arjuna, who gained most from his teaching, did nothing whatever to save him, though it is said he made an unsuccessful attempt to rescue some of the women Krishna had loved to such good effect for the world's benefit. Hiding in the forest from mysterious enemies (who may have been set upon him by Arjuna himself; all forms of the story are very obscure on this point), he was shot by a hunter in mistake for a buck and ascended into the sky, filling the great vault with shining glory.

In some ways, as has already become apparent, this Krishna of India was one of the most hugely Falstaffian of all such characters so far examined. In addition, his scorn for man-made law, the law of the conqueror, even when raised to the dignity of religious dogma, was almost as tremendous as his feats of love. There are many tales of him as a fabulous baby and incredibly naughty child. We are not told that, like Falstaff, he was born with a grey head, but he certainly had "something a round belly", which he was always further expanding by continual thefts of butter. To clothe his beggarly rout of cowherds he stole clothes from the usurping king's washermen, but the theft for which he is most famous was that of the milkmaids' clothing when they were bathing. Their garments he carried up a tree, where he sat, a veritable Yaksa, commanding each girl to appear in undisguised nakedness before he would throw down her sari.

This scene is a favourite of Indian artists and theologians, who interpret it as meaning that man cannot and must not hold back anything from God. Indeed no milkmaid and no other woman, married or single, could or ever wished to deny Krishna. Maenad-like, all loved to dance with him in a mystic circle, a dance which made all India spring into bud and blossom, and which ended by Krishna dividing himself into a thousand indistinguishable Krishnas for the purpose of giving himself personally to every lover in equal measure and at the same moment – a form of lovemaking which is also susceptible of symbolic interpretation. One of the places in which these deeds of Krishna are most delightfully and voluptuously described is the tenth chapter of the *Bhagavata Purana*, translated into Hindi as the *Prema-Sagara* or *Ocean of Love*. In this book King Pariksit, hearing of this last miracle from the saint Sri Sukadev Ji, is shocked, exclaiming,

> "If Sri Krisna Chand, indeed, took incarnate form and came into the world to slay asuras [demons of darkness] and remove the burden of the earth, and to give happiness to good and pious people, and to promote the course of virtue, why did he dance and sport with the wives of others? This indeed is the act of a libertine, to enjoy the wife of another."
> Sukadev Ji said, "Listen, King! You do not understand this mystery. ... What are not the powerful doing? They, indeed, by acting interfere with destiny. ... Who knows the true meaning of their course of action? They indeed do nothing for themselves."[5]

In fact, the point missed by literal-minded people, including perhaps the critics of Falstaff, when trying to estimate activities of any Falstaff-persona, is that these characters often give of themselves, even unto death, simply for the good of mankind. This mission of theirs involves denying and even disestablishing, at least for a time, the worship of the gods that be. We shall come to this point in a moment, but first, I wish to quote from the book just mentioned a denunciation of Krishna worship by a peevish Indian monarch which makes one think of Dover Wilson denouncing Bradley's apotheosis of Falstaff.

> He who, having been born in Braj, ate the orts of the cowherd lads has received in this assembly greatness and lordship. All are thoughtlessly calling him great; they are giving the power of the lord of the gods to a

black crow. He who made friends with low fellows and women of loose morals has been constituted by this assembly the very holiest; he who stole from every house milk curds, buttermilk, and butter, his praise has been sung by all in unison; ... he who by force and fraud has enjoyed other men's wives, him all have unanimously accorded the first forehead-mark; he who abolished the worship of Indra in Braj has been raised to the rank of god; he whose genealogy, parentage, family and duties are obscure and unsettled, him have all honored as the Invisible and Indestructible One.[6]

The Indra mentioned above was, we remember, the chief war god of the conquering Aryans, and Krishna's successful attack on his worship points to the main concern of the present chapter, the scorn of all Mock Monarchs for the currently accepted religion of the conquerors. It seems to have been required of all Substitute Kings that during the Saturnalia they make fun, probably according to an accepted libretto, of the rites, dogmas, and even the god of the religion that has supplanted the fertility worship of which they themselves are among the few remaining hierophants. Falstaff and his crew love to boast that they have even forgotten what the inside of a church is made of, and the only rosary they choose to tell over again and again is that of deeds which the established church denounces as vices. They call themselves "Ephesians ... of the old church",[7] and speak of allegiance to a Diana-like goddess. Falstaff swears jestingly "by the mass",[8] perhaps punning on the size of his own stomach, and when he swears falsely that his sword was hacked like a handsaw at the battle of Gad's Hill (it has been hacked, but by himself against a stone), he raises the battered blade, probably hilt upward, with the solemn words *"Ecce signum"*.[9] These are the words spoken during the Roman mass at the raising of the cross. After he has made sure that the gold stolen at Gad's Hill has been safely brought to the Boar's Head, Falstaff invites his crew to a night of revelry, drinking, and extemporary play-acting (mumming?) with words which parallel those spoken by Christ in the long vigil in Gethsemane on the night before the Crucifixion, "Watch tonight, pray to-morrow."[10] Several times Falstaff blames the decline of the good life of ritual robbery, revelry, and wenching on the rise of psalm-singing, as when he attributes his own decline into old age to a gullible "hallooing and singing of anthems"[11] or when he exclaims ironically in the Boar's Head, "God help the while! a bad world, I say. I would I were a weaver; I could sing psalms or anything."[12] To this reader, at any rate, it seems unnecessary to explain such passages as the nostalgic Lollardy of a Lord of Misrule whom Shakespeare first named Oldcastle. Falstaff and all his entourage, in addition to Dame Quickly, find prayer-given people peevish (*"Quick.* His worst fault is, that he is given to prayer. He is something peevish that way"[13]), and like that minor Falstaff, Sir Toby Belch of *Twelfth Night*, they would try, if forced to go to church, to relieve the tedium and melancholy of the obligation by dancing thither and back (*"Sir To.* Why dost thou not go to church in a galliard and come home in a coranto?"[14]). When Falstaff talks of repentance, it is always in a highly ironical vein, as when he tells Hal to "repent at idle times as thou mayest; and so, farewell."[15]

But these attacks on the church by Falstaff and his followers sound like good-natured echoes of that famous anticlerical Sacaea of the Middle Ages, in which "sacred things were profaned, laws relaxed, and ethical ideals reversed under the leadership of a Patriarch, Pope, or Bishop of Fools",[16] when compared with Krishna's onslaught on Hinduism. In the Sacaea of the Middle Ages there was, as everyone knows, a momentary overturn of all sacred customs, the transformation beginning with the singing, over and over and with a fresh sense and emphasis, of the significant words from the Vesper Magnificat: "He hath put down the mighty from their seats and hath exalted the humble and meek." For the period of the celebration the clergy formally shed their authority by delivering the *baculus* or staff of office to a despised subdeacon who then, as the Bishop of Fools or Abbot of Unreason, presided over a blasphemous censing of the church. This was followed by a burlesquing of the solemn mass in which the celebrant, instead of pronouncing the *"Ite missa est"*, brayed three times like an ass while the people responded with howls and shouts of derision. These are lengths to which Falstaff and his Ephesians did not go, but they fall whole lengths short of Krishna's attack on Hinduism.

There are peculiar reasons which make Krishna the best known of all Mock Kings and yet, in spite of his famous dancing, lovemaking, thievery, and irreverence, somewhat hard to recognise in this role. If we assume, as some mythologists do, that the *Mahabharata* was first of all the libretto to a great seasonal drama which was later written down as a story and expanded by the addition of all kinds of folklore, then the first picture of Krishna must have been that of a not untypical Substitute King educating a prince (Arjuna) for his fertility duties, presiding over a seasonal battle, and dying in the end to increase the pupil's strength, or, as we have come to understand this phenomenon, dying into the life of the young prince – that typical series of episodes which constitutes a symbolic account of how the declining sun of winter renews its youth and restores fruits and flowers to the barren womb of earth.

But clearly the Krishna of the *Mahabharata* is more than this typical Falstaff-persona, largely because of a theological poem interpolated into the epic after it had assumed something like its final form. This interpolation is the famous *Bhagavad-Gita* or speech which Krishna makes to his pupil Arjuna on the night before the battle. This, often called the chief scripture of India, is on the face of it not a lesson in fertility lore but a defence of the caste system and of the violence religiously enjoined on the warrior group. It seems that around the time of Christ, Hinduism was fighting desperately, perhaps for its life, against the inroads of Buddhism, which discouraged or ignored caste and preached non-violence toward all forms of life. In order to regain its hold on the lower castes, Hinduism had to resort to extreme measures, and a Brahmin priest, it is thought, hit upon the expedient of making the widely popular figure of the epic poem – Krishna the companion of cowherds and milkmaids, lord of animals, tremendous eater, drinker, and lovemaker, who taught Arjuna fertility wisdom because he was himself the deputy on earth of some ancient Dravidian sun-god and was willing to give his life for Arjuna, his nephew by marriage – hit on the expedient, I say, of making this black sun-hero confirm the most *outré* beliefs and dogmas of Hinduism! This was indeed a clever idea, but it was bound to backfire, sooner or later, because the great dark demi-god was too thoroughly associated with Dravidian wisdom to be made to stand convincingly for the Aryan rejection of that wisdom. Krishna had to be silenced, as it were, to pre-empt both points of view, no matter how discordant or incompatible. He had to be made to say that the caste system was his own invention and dear to his heart, and yet allowed to affirm that he held no group of men dearer than any other.

In Hinduism before the *Gita*, the careful and unquestioning performance of caste duty had been held to help a low-caste man to be reincarnated a little higher in the social scale until finally he became a Brahmin, after which achievement he could escape entirely from the round of existences into direct and everlasting union with the Ultimate Reality which underlies phenomenal life. This theory was a neat way of persuading people to put up with their caste disabilities and perform their caste duties without complaint, for however little they liked them, their lot was bound to improve till some day they themselves would become a portion of the disembodied Truth. Now Krishna, while confirming the caste system, took the sting out of social distinctions and abolished the advantages of Brahminism by declaring that any person of any caste who performed his caste work disinterestedly, that is, without attachment to results or to rewards, without any motive except the love of Him who commands that all shall work, each after his fashion – this person could be united directly, both in this life and forever after, with God.

But God in what sense, in what form? It was here that a difficulty (for Brahminism) arose. In order to give Krishna's approval, partial as it was, of the caste system's incontestable validity, it was necessary for the Brahmin poet of the *Gita* to equate the sun-hero with the Supreme Reality, and this fact gave *every* statement of his, both in the *Gita* and elsewhere, the quality of an unimpeachable divine commandment or pronouncement. Thus in order to save Hinduism the Brahmins were forced to entrust their fortunes to a fertility god of the Dravidians, the whole sense of whose well-known and well-loved life tended to deny the tenets which his voice, speaking at Kuruksetra, was made to affirm. After all Krishna was, as we have seen, the traditional enemy of Indra, the Aryan war-god, and had always blasphemed against him and decried his worship. Now the tables were turned, and the

Mock King's scorn of the rites, forms, ceremonies, and gods of orthodox
Hinduism became the word of the living God, at least for those Indians who
flocked to his standard, and these were indeed so many that Buddhism in
time entirely lost its hold on the people of the peninsula.

As we have seen, the remission of law at the Saturnalia, the exaltation of
slaves over their masters, and the appointment of a temporary king over a
topsy-turvy society were designed to just one end: to reinvigorate the
processes of nature by reviving old customs, righting old wrongs (at least for
a time), and restoring to the dispossessed and to their gods (for a season, a
dangerous season) the power and worship they had once enjoyed. For early
men there was always the possibility that the old gods and their representatives on earth, their priests and kings, might just be the only possessors of
the magic influence needed to restore the ruddiness of the sun, the greenness
of the earth – always a chance that the invaders' gods would be impotent in
the new land. For this reason the Mock King was called in and allowed,
perhaps compelled, not merely to insult and rob the ruling monarch but to
mock the regnant gods. It was never contemplated that he would replace
them, however, nor did this happen except in one country, India, where the
Mock King was asked, quite inappropriately, to confirm the tenets of the
conquerors' religion. This he did, out of one side of his cosmic mouth, but
out of the other the irrepressible fertility deity denied what he had just
affirmed. Caste is fine, he said, in fact indispensable, but I, God, generally
dispense with it. Brahmins come to my bosom through studying the scriptures and the practice of asceticism, but the Sudras, those heavy-laden
workers, may come to me just as easily by performing their daily tasks –
may come, in fact, more easily, for I, Krishna, the Supreme God with a
farm-boy background, I the Divine Lover of women, prefer the Way of
Work to that of No-work or withdrawal from life.

We can readily imagine how glad most Indians were to hear that "a man of
deep insight looks with the same eye upon a Brahmin well versed in the
scriptures, upon a cow, or an elephant, or a dog, or an outcaste". Jnanesvar,
a twelfth-century follower of Krishna in the Maratha country, turned this
passage into a hymn which is widely sung to this day in India. Speaking of
the man of insight who knows God because God is in him and knows him,
Jnanesvar wrote:

> His heart, O Arjuna, no bias knows:
> On all an equal aspect he bestows
> Friends let them be or foes. ...
> Ah, sweetly, sweetly does the moonlight fall
> Alike upon the monarch and the thrall –
> So he the same to all.[17]

Under the influence of Krishna's assurance that each and every man can be
joined with him in this world and gain release from endless incarnations by
doing his daily task without attachment or self-seeking passion, Indians

began to find such bliss in this world, such mystic union with the Divine through love and work performed on earth, that they began actively to fear total absorption into the Godhead, for as Ramakrishna, a nineteenth-century saint, said, "Who would wish to become sugar if he could always be eating sugar?" For Krishna's followers, the blight of caste, now broken though the system remained literally in force, life became a year-round Saturnalia under a Mock King who had miraculously become the supreme deity:

> They bathe in Wisdom; then their hunger stay
> With Perfectness; lo, all in green array,
> The leaves of peace are they.
>
> Buds of Attainment these; columns they are
> In Valour's hall; for joy fetched from afar
> Each in a full water jar.
>
> So dear the path of Love-Work, they despise
> The Great Release; e'en in their sport there lies
> The wisdom of the wise.
>
> With pearls of Peace their limbs they beautify;
> Within their minds as in a scabbard I,
> The All-indweller, lie.[18]

It is Krishna, of course, who is speaking, and this is another popular hymn paraphrased by Jnanesvar from a passage in the *Gita*. In the Maratha country, at least, Krishna became an active opponent of asceticism and life-denial, as is shown in the story of Gora the potter who, rapt in yogic contemplation, trampled his baby son into the clay he was kneading with his feet and, having decided that women were an impediment to the spiritual life, took an oath never to lie with his two wives. When, by placing the hands of their sleeping husband on their breasts, they tricked him into believing he had broken his vow of chastity, he managed to amputate the offending members at the wrist. Handless now, Gora, having renounced both love and work, could give himself up entirely to the practice of yoga. But one day at a celebration in honour of Krishna, he wished to be able, like all the other worshippers, to wave a flag in honour of God, and prayed for a miracle. It happened, but accompanied by a solemn voice from heaven which said to Gora:

> "Go home now and play the fool no longer. Think no more of your
> insane vow, but be kind to your wives and make the face of your
> murdered boy – I herewith resurrect him – shine with happiness. My
> worship is action, physical yet spiritual, simple yet profound, eternal
> but here and now."[19]

From stories like this and songs like Jnanesvar's it is clear that in one way or another Krishna did bring to India, and for ever, we may suppose, the Golden Age that every Mock King seeks to bring back for a week or so; also, that this wondrous deity was quite equal to the task of providing green pastures not merely for herds and flocks but also for the human spirit reaching for ecstatic union with the Divine through love and love's labour, for an experience of timeless and infinite Truth, but not in a sphere beyond time and place.

The Indians think of Krishna as one of the avatars or incarnations of Visnu, god of the nourishing light of the sun. Visnu, as we have seen, had several avatars, many in half-animal form, to at least one of which, the boar or *varaha* avatar, we have called special attention. When Visnu descended to save mankind and the physical world at Kuruksetra, his golden fire became incarnate in the glorious human form of Krishna who is so beloved in India. But we are told that still another deity, no avatar of Visnu though often worshipped in Hindu temples in company with Visnu's animal incarnations, and said in certain versions of the saviour lineage to be a son of Krishna himself, is even more beloved by modern Indians. I mean, of course, the happy, elephant-faced Ganesa, who is often hailed as "Remover of Obstacles", an epithet by which Krishna himself is referred to in the *Mahabharata*. Alice Getty begins her book on Ganesa thus:

> Ganesa, Lord of the Ganas (followers, troops, or crew of revellers), although among the latest deities to be admitted to the Brahmanic pantheon, was, and still is, the most universally adored of all the Hindu gods, and his image is found in practically every part of India. ...
>
> Certain authorities believe that Ganesa was originally a Dravidian deity worshipped by the aboriginal populations of India who were sun worshippers; and that Ganesa on his *vahana*, the rat, symbolised the sun-god overcoming the animal, which, in ancient mythology, was a symbol of the night.
>
> It is not known whether Ganesa is to be looked upon as an original or a derivative deity, but it is probable he was primarily the totem of a Dravidian tribe. The primitive effigies were often animal-headed; and the elephant, being the largest animal in India as well as the shrewdest, would assuredly have figured among them.[20]

Though Ganesa is often represented as being the son of Siva and Parvati, gods into whose symbolism we have no space to go here, this seems very unlikely inasmuch as these deities, because of divine vows, were pledged to abstention from sexual intercourse. To be sure, there are several accounts of the fashion in which Parvati managed, without Siva's help, to become the mother of the elephant-headed god. Sometimes she is said to have done it simply by rubbing her body gently, or by mixing together unguents she had used with certain impurities from her body, or by softening these same impurities with the oil and ointments from her bath. Another story, the one that interests us here, insists that Ganesa was a manifestation of Krishna given by that god to Parvati when she was stricken by grief because she could have no child by Siva.

One day, plunged in deep grief ... she heard a voice from the heavens telling her to go to her private apartments where she would find her son (who was in reality a manifestation of Krishna). Great was her joy on hearing the message; and repairing to her private apartments, she found a beautiful youth whom she and Siva accepted as their son. In honour of the event, they invited all the gods to a great feast for the purpose of looking upon the wondrous youth. Sani [Saturn] was the only god who kept his eyes fixed persistently on the ground. Parvati reproached him with this and bade him gaze upon her beautiful son. Hardly had he raised his eyes when the head of the youth separated from his body and disappeared into Goloka, the heaven of Krishna.

The gods in despair threw themselves on the ground weeping and wailing at the disaster, but Visnu ... flew away to the river Puspavadra, where he found an elephant asleep with its head turned to the north; cutting off the head, he flew back again and placed it on the headless child (Bala-Ganeśa), who sprang into life ...

The devotees of the Krishna–Ganeśa cult represented Bala-Ganeśa in the attitude of the child Krishna crawling with one hand raised and the other posed on the ground, but with this difference – that the child Ganeśa was represented elephant-faced and with four arms. In their religious ardor they took over the *Bhagavad-Gita*, inserting the name of Ganeśa wherever occurred that of Krishna, and called it *Ganeśa-Gita*.[21]

Ganeśa, as we have said, means Lord of the Ganas or Hosts or Troops, and these motley followers may have been diverted into his service from that of his putative father, Siva, who is sometimes said to have been followed by a wild horde of women, barbarians, and Sudras. This is possible but unlikely, for a verse attributed to an ancient version of the Laws of Manu runs, "Siva is the god of the Brahmins while Ganeśa is the god of the Sudras".[22] It is therefore likely that the Dionysiac group belonged to Ganeśa from the beginning. If the elephant-god is really the deity of the *declassée* and underprivileged, it is only fitting that many of the great lines of the *Gita* declaring the equal worth of Brahmins, elephants, dogs, and outcastes should be trumpeted through his trunk, and that he should be identified with Krishna as an enemy of caste, social division, and religious privilege. His war on the ungodly–godly is unceasing. Like Falstaff he loves to plan midnight robberies, but the object of his favourite thievery is an odd one, illustrating his intense scorn of other deities, their rites and observances, and of the merit which is acquired by faithful devotion to them. If not propitiated before all other gods, Ganeśa the Thief robs pious worshippers of the merit they have stored up by meticulous and sedulous devotion to other deities. This is a form of robbery that would undoubtedly have delighted the heart of old Jack Falstaff, who hated psalm-singers and had forgot what the inside of a church is made of.

It is as a deity of the dispossessed and broken-hearted that Ganeśa opposes other gods and labours to promote the fertility of the earth, it being strictly for ritual purposes that he overeats, drinks, and dallies with his Sakti or wives. Still, he does eat, or rather, drink! There is on a stupa or small temple in Sri Lanka a curious bas-relief which shows Ganeśa being waited on by six or seven of his pot-bellied train. Of these, only one, it seems, is bringing the god a handful of grain or rice; all the others are burdened by what look like jars of wine – an icon that reminds us inescapably of the scene at the Boar's Head in which an itemised tavern-bill is found in Falstaff's pocket as he snores behind the arras, a document over which Hal exclaims, "O monstrous! but one half penny-worth of bread to this intolerable deal of sack!"[23]

Perhaps we should remember, in extenuation, that in their drinking both these fat creatures are seeking to bring to earth what no other god has ever been interested in: a heaven here and now. Their quarrel with conventional religion centred, it seems, about just this point. Unlike the gods who preached the superior glories of an after-life, these wanted to make of earth itself a Paradise. If this occurs Ganeśa, twin of the old Wealth God Kuvera, will preside over the new Golden Age, standing under an Eden tree made of nine jewels and flanked by his favourite girl friends, Buddhi and Siddhi. There he will be worshipped for having done more, perhaps, than any of his fellow-Falstaffs to ease the tensions and hate, fostered by false gods of power and conquest, that sour the social and political life of man and dry up the fruitfulness of the earth itself. Perhaps on that day, with the recognition that the human psyche in all times and in all places has loved to elaborate myths, images, and ideas so alike as to be indistinguishable, Falstaff himself will be remembered when men pray:

> I adore the elephant-faced Ganeśa, the Incomprehensible with ... the capacious belly ... King of all Beings, the Eternal ... blood-red of hue ... Remover of all Difficulties.[24]

VIII
Ts'ai Shen of China,
Who Had a Philosophy of "Good Sherris-sack"

One of the first associations that come to mind at the mention of Falstaff is his devotion to sack, his unremitting intoxication, but while we have noted in every one of the Falstaff-personae so far treated an enormous capacity for drinking, we have not discussed the inwardness, the true meaning, of this phenomenon. I have described and, as well as I could, sought to account for his hot round figure, his "beastliness", his "activity of youth, activity of age", his sexual fury, his scorn of regnant law, his blasphemies against established religion. We have traced the appearance of this powerful figure back to the youth of the race, to primitive beliefs and historical activities which turned into religious rites accompanied by liturgies that furnished the libretti for the first dramas and enjoyed their most sophisticated and perhaps climactic literary development in the pentalogy from *Richard II* to *Henry V*.

But we are only now approaching what must have been the heart of that ancient rite – the battle of the Mock King against the powers of darkness that threaten his heavenly father and his all-too-human pupil around the winter solstice. Besides actual–symbolical fighting, the Mock King fought the fiends of infertility by heavy drinking, fought desperate battles with them even as he sat noisily "boozing" in whatever Boar's Head he frequented. I have saved the consideration of this point until we had journeyed as far east as our study can take us, for it was in China that ritual drinking seems to have been best understood, or at least most overtly reasoned about. I will

Ts'ai Shen — Chinese God of Wealth

Courtesy of the Horniman Museum

say a word here, also, about ritual overeating, for the two go together. Nowhere more than in the poetry of China do we find spirituous indulgence raised to a spiritual obligation; nowhere more than in the art of China do we find fat, bearded sages feasting to surfeit. What, after all, is the explanation for these gor-bellied creatures, these bags of guts, bombards of sack?

Many of the heroes of Chinese sagas of overeating and overdrinking have come down to us as real men – as all Falstaffian figures were, perhaps, in the beginning, though most of the tales, even those that date from the comparatively late dynasties of Tang and Sung, are more than tinged with myth. China seems simply to have swarmed with avatars of a god of good crops and good fortune. All the Falstaff-personae I am about to describe, real or perhaps really legendary, seem to have been epiphanies on earth of Ts'ai Shen, which means simply the God of Wealth, perhaps the most widely venerated deity of China, and directly identified, at least in Chinese Buddhism, with Kuvera of India.

> As to the devotees of the cult of the God of Wealth, probably all China worships him except, it may be, good Christians, Mohammedans, and also Europeanised Chinese. Certainly the God is venerated by the entire rustic population, which welcomes him on New Year's Eve with extravagant display of reverence. All trades are of course his special concern, and his shrine is prominent in every shop ... but apart from the commercial classes, persons of every other calling worship the God with sincere devotion, their outspoken materialism thus merging into a kind of religious mysticism. Perhaps the less honourable the calling, the more devout the worshipper: certainly the most earnest of his devotees are to be found among the humblest class.[1]

It is hard not to sense immediately that we are in the presence of a very ancient deity with a train of noisy, ragged worshippers, who manifests himself in the cold season in order to help sun, man, and earth through the sharp pinch of winter's cloture. We are told that simple folk in China love to have pictures of the great, fat, bearded deity, dressed in a bright red cloak which is sometimes lined like that of Santa Claus with white fur, hanging on their walls and inscribed with the words, "Truly a living Ts'ai Shen is coming to our house". In Chinese this formula is written in nine characters, each composed of nine strokes, and people "like to fill in with ink one of these strokes every day through the eighty-one days of winter cold".[2] The phrase "a living Ts'ai Shen" may mean, of course, a rich relative loaded with gold and jewels, and it usually does mean just about this to simple country people, but it may also mean an avatar of a god who performs a protective, foot-warming, fertilising role on earth. Many of the great scholars, prime ministers, and warriors of China have been identified as incarnations of Ts'ai Shen, and we can immediately sense, now that we have progressed thus far in our study, that these avatars could have acted as tutors, defenders, and not infrequently as victims of the monarchs of China. They did.

Right down to the twentieth century the Chinese emperor played, quite self-consciously, a Divine King role. Already in the famous Chinese *Annals* known as "The Great Law", edited, Père Wieger thinks, around 1050 B.C., we have a description of the role of the emperor in promoting the fertility of the soil:

> It is the duty of the government at all times to watch carefully the phenomena of nature, which are the echo in the world of nature of the order or disorder in the world of government. The government is bound to watch the phenomena of nature in order to be able immediately to amend what is in need of amendment. When the course of nature goes its proper way, it is a sign that the government is good, but when there is some disturbance in nature, it is a sign that there is some sin in the government. With the help of fixed tables it is possible to learn from the disturbance in nature what is the sin that caused it. Any disturbance in the sun accuses the emperor. A disturbance around the sun – the court, the ministers; a disturbance in the moon – the queen, the harem. Good weather that lasts too long shows that the emperor is too active. Days which continue to be cloudy show that the emperor lacks under-standing. Too much rainfall shows that he is unjust. Lack of rain shows that he is careless. Too great a cold shows that he is inconsiderate of others. Stormy wind – that he is lazy. Good harvest proves that everything is all right; bad harvest – that the government is guilty. When the pear-tree blossomed in the autumn, the court had to be warned that there was some hidden disorder there ...[3]

At several times in Chinese history the special ceremonials for reinvigorating the sun and nature at the midwinter crisis were conducted in a specially constructed temple known as the Ming T'ang or Hall of Light, in which the Chinese emperor wrestled on the shortest night of the year with the powers of darkness in order to guarantee his land and people a prosper-ous year to come. When he failed for two or three years in succession to ensure good crops (the sun always managed to recover its youth, but the crops were another matter), he was sometimes deposed along with his line; sometimes he committed suicide in favour of the heir-apparent in order to keep his dynasty from being overthrown. Though the Ming T'ang itself fell from time to time into disuse, the midwinter ceremony was always per-formed, it seems, in one holy place or another, at the Temple of the Altar of Heaven or in the Temple of Prayer for the Year, and W.E. Soothill could write as late as 1912 that

> this supreme act of worship, with its accompanying sacrifices, is the sign and symbol of the imperial office. Only the emperor, the High Priest of the World, the Son of Heaven, may perform this great sacrifice, which has existed from all historic antiquity. ... It falls to his lot to pay his duties in the depth of winter and the dead of night. Then the cold is so intense that, as one who has often officiated there told me, even high wadded boots and the thickest furs fail to keep strong men from chilling to the marrow, and in some cases going to their graves. It is at the winter

solstice that the sovereign sheds the blood of sacrifice, when the dying
sun has reached the lowest ebb of its vitality and is again to renew its
youth.[4]

High Priest of the World, with the welfare of mankind dependent on him,
the Chinese monarch naturally adopted every possible expedient to avoid
failure. The chief of many expedients was, it seems, to surround himself
with living Ts'ai Shens in the forms of scholars, ministers, poets, and
warriors in whom some of the calorific virtue inherent in the deity of gold
and grain was thought to have been incarnated. Perhaps nothing shows the
democratic nature of Chinese culture better than the multiplicity of Ts'ai-
personae available to a worried emperor in time of seasonal crisis. As we
shall see, there is reason to suppose that at least some of these Falstaffian
figures, like those in other countries, were scions of deposed or degraded
royalty, but there were political clemency and the ramifying Chinese family
system to guarantee whole crops of inheritors of fertility *mana*, while the
Chinese belief that the law of Heaven, too, is implanted in every wise man's
breast, making a natural nobleman of him, served to swell the emperor's
Falstaffian friends or helpers by the dozen. Not, of course, that the career of
a Ts'ai Shen or *aide-de-camp* to the frost-embattled emperor was easy or
even safe. Nevertheless, these Chinese bearers of the torch within seem to
have done everything in their power to spread their inner fire over the whole
creation, by eating, drinking, dancing, lovemaking, and scoffing at conventional concepts of law and religion. All such "living Ts'ai Shens" constituted
a band of tutors, helpers, and soldiers of the king in his critical warfare.

Some, including his ministers and his noblemen, helped him by ceremonial practices such as the famous contest in archery about which we read in
the section of the *Li Chi* or *Record of Rites* called the "She-I" or "Meaning of
Archery" and in the fifth, sixth, and seventh sections of the *I-Li* or *Book of
Etiquette and Ceremonial*.[5] Others, including his favourite poets and scholars, seemed to have helped him fight the forces of darkness by carousing at a
distance – and not merely on the critical night of the year, but at all times
and all places. "In ancient times ... the archery pavilion attached to the Ming
T'ang, called the *She Kung*, was of much importance. ... Before the Great
Sacrifice, the Son of Heaven held the state archery tournament at the Ming
T'ang"[6] and the successful archers, for their help in the success of the winter
sacrifice, became "feudal lords, principal officers of state, and officers in
general".[7] They had hit the bull's eye, or rather the bear, stag, tiger, or boar's
head painted in the centre of the communal target. In these animals we can
recognise sun-associated beasts often sacrificed, along with the beast-
associated Mock King, at the period when the Old Sun renewed itself by
dying or passing into the New. These targets were always set up at the
southern end of the Archery Pavilion, i.e., in the quarter of the sky through
which the ageing sun cuts its diminished arc. That these shooting bouts were
ceremonial is clearly indicated by their accompaniment by music and songs
of fruitfulness entitled "The Southern Steps", "White Blossoms", and "The

Millet's in Flower".[8] It was also *de rigueur* that the archers, before engaging in the contest, would drink "all they can carry"![9] It is recorded that winners in these contests helped the emperor soon after with the great midwinter sacrifice, though what they did is not exactly clear. There is some reason to suppose that they may have spent the longest night of the year shooting arrows into the Black Night, for we know that the royal archers in a body used to give the black beast which caused solar eclipses this somewhat absent treatment; or it is possible that they actually killed the sun-animals when the emperor's all-night rite called for "the blood of sacrifice". Neither of these actions would have been made impossible by a high degree of intoxication. These feasts are something of a digression, but they help to make clear that the winter battle we have so often seen associated with the real one was essentially ceremonial and symbolical. They point up the role, not particularly stressed so far, of the Falstaffian tutor as fighter, soldier, officer, or minister co-responsible with the emperor for winning the war of the solstice, the battle of the grain.

It seems that not infrequently, in early times at least, the emperor's real minister and perhaps others of his midnight battlers were themselves, somewhat in the fashion of Mock Kings at the end of the Saturnalia, sacrificed at the end of the campaign. In fact, the first great avatar of Ts'ai Shen whom we hear of in Chinese history was the famous Pi Kan of the *Shu Ching* or *Book of Documents*, who was tortured and killed by the last ruler of the Shang dynasty: "for reasons which it would be difficult to trace, they [the Chinese] ... deify ... Pi Kan, who suffered unspeakable tortures at the hands of a degenerate monarch."[10] A good deal of indignation at this act is expressed in the Confucianist *Book of Documents* and the *Analects*; however, so many later emperors treated their prime ministers just as cruelly, especially in times of danger to the land and the dynasty (remember that when Pi Kan was killed the Shang was on the very verge of downfall) that we can only conclude the death to have been a ritual one. We are told, of course, that the last of the Shangs fell precisely because he tyrannised cruelly over his "reprover and helper" and ended by cutting out "the heart of the worthy man",[11] but it is more likely that he did just this in order to keep from falling. It is said that the tyrant maliciously tore out Pi Kan's heart in order to see if a sage's heart was really different from other men's, but it is more likely that, the heart being the seat of Tao or the Way of Heaven which makes all things flourish, he was seeking to possess himself of a talisman against infertility and doom.

It would have been nobler of him, of course, to have taken or at least to have offered his own life for the safety of his people, as did King T'ang of the Chou Dynasty when a great drought and famine attacked China in 1766–1760 B.C.:

> T'ang said, "If a man must be a victim, I will be he." He fasted, cut off his
> hair and nails, and in a plain carriage drawn by white horses, clad in

rushes, in the guise of a sacrificial victim, he proceeded to the forest of mulberry trees, and there prayed, asking to what error or crime of his the calamity was owing. He had not done speaking when a copious rain fell.[12]

The reference to the white horses is perhaps of some interest to us, for Ts'ai Shen is often represented in art as riding on a white horse or accompanied by a white horse laden with treasure, and all his incarnations on earth – ministers, poets, and generals – are represented as riding on white horses. This fact points to the likelihood that King T'ang's horses were representatives of the animal most often associated with the sun-god.

But we are much less concerned here with the so-called Military Ts'ai Shen, whose avatars were soldiers, archers, and ministers, than with the Civil Wealth God, whose essence was incarnated in poets, scholars, and peaceful saints, chiefly Taoists. The first great Ming T'ang or Hall of Light is supposed to have been built by Huang Ti, the famous Yellow Emperor (his traditional dates are 2692 to 2598 B.C.) who is, further, supposed to have developed the theory and practice of the seasonal ceremonies that took place there. It seems that the whole ritual of the Ming T'ang was largely associated with Taoism and Taoist practitioners, though the Confucian classics contain many specifications for the building of such a Hall of Light. It is quite possible that Taoism, even as it exists today, was a development of beliefs and practices which constituted what we may call the earliest religion of China. At any rate, the Taoists considered themselves the guardians of the secrets of China's ancient animism, which held that the life of nature can be stimulated, controlled, and used by the Knowing Man, i.e., one who knows that his life is identical with that in nature and performs mimetic rites that affect nature by sympathetic magic. That the emperor was able to win the war of the solstice, the battle of the grain, was – according to the Taoists – because he had been taught the secrets of mimetic warfare by studying with Taoist priests such subjects as astronomy, geomancy, and alchemy, which they alone claimed to understand. Some tales represent them as willing to impart these secrets to him only at a good price, though others show them going to usual extremes of self-sacrifice for the good of mankind. In any case, and in all known instances, they adopt the hieratic tone so common to ostensibly disreputable Falstaff-personae and act as if they were indeed descendants of the original divine-right rulers of China. In art they are always represented as enormous, fat, whiskery men, dancing, drinking, or riding on white stags, tigers, or horses. When hired by the king either as sages, ministers, or poets, they constitute a whole stable of Falstaffs retained by the monarch to help him keep the land and people of China in a flourishing condition. These Taoist sages are known as Hsien or Immortals, and their lives and remarkable feats on behalf of the empire are recorded in many books, from some twenty-eight of which Lionel Giles has compiled his charming *Gallery of Chinese Immortals*. Here we have dozens of stories of fat sages who feast and eat and drink and steal and fornicate and make fun of Old Father Antic in order to help the emperor in his time of trouble. Then, the day (literally) having been saved, they are not infrequently treated with ingratitude, stoned, and even beheaded.

I am thinking especially of those Hsien or Immortals that aided Duke Ts'ao Ts'ao who, more dastardly than the last king of Shang, martyred his saintly saviours in a very systematic and businesslike way. Not, of course, that a Hsien can really be killed, but Immortals have mortal necks which can be severed easily for the general good. In such cases either in the spirit or the body (quite often in both), they ascend straight from earth to an island heaven called P'eng-Lai, where they live like the Hsien Shen Hsi in a celestial palace

> composed of an insubstantial luminous haze shot through with an indescribable variety of colours. There were hundreds of attendants, mostly female. In the gardens grew trees bearing gems and jade, and all the different kinds of *chih* plant in great profusion. Dragons and tigers gambolled in our midst. ... After a while a bevy of fair maidens brought in a golden table with jade goblets and set it before me saying: 'This is the divine elixir. Whoso quaffs it shall be exempt from death.'[13]

This Taoist heaven is clearly a realm of eternal summer to which all the old white-bearded suns, their work on earth done, are allowed to retire and from which it is suggested they can return from time to time to help to stimulate the productive life – in nature when it is harried by frost and darkness, in man when he is pinched by the frosts of hate and civil war. Quite literally, old sun-figures never die: they fade away, but do not entirely vanish. Their influence for good goes on, and from time to time they are allowed to descend to earth or at least to speak and act from heaven for mankind's benefit.

Immortals, both the purely legendary and those historically identifiable, often organised themselves into clubs or coteries in order to give the maximum help to the emperor by mass as well as massive eating, drinking, and lovemaking in times of danger. Famous among such groups were the Six Idlers of the Bamboo Brook, the Eight Immortals of the Wine-cup presided over by the famous eighth-century poet Li Po, or the Four Sages of Mount Shang. All of these admittedly wise men, wise-beyond-wise, seem to have punctuated their deep draughts of wine with shouts and roars which probably created a hubbub not unlike that for which the Chinese sages so exuberantly overate, drank, and fornicated. When the news of the revolt of Glendower, Hotspur, and Douglas arrived, Falstaff, looking up wide-eyed and coyly (or so we may imagine) at Prince Hal, asked him if he was not frightened by this triple-headed monster of darkness.

> *Fal.:* Tell me, Hal, art thou not horrible afeard? Thou being heir-apparent, could the world pick thee out three such enemies again as that fiend Douglas, that spirit Percy, and that devil Glendower? Art thou not horribly afraid? Doth not thy blood thrill at it?[14]

The Prince insists that it doesn't, but Falstaff immediately suggests that they stage a kind of mummers' play in which Falstaff will play the role of the infirm Henry IV, though Falstaff's throne be only "this chair ..., this dagger my sceptre, and this cushion my crown". During this scene he praises himself to the skies and tells Hal, as his son, that there is "virtue" in that "goodly, portly man ... that Falstaff; him keep with, the rest banish". From this scene we get the impression that Falstaff, while apparently taking his ease in his inn, is actively substituting for the sick king during England's trouble, and that in this Mock King role he is prepared, by powers peculiar to him though obscure to Hal, who is here being laughed at, to defend the prince from a coalition of enemies clearly equated with the forces of darkness. Percy is volatile as an imp from hell, Douglas a frightful were-wolf, and "damned Glendower" a "great magician"[15] who can spend nine hours reckoning up the names of devils who are his lackeys, "call spirits from the vasty deep", and command the Devil himself; who loves to remember that at his birth "the front of heaven was full of fiery shapes" and a hundred supernatural signs which marked him "extraordinary ... not in the role of common men".[16]

To protect the prince against this coalition of demons, Falstaff proceeds in a strange way – strange, that is, to us, but one that would easily have been understood in the China, and probably the England, of Shakespeare's time. He simply gets drunker and drunker until he falls asleep behind the arras. He shows no eagerness whatever to be off to the battle of Shrewsbury, yet implies continually that if this war is to be won it will be by the expenditure of his yeasty prowess. At one point he exclaims, "Well, God be thank'd for these rebels, they offend none but the virtuous. I laud them, I praise them",[17] a passage which can be interpreted to mean that the rebel fiends, being powerless against the so-called disreputable Falstaff, who is a kind of devil himself, simply give him a chance to display his own peculiar magic. At his peculiar career, his mission, Falstaff works unremittingly by eating and drinking Dame Quickly out of house and home. When the prince rushes off to Shrewsbury shouting,

> The land is burning. Percy stands on high,
> And either we or they must lower lie,

Falstaff counters with an ironical sentiment which may, however, constitute a much more serious threat to devils incarnate:

> Rare words! Brave world! Hostess, my breakfast, come!
> O I could wish this tavern were my drum.[18]

Apparently the resounding board at the Boar's Head was, in truth, an effective charm against the black rebels, for they lost the ensuing battle; strangely enough Glendower, for all his boasted valour and wizardry, never turned up, and the mighty Douglas fell accidentally from a cliff. Some greater magician had, perhaps, outmagicked these monsters, undermined their power from a distance, long before the battle was joined. "Here's that can sack a city!"

I indulge in these fanciful speculations because of the well-known power of Chinese Hsien to foil demons of division and darkness, not by rushing directly to the monarch's rescue, but simply by increasing the size of their banquets and the number of their potations. It is also true, oddly enough, that demons in Chinese stories usually attack in trios, as we can see in seven of the adventures related in the famous folkloristic novel *Hsi Yu Ki*, written by Wu Ch'eng-en and partially translated into English by Arthur Waley as *Monkey*.[19] Had we time for it, we could find in the loved monkey-hero of the prose epic, in this Bes of China, this magical foe of malevolent spooks, this colossal boaster (and performer) who once stormed heaven itself, acquiring the title "Equal of Heaven", one of the world's most delightful memories of a Mock King.

It is possible that Sun the Monkey is derivative from the famous Hanuman of India, the animal-like tutor and helper of Rama in the great Indian epic known as the *Ramayana*. Rama's wife, Sita, the princess born of a furrow, daughter of Mother Earth herself, had been stolen by the demons of Lanka (modern Sri Lanka), the powers of darkness, and without the advice, the wisdom, and the direct aid of Hanuman, this beautifully personified growth-of-the-soil would never have been rescued from the land "down under". In India today it is common to picture Hanuman as distinctly plump when not grossly fat, and in the ballet representations of scenes from this fable which are popular in Thailand, Monkey is represented of such gigantic proportions that he can conceal his protegé Rama and an attendant army in his mouth. It is possible that Hanuman, helper of Rama (or sun-prince; later, an avatar of Visnu) owes something to Egyptian Bes, often represented in art, as we have seen, in the form of a fat ape who played guide and guardian to every young Pharaoh (each an avatar of Sun-Horus) in his struggle with darkness personified as Set.

From India to Thailand there is perhaps no more beloved figure than this wondrous monkey who gave so generously of his energy, his wisdom, and his life for the rescue of plant life in the form of Sita. The scenes in which Hanuman occurs, on the stage or in poetry or prose, sometimes lean toward comedy but are never really frivolous. They have the same underlying, if not easily understood, sense of serious ramifications which attaches to the great comic scenes dominated by Falstaff. In India, in fact, Hanuman's service to Rama has caused him to be raised (perhaps "restored") to high status – to godhead. It is for love of him that Indians have made monkeys practically sacrosanct and immune from harm. I have in my possession a modern Thai tea tray and coasters decorated with the monkey Hanuman, showing the flaring hair, the arching eyebrows, the flattened, gangster-like nose, the fat cheeks, and the thick-lipped mouth of Bes, all very horrifying yet very fascinating and clearly celebrating him as the best-loved figure in Thai folklore, just as Monkey Sun, probably his descendant, is perhaps the most popular figure in Chinese folk art and literature. Which brings us back to Ts'ai Shen, with his many incarnations in feral and human form.

Before discussing how the life of the great poet Li Po can be explained as a continuous exhibition of long-distance conjuring in behalf of king and country (this time I am going to treat a famous historical figure rather than a half-animal demi-god as the typical Falstaff-figure), I will say a word or two about a few Chinese Immortals, pointing out one or two ways in which each recalls the Falstaff-persona. Perhaps we may be permitted to assemble a drinking coterie of our own, not *The Eight* but still a group of Eight Immortals of the Wine-cup, six more or less legendary and two well-known as poets, the whole group to be completed and presided over, as were *The Eight*, by Li Po himself.

1. Tung-fang So began life as a common schoolmaster but was regarded by some of his contemporaries as an inspired sage. "His behaviour showed such a strange combination of depth and shallowness, openness and reserve, that no one knew exactly when he was speaking from his heart or when he was merely jesting."[20] By extravagant boasting he managed to rise high in the emperor's favour, and by merely insisting that he had the right qualities for the job – "So's words were lacking in modesty and extravagant in their self-praise" – he became his majesty's chief minister. His idea of working at his career was to keep "a troupe of singers and actors". He "did not concern himself with State business", yet the kingdom flourished throughout his days and his "contemporaries all described him as the prince of good fellows and irresistible in argument".[21] On a famous occasion he rescued Emperor Wu Ti of the Han from a monster whose terrific black body, thirty or forty feet in length, was blocking a mountain pass, by pouring so many gallons of wine over it that the insoluble apparition melted away.

> The emperor asked Tung-Fang So to explain the phenomenon, and he replied: "This may be called the product of an atmosphere of sorrow and suffering. The spot on which we stand must have been the site of a dungeon under the Ch'in dynasty or else the scene of the labours of a multitude of transported criminals. Now, wine has the power to banish grief, and that is why it was able to dispel this phantom." "Oh, man of much learning," exclaimed the emperor, "to think that your knowledge can extend as far as this!"[22]

Such virtues in wine, considerable as they are, cannot of course equal those detailed in Falstaff's famous description of the operation and virtues of sack, but it is significant that both these Immortals, one eastern and the other western, acclaim wine as the sovereign solvent of the morally murky atmosphere generated by ambition, cruelty, and injustice. It may be that because few people recognised so far what he really was – the Spirit of the Year-star – he was able to enjoy a peaceful passing from life in the Chinese Avalon. Most Hsien are banished or beheaded.

2. Liu Ken's "body was covered with a shaggy growth of hair over a foot long, yet his complexion was that of a boy".[23] On one occasion a governor who regarded Liu as a mischievous wizard summoned him before his

tribunal meaning to have him beheaded, but this proceeding by Old Father Antic backfired with the result that the governor and all his immediate family lost their lives. Liu was addicted not only to drink but to drugs, explaining that "For every aspirant to hsienship an essential thing is the assimilation of drugs. But some drugs are better than others, and there are several grades of Hsien. He who is unversed in the mysteries of sexual intercourse, in the art of controlling his breath, and in physical exercises, as well as in the science of celestial drugs, can never hope to become a Hsien."[24] It is not at all clear that Falstaff measured up to certain of these requirements for an Immortal and here again his Chinese counterpart made a comparatively easy exit from earth. Liu was able to do much good in the world before he too passed peacefully, but not permanently, on.

3. Of Kuan Lu we are told that "his features were coarse and ugly and his manners lacking in dignity. Much addicted to wine and good cheer, and fond of his jokes, he would associate only with congenial spirits. ... All his sayings and repartees were highly original, and his seniors were unable to get the better of him in argument."[25] Kuan Lu was not himself a soldier but frequently accompanied the emperor's army on its marches, apparently guaranteeing victory on some occasions and on others, when his own magic could not counteract that of enemy demons – the Green Dragon that had no feet, the White Tiger that held a corpse in his jaws, or the Red Bird that wailed and lamented – predicting defeats which always ensued. Appointed to an assistant governorship by the emperor, he met an untimely end, perhaps by rejection, but not before himself saving a beautiful youth from early death.

4. Like Falstaff, Chiao Hsien was clearly a "latter-spring! ... All Hallown summer!" – that is, a force of vernal energy in the dangerous days of winter. Of him we are told that when there came a great snowfall, "Hsien's hut collapsed, and a party of rescuers, seeing no trace of him, feared that he must have frozen to death. But on digging their way into the hut, they found him fast asleep under the snow, with a ruddy face and breathing freely, just like one lying drunk in the height of summer."[26] He was indeed drunk, and it may be that in this little episode we come upon one of the more plausible explanations for the heavy drinking of Falstaff-personae in all parts of the world. Wine is a catalyst of perpetual thaw, making all seasons summery. In China the wine jar is often called "a jade kettle with a purchase of spring", meaning that "wine ... makes men see spring at all seasons".[27] In order to account for the magic power of the drunken Chiao, we should perhaps substitute "be" for "see", for in his intoxicated state he was a powerful breath of spring, a shaft of sun which warmed the frozen earth and tempted bare boughs to put forth blossoms. We are told that Chiao lived, "now old and now young, for more than two hundred years. At last he parted from his fellow men and went no one knows whither."[28] As Falstaff puzzles his critics, Chiao Hsien puzzled the less imaginative among those who knew him, and never more so than when he made fun of the fact that "the world in general

desires ... honour".[29] The following description of Chiao's nature and deathlessness makes one think of Bradley, or some other elevated if frustrated western "scholar", praising the "out of all compass" knight:

> No man is able to fathom his thoughts; the breadth of the Four Seas cannot encompass his mind. ... Danger and stress cause him no qualms, honours and affections [of the common kind] do not entangle his spirit. ... He has planted his feet in the domain where no hurt is, and has established himself in the realm of independence. His length of years ... cannot be reckoned by the oldest acquaintance. He has been one and the same ever since the time of the Emperor Fu Hsi [i.e., the Yellow Emperor, putative founder of Taoism and builder of the first Ming T'ang or Hall of Light by which darkness was magically routed].[30]

5. When speaking of the Hsien's reputed power to help restore springtime to the magically communicated beat of his inner alcohol lamp we must not overlook Ma Hsiang, who was famous for his "grog-blossom nose".[31] We cannot be surprised to hear that in addition to this cherry bloom, "he had an ugly face ... and a very large mouth", characteristics that we have noticed in Falstaff-personae from Bes to Kuvera. He seems to have been the father of a feat of fertility magic still popular among Oriental prestidigitators.

> So Hsiang placed a porcelain bowl on his mat, filled it with earth, and sowed a melon seed. In a few moments a melon plant was spreading in every direction and put forth flowers and fruit. These were picked and handed to the assembled guests, who pronounced them to be delicious, and much superior to ordinary melons in flower.[32]

Ma Hsiang fought the powers of darkness in the form of pests and rodents which prey on men. We are further told that "Ma Hsiang had all the outward appearance of a lunatic. He was in the habit of buying wine on credit from a wine shop in the street of the White Pagoda." A famous poem in China, supposed to have been written by Ma Hsiang himself, begins

> In days gone by I followed Wei Po-yang as my Master,
> And spent half my time lying tipsy on a gilded couch;
> He chid me harshly for my slothful ways,
> And back into the world I went, still a frenzied lover of wine.[33]

Better than his master he knew that his fondness for drink was the true source of the power by which he benefited emperors, land, and people, and he never ceased singing the praises of good liquor, "precious as jade-juice".[34] Like most good Hsien who are not beheaded, he was banished at last and died in exile broken-hearted but dreaming of greenery.

> With smiles we disguise the bitterness in our hearts,
> Our hair turns white with the anguish of separation.
> Happily, a refuge awaits me in cloud-land:
> The illimitable green hills shall be mine![35]

6. Here I could tell of many Hsien who loved, when on their death bed, to play with flowers and babble of green fields, but I will content myself with mentioning briefly Lan Ts'ai-ho, one of the eight Official Taoist Immortals, who differs from the others only in usually being represented in art as beardless. He is said to have loved to hop or dance about on one foot (an idiosyncracy of, among others, Bes, Silenos, and Ganeśa), "singing crazy songs which he improvised as he went along".

> In summer he stuffed his gown with cotton-wool, while in winter he would sleep in the snow with vapour rising from his body like steam. When drunk, he used to sing and caper, and was followed by crowds of people. ... The cash which he received as alms he would thread on a string and trail behind him as he walked. If any were lost, he would pay no heed. He used to give his money to the poor, or spend it in wine-taverns. It was from a wine-tavern that he eventually soared up to the sky ...
>
> This strange being is usually shown with a basket full of flowers and plants associated with longevity, such as chrysanthemums, plum-blossoms, sprigs of pine and bamboo.[36]

All these half-legendary Immortals could be and often were identified by the Chinese as incarnations of Ts'ai Shen, the Wealth God, but it was and still is also customary to denominate real men who bring prosperity to a community in the form of grain or gold the New Year deity's sons or avatars on earth, and it is my conviction that many of the great poets and scholars of China quite consciously saw themselves playing in life the magic role of Taoist Immortals. There seems to be no other plausible explanation for the identical pattern which their lives so often took: as strange child, drunken friend and adviser of emperors, master of ceremonies at great seasonal banquets; as minstrel who sought in his poems to evoke the powers and beauties of absent spring or to hearten the king's army to pepper with arrows the heart of the Black-cloud Enemy (so-called even when he appeared on the northwestern horizon in the shape of a very real foe); as, later, an exile banished from his sovereign's favour who lived a so-called hermit's life while still drinking all he could lay his hands on in the company, as in his heyday, of a pair of beautiful concubines; and finally, as a deserted old man still true, though dying, to his great vocation of prospering king and country by murmuring to the end broken incantations about trees, flowers, waterfalls, blossoms, and green fields.

It is amusing to see how students – ancient (but not too ancient) as well as modern, Oriental as well as Occidental – have laboured to make the lives of the great Chinese poets read like those of mere men. It cannot be done. The fact that the short original biographies on which all later ones must be based follow such a strict pattern should, it seems to me, have discouraged a literal approach from the beginning. The schematisation which they force on would-be biographers, a counterpoint endlessly repeated, makes realism impossible. The Chinese biographies occurring in the old dynastic histories were classified under headings such as "Loyal Ministers, Rebellious Officials, Filial Sons, Great Confucian Scholars", but the biographies of the important poets were usually "put in a rather strange category – that of *yin i* – the 'hidden and aloof' ".[37] These, W. Acker thinks, "seem to have been people of great ability, men whose gifts were so great that they should by rights [sic] have played a significant role in their age but who because of some unfortunate trait of character or some strange idiosyncrasy could not bring their great talents to bear in a practical way".[38] This, it seems to me, is to get the whole conception upside down, for nothing seemed to the Chinese more practical than that the emperor, aided by his entourage of noble archers and abetted by his stable of revelling poets, whether present or absent, should carry out successfully the great ceremony at the Ming T'ang so necessary to avert famine and civil war and keep the Chinese for another year well fed and happy.

7. Take the story of Tao Ch'ien, a poet of the fourth and fifth centuries, as given in the old histories. His very name is suggestive of symbolism, Tao meaning the Way of Heaven or God and Ch'ien meaning Hidden-in-the-Depths, while the courtesy title given him by his friends on his coming of age was Yuan-ming, meaning Light of the Abyss. In other words, his name in translation means Poet Secret Way, Light in Darkness. The dynastic history tells us he was

> aristocratically off-hand in his demeanour and unconstrained in his manner. He relied upon the Real and was self-contained, so that his neighbours and fellow-townsmen thought highly of him. [Nevertheless, afraid that people would not understand his activities and inactivities] he once wrote the *Story of the Master of the Five Willows* in order to render an account of himself.[39]

He was offered a dozen official positions, most of which he declined, choosing rather "to play and sing". Later, having accepted the governorship of Peng-tse,

> in his official capacity he ordered that all the public lands of the district be sown with glutinous millet [suitable for brewing wine] "which should be just enough to keep me drunk" … When, however, his wife and children begged that he should have some land sown with plain millet, he had a hundred and fifty acres sown with glutinous millet and fifty sown with plain millet.[40]

"O monstrous!" as Hal would have exclaimed, "but a halfpenny-worth of bread to this intolerable deal of sack!"[41] When Old Father Antic in the form of a Censor arrived in his district, Tao Ch'ien refused due obeisance, saying, "How can I bend my waist for five packs of rice and earnestly pay court to such a rascal?"[42] Shortly after, he gave up his position to spend all his time with five or six friends who constituted, apparently, a cell of poets who worked in their own self-sacrificing way for the emperor and the Central Flowery Kingdom.

> Sometimes when he had wine he would invite them, or he would ask them to go with him to some party where wine was being served. Even if he did not know the host at all, he would enjoy himself with the utmost gaiety and not return home till he was drunk ... whenever he got drunk, he would become as one inspired and make incredible conversational hits.
>
> Also he had no heart for making a living and left management of his household entirely to his children and servants. Whatever they did, he never showed approbation or disapprobation: only, if there was wine he would drink it; if there was none, he would still go on humming verses to himself incessantly. He once playfully gave himself the name *Hsi Huang Shang jen*.[43]

Hsi Huang was another name for Fu Hsi, the famous Yellow Emperor who built the first Ming T'ang, while "Shang jen" is a Buddhist term meaning "an adept". Tao's pet name for himself meant, therefore, Skilled-in-the-Secrets-of-Governing-the-Seasons.

Of Tao Ch'ien the dynastic history also tells us that while he could not play music, he treasured a lute that had no strings; and that whenever friends came and while wine was flowing, he would take this lute in his hands and stroke it saying, "All I care about is the meaning within the lute."[44] I suppose he meant to imply that the "meaning within the lute" – the melody of winds, the patter of rain, the ripple of millet, the roar of the sun – is made explicit by poets, and that it was his mission on earth to promote natural processes not only by acting the fool but by writing. It is to be noted that in China, even more particularly than in Islam, it was of the utmost importance that the prince's drinker–jester–friend be a poet celebrating the glories of the springtime earth. About A.D. 300 Lu Ki, China's first great literary critic, defined "the pleasure of writing" as follows:

> There is joy in this vocation; all sages esteem it.
>
> We wrestle with non-being to force it into being; beat silence for an answering music. ...
>
> ...
>
> The scent of sweet blossom is diffused; the thrust of green twigs is budding.
>
> Laughing wind will fly and whirl upward; pregnant clouds will arise from the forest of writing-brushes.[45]

There is a clear implication here and elsewhere in Lu Ki ("literature is the equal of clouds and rain in yielding sweet moisture"[46]) that poetry itself helped to stimulate the powers of nature. The emperor himself, like the

Emperor of Japan in our time, was expected to write nature poetry. If he could not, it was necessary for his stable of poetic favourites to work all the harder.

There was still another way in which poets were expected to help the emperor in his love affairs with nature. This was in the matter of ritual visits to certain great sacred mountains of China which were considered focal centres of the *élan vital* that permeates man and the cosmos. To this power of nature, quite appropriately personified as a fairy or dryad, the emperor on his ritual visit made love (symbolic? actual?) in a Chinese variant of the Divine King–Earth Mother *connubium*. A great poem on such a royal pilgrimage to the Kao T'ang mountain was composed by Sung Yu, a famous court jester and minister who flourished around 280 B.C. The poem, called "The Kao T'ang Fu", tells of an old king who, on the sacred mountain's top, lay with a girl who at parting told him, "My home is on the southern side of the Witches' Hill, where from its rounded summit a sudden chasm falls. At dawn I am the morning cloud; at dusk the driving rain."[47] After describing this mythic adventure Sung Yu, the author, promises to take the present king, his master, in search of a similar experience on the same mountain, which he describes as an incredible storehouse of natural force that glitters in crashing waterfalls, shimmers in waving pine forests, and flashes in half-hidden, half-revealed animal life. After a hundred-odd lines of astonishing poetic virtuosity, Sung Yu ends the poem by assuring the king:

> Thereafter shall my lord the King deal kindly for ever with the thousand lands, sorrow for the wrongs of his people, promote the wise and good, and make whole whatever was amiss. No longer shall the apertures of his intelligence be choked; to his soul's scrutiny all hidden things shall be laid bare. His years shall be prolonged, his strength eternally endure.[48]

In other words, the education in wisdom and love that the jester desired for the king is represented as emanating directly from nature itself; we can now understand why it seems to have been so necessary for an emperor, much busied in his capital, to make sure that his poetic *aides-de-camp* spent much of their time wandering in so-called exile among sacred mountains, hymning the divine force concentrated in these great powerhouses.

It is also interesting that in Sung Yo's poem the drinking, poetising, lovemaking, and mountain-roving into which the great poets sought to initiate their royal friend, or which they themselves performed for him by proxy, were specifically designed to make the ruler understand and deal kindly with his subjects – to sorrow for their wrongs – by liberating his intelligence and laying bare the fact that the good of mankind consists in the leader's practice of lovingkindness rather than in the politician's pursuit of power and honour. Falstaff is probably a much less complicated character than these Chinese jester–poets, but he has his poetical side and, as we have

repeatedly pointed out, a strange affection for flowers and fields. Like the
Chinese poets, he loved to hear the chimes at midnight and to think of
himself, hot ball that he was, as a forester of Diana, "minion of the moon".[49]
He thought of himself as a "true spirit" of Windsor Forest, an antlered man
striving in a play performed during the winter season (so we are told) to
stimulate the life in frozen fields by composing little Chinese-like poems in
prose:

> *Fal.:*   Let the sky rain potations; let it thunder to the tune of "Green
> Sleeves", hail kissing-comfits, and snow eringoes; let there come a
> tempest of provocation ...[50]

If we change "potatoes" to "potations", as I have done here, we can see that
this invocation is as carefully composed in its choice of similitudes as any
Chinese stanzas, the stimulating wine being compared to rainfall, the tiny
lozenges for sour breath to hailstones, and the candied sea-holly root or
eringo, the true aphrodisiac of the poem, nourished in the very element in
which Aphrodite was born, to foam-flakes or snowflakes. Again, Falstaff's
famous description of the virtues of wine can be parallelled in many a
Chinese poem in praise of drinking. It seems to be the old grey-bearded
devil's intention to teach the essentially crazed and truly corrupt prince, who
has evidently inherited the cold, treacherous power-madness of his father,
to deal kindly with the land, grieve for the wrongs of his people, and think
clearly about true values by ridding himself of the weedy, muddy notions of
honour that choke the conduits of his brain. Prince John of Lancaster had
coldly tricked and sent to their deaths hundreds of Englishmen, both high
and low, who had not unjustified grievances against the crown; it is just
after this betrayal that Falstaff makes his great Chinese-like speech against
"the young, sober-blooded boy" who loves few people and who cannot be
made to laugh – "but that's no marvel, he drinks no wine. There's never none
of these demure boys come to any proof." However they may succeed in a
worldly sense, they are essentially bad for the country and the people,
actually "fools and cowards" who endanger their subjects and the very
scheme of things. Their trouble is lack of "inflammation".

> *Fal.:*   A good sherris-sack hath a two-fold operation in it. It ascends me
> into the brain; dries me there all the foolish and dull and crudy vapours
> which environ it; makes it apprehensive, quick, forgetive, full of nimble
> fiery and delectable shapes; which, deliver'd o'er to the voice, the
> tongue, which is the birth, becomes excellent wit. The second property
> of your excellent sherris is the warming of the blood ... It illumines the
> face, which as a beacon gives warning to all the rest of this little
> kingdom, man, to arm ... So that skill in the weapon is nothing without
> sack, for that sets it a-work; and learning, a mere hoard of gold kept by
> a devil till sack commences it and sets it in act and use. Herefore comes it
> that Prince Harry is valiant; for the cold blood he did naturally inherit of

his father he hath, like lean, sterile and bare land, manured, husbanded, and till'd with excellent endeavour of drinking good store of fertile sherris ...[51]

How often have we been told that Hal, especially as Henry V, had the common touch, was one with the foot-soldiers of Agincourt, pained by their pain, contributing to the knockabout jests which amused them. Grudgingly Wilson and company admit that this common touch must have been picked up in the course of the degrading revels at the Boar's Head. The question these critics should have asked themselves is: Can degrading experiences really exalt the character? Or, to probe deeper: Could Henry have won the great historical–allegorical battle and finally restored to its original order and beauty the garden which had gone to weed in Richard II's day without having gained precisely those qualities of warm sympathy, clear intelligence, and warm-heartedness which Falstaffs, east and west, agree are produced in the brain by plentiful drinking of fertile sherris? It is said of Socrates that, however much he drank, he never became intoxicated; but it is also true that it seems, often, to have been after drinking bouts that he was visited by his *daimon*, thus escaping while still in the flesh from time into eternity, from pleasure into ecstasy, an entranced Hsien or Immortal who made the very snow he walked on warm. Here in this east–west, Socratic–Rabelaisian ("*De vin on devient divin*") concept of wine-drinking, lies the real clue to the dignity of the drunken Falstaff-persona, to the majesty of his pronouncements, to the depth of his scorn for ambition and honour, to his hatred of injustice masquerading as equity, of religion puling psalm-sentiments which it has no intention of re-enforcing?

8. Let us end this chapter with a brief glance at the life of Li Po, perhaps the most famous of all Chinese poets, a biography of whom by Arthur Waley appeared in 1950 in the "Ethical and Religious Classics of East and West". The editors of the series seem to have felt that it was necessary to preface this book with an apology for its inclusion inasmuch as they can find little or nothing which, by their standards, is either ethical or religious in the life of this poet.

> Li Po himself was not a man of high character; on the contrary [says Dr Waley] "he appears in his works as boastful, callous, dissipated, irresponsible, and untruthful"; in particular he was a drunkard. Though a Taoist, he seems to have understood little of Taoism as a mystical philosophy but rather to have sought in Taoism and Buddhism an escape from his earthly troubles. Yet from an ethical point of view, such a man is valuable as a contrast to men of higher type. The mountain peaks can only be recognised by looking at the foothills.[52]

Such deep-seated misunderstanding of the East by a group of men dedicated to promoting "a deeper understanding and appreciation of other peoples and their civilisations, especially their moral and spiritual achievements",[53] is heartbreaking. It may be said to the editors' credit, however, that they did include this book, even if for the wrong reasons, in a series designed to give "a clearer insight into the fundamentals of ethics and religion" and to satisfy "a general desire to know what the greatest minds, whether of East or West, have thought and said about the Truth of God and of the beings who (as most of them hold) have sprung from Him, lived by Him, and returned to Him".[54] In including this book in their series they did better than they knew. They were really regaling us with the story of a saint, no matter how impossible it was for them to discern the true gold in one whose life strangely resembled that of a well-known "old white-bearded Satan", and it may even be that what they have done marks a little step forward on the road to a better understanding of Falstaff himself.

The very first thing we learn about Li Po is that at the age of fifteen, apparently at the urging of his father, he wrote a *fu*, a dithyrambic ode, half-prose, half-poetry, to celebrate the rebuilding in 687 at Lo-yang of a colossal Ming T'ang over three hundred feet high. For many years the use of such a building, if not the winter rite itself, had been allowed to lapse, and Li Po's poem, called "The Ming T'ang Fu", celebrated both the rehabilitation of the temple and the significance of the ceremony. It is of interest to note that Li's family believed itself descended from Li Kao, who had founded a local dynasty in the extreme west of China around A.D. 400. "The T'ang emperors also claimed to be descended from Li Kao, though they seem to have belonged in reality to a quite different family."[55] It is therefore quite feasible that Li Po thought of himself as a disinherited prince, perhaps the true vessel of the fertility magic of a divine line, and it is not impossible that he was for a long time welcomed at the court and throughout China as a kind of adjunct or Substitute King on whom the growth of the crops and the peace of the empire not a little depended.

Like Tao Ch'ien, Li Po was certainly "aristocratically offhand in his demeanour and unconstrained in his manner," and he made much, throughout his life and in his poems, of the occasion when one Ho Chih-chang, a long-time Vice-president of the Board of Rites, "in his old age ... more and more tipsy, disorderly, and eccentric, had hailed Li Po at their first meeting as a Banished Immortal".[56] Li emphasised that Ho, in so recognising him, had simply recorded a fact, for a Banished Immortal was just what he was, i.e., one who for misbehaviour in the Taoist Heaven was being punished by being made to live on earth for a certain period as a quite naturally "wayward and extraordinary" human being.[57] It is true, of course, that Immortals sometimes sought incarnation or reincarnation for the purpose of guiding an awkward or cruel prince and helping suffering mankind, but this was not the case with Li. The more specific title for a Banished Immortal was Minister Abroad of the Thirty-six Emperors of Heaven, and it was up to him to stimulate the divine harmony of heaven and earth, to promote the divine purpose of fruitfulness and multiplication, by unremitting eating, drinking, dancing, writing of poetry, making of love, ascending of sacred mountains, and perhaps dying as Li did, in an attempt, as the moon's minion, to embrace his sacred lover as she fled before the prow of his boat along the Yellow River. At any rate, this is exactly the life Li led.

At Cha'ng-an, the great capital of the T'ang Dynasty,

> Li Po was not given an official post, but joined a pool of distinguished poets who were kept at the Han-lin Academy, ready at any moment to attend the outings and festivities of the Court and celebrate them in verse. He was handsomely treated: "I rode a colt from the Emperor's stable, my stirrups were of filigree, my saddle was studded with white jade, my bed was of ivory, my mat of fine silk. I ate out of a golden dish."[58]

Perhaps because of his real or imagined royal lineage, he did not serve the emperor as a scholar or official, but only in those employments where his magic inheritance and poetic skill could help. He loved to preside over drinking parties, and headed a drunken company of his own known as the Eight Immortals of the Wine-Cup. During the rebellion of An Lu-shan, he sought to "play the part of Chi Meng, the legendary knight-errant and gambler, who was worth to whatever side he joined 'as much as the conquest of a whole kingdom' ".[59] For years he was interested in alchemy, which he seems to have understood as an attempt to assimilate into his warm body the golden sun-power to the end that he might defend and magnify the sun in its days of danger. Though he had four wives and three or four children, he spent much of his time travelling about the emperor's dominions climbing sacred mountains and making love, perhaps publicly, to two of the most beautiful girls in China. A certain Wei Hao has left us an account of these apparently ritualistic activities:

> Sometimes he used to take his singing-girls, Chao-yang and Chin-ling, with him on his travels ... and wherever he arrived, on his fine steed, with these lovely concubines in his company, the Governor of the place would always come out to meet him. When he had taken some gallons of wine and was already pretty drunk, his page boy, Cynnabar, would play The Waves of the Blue Sea ... However badly a party was going, from the moment Li Po became toastmaster, everybody was in high spirits.[60]

Wei Hao has also left us a thumbnail portrait of the poet with his eyes in a fine frenzy rolling – "the pupils flashed; they were immense, like those of a hungry tiger". Elsewhere his eyes are compared to two suns and, strangely to our way of thinking (or are we so surprised now?), he seems to have thought that in the various activities described above he was imitating ancient deities of irrigation and agriculture.

During the rebellion of An Lu-shan, a time of political trouble following fast on a series of disasters including drought, a fire and a typhoon, floods that lasted for weeks and a hurricane that seemed about to seal the fate of the dynasty, Li Po was very anxious to help his monarch to tranquilise the Tartar Sands (kill the Turkish Knight!). For this purpose he joined Prince Lin, who was connected with the royal family. Unknown to Li Po, Prince Lin was less interested in liquidating An Lu-shan than in trying to seize the government for himself. In any case, the Prince was very happy to have on his side the most famous poet in China, who now chose to reveal what had remained hidden from society for forty years, though not concealed in his poems: that he was a mighty man in the military line, especially when the problem was that of fighting the powers of cold and evil. He disclosed that, concealed at his waist, he carried the fabulously indomitable sword Dragon Pool, made of gilded work. Significantly, however, his notion of winning the war was to preside over the drinking bouts of Prince Lin's officers while writing poems such as that called "Watching the Dancing Girls at a Banquet on Board Marshal Wei's Transport; Written When with the Fleet". When Prince Lin's true purposes were discovered Li Po, though innocent of rebellion, was arrested and thrown into prison, where "as in darkness beneath a down-turned bowl"[61] he alternately wept and remembered with joy those naval exploits when the "tankard passed round on a dish of green jade".[62] At last freed, if not entirely exonerated, with the help of Sung Jo-ssu, Assistant Director of the Censorate, Li wrote poems intended to guarantee the success of his new patron's military efforts against An Lu-shan, which happened quickly now. We know now how effective a drum the wine table can be when there are demons to be exorcised.

During most of the eight years of the rebellion Li was a homeless refugee, yet it is pleasant to remember that he never once lost his status as Minister on Distant Service of the Celestial Principalities, and that he never refers in his poems or letters to any difficulty encountered in getting enough to eat or, especially, to drink. To the end of his days, whether in prison or banished by accident or design from his monarch's face, he continued in his own way to fight the sacred war, immortalising in poems designed to promote the good of man and nature the literally magic days of his youth when

> We galloped to the brothels, cracking our gilded whip;
> We sent in our writings to the Palace of the Unicorn;
> Girls sang to us and danced hour by hour on tortoiseshell mats;[63]

the literally magic nights when

> On the southern lake the autumn moon shone pale;
> Prefect Wang invited me at night.
> In his damask tent Secretary Chang lay drunk.
> In their gauze dresses, the dancing girls were gay.

The sound of flutes was shrill from shore to shore,
The singers' tunes mounted the cloudy sky ...[64]

It was on a similar moonlight night that Li, now a banished old man, met his death, or so the story goes, while seeking, in the depths of divine drunkenness, to embrace the reflection of the moon in the Yellow River, thus rounding off a life of perfect Falstaffian service and self-sacrifice. At least, it can be considered so by all who, like the Chinese and the ancient Greeks, stand in awe of the mysterious heart-warming and brain-reorienting effects of wine. The story of his death is admittedly mythical, but no more so, as far as I can see, than the story of his life. In an old Chinese version – the incidents are not too unlike those of Falstaff's summons to Arthur's bosom to throw some light, perhaps, on Sir John's death-scene – the story runs as follows:

The moon that night was shining like day. Li Tai-po was supping on the river when all of a sudden there was heard in the mid-air a concert of harmonious voices, which sounded nearer and nearer to the boat. Then, the water rose in a great tumult, and lo! there appeared in front of Li Tai-po dolphins which stood on their tails, waving their fins, and two children of immortality carrying in their hands the banners to indicate the way. They had come in behalf of the lord of the heavens to invite the poet to return and resume his place in the celestial realm. His companions on the boat saw the poet depart, sitting on the back of a dolphin while the harmonious voices guided the cortege. ... Soon they vanished altogether in the mist."[65]

IX
Ilya of the Slavs,
Who "Fought a Long Hour
by Shrewsbury Clock"

Half a dozen times we have seen the seasonal conflict which the fat tutor helped his pupil to wage represented as a real war. Early man was not able, we are told, to entertain ideas not welded to facts which inspired them; neither was he able to conceive of facts as anything but counters or symbols for ideas. This is the way our forefathers' minds worked, they say, but this is also the way our minds work when their activity is rich with meaning. When facts mean nothing but themselves, they mean practically nothing at all, or so the symbolic logicians tell us, while concepts which are pried endlessly loose from the facts that gave rise to them fall, as far as mental satisfaction goes, stark-dead. In the story of Dionysos overcoming a dark eastern king with the help of Silenos, the battle may have been in the first place almost purely ritual-symbolic; yet when Alexander the Great conquered western India, Dionysos' old conflict was quickly given a local habitation and a name, while, conversely, Alexander was soon equated with Dionysos as an avatar. Thus an intensely real and definitely historical event gave to and took from seasonal myth a rainbow aura. Enkidu fighting the powers that make for infertility is almost bound to be represented in literature and art, even in liturgy and sacred drama, as quite a real conflict, while real enemies, who physically threaten the peace and fruitfulness of the land, are almost bound to be identified with fiends of night, hail, and death. Thus phrases like "the children of light" and "the children of darkness" have for thousands of years had connotations both literal and metaphorical, while wars have

often been thought of as at once hopelessly factual and hopefully symbolical. The bleak encroachment of winter is identified if you are English with
Muslim or French enemies personified as Turkish Knights or the Kings of
France, while St George medicines winter's sadness on a mummers' battlefield called Jerusalem or Agincourt, and his guide and guardian becomes,
literally, a recruiting officer.

In this brief chapter I hope to say something about the role of the
Falstaff-persona as recruiting sergeant and actual man-at-arms. In the last
chapter we saw him fighting the demons of cold and darkness by magical
drinking at long distance – by miraculous absent-treatment. In this chapter I
shall treat the Falstaffian figure who, rousing his ponderous body from its
ease at his inn, betakes himself to hand-to-hand conflict with the enemy, or
at least to egging on and protecting his pupil in wars depicted as real though,
in significance, nine-tenths mythic. At least, the result of victory in such
battles is not so much the annihilation of any recognisable human enemy as
the sudden bursting of a wasteland into leaf and spike, the restoration of
order and loveliness to a garden choked with nettles.

I propose to treat this theme in relation to a demi-god or ancient deity of
Slavonic legend, Ilya of Murom, who was not much of a teacher, to be sure,
but who performed incredible feats of valour against the Black Tartars for
his prince Vladimir, whose endlessly reiterated epithet is "Little Sun". For the
first time in this study we have moved into regions where the decline of the
sun meant the triumph of sleet, snow, and ice – where men without the aid of
fire could hardly manage to exist through the winter debacle. It is, therefore,
not surprising that the helper and saviour of the sun should be a creature
enwreathed in flame as well as a man of infinite capacity for food, drink,
lovemaking, and the usual irrepressible disgust with accepted forms of law
and religion.

As far as I know, nearly all the Falstaffian figures of the north have in
them flames of a fire-god as well as the declining embers of a benevolent Old
Sun. Like Falstaff, Ilya had a childhood though in the *bilyny* (epic songs) he
is always called "the Old Cossack". Of his babyhood we are told enough to
tempt us to make guesses about our fat knight. For the first thirty years of his
life he sat upon the oven in his father's cottage, an ugly creature with neither
arms nor legs, or with extremely skinny extremities such as those we see in
certain icons of Bes and Kuvera. After the period (days, rather than years?)
symbolic of the time during which the New Sun gathers strength for a
decisive battle with the devils of darkness, Ilya receives the power to rise and
walk from three mysterious strangers, one of whom (I am here drawing on
the group of *bilyny* known as *The Cycle of Vladimir* or *of Kiev*) is identified
as Christ, who here appears as an aged sun-god handing over his remaining
warmth to a successor. Characteristically, he transmits it in the form of an
alcoholic drink, the first draught of which leads Ilya to exclaim, "I feel a
great strength within me so that I could even move the earth".[1] In fact, this is
exactly what Ilya is supposed to do – to move the earth, as its lover, to new

births of grain and fruit – but now Christ gives him another drink intended to diminish by half the potency communicated by the first drink. From childhood Ilya's thirst, the most mighty in all the lore of Falstaff figures, compelled him to swallow so many gallons of wine at a single gulp that if the power communicated by Christ's gift had not been diminished the earth, we are told, would have been unable to bear his embraces. Other stories of Ilya tell that he received his miraculous strength not from Christ but from Svyatogor, an old sun-hero who "taught Ilya all heroic customs and traditions",[2] including, of course, drinking and lovemaking, the latter of which Ilya practised with Svyatogor's "fair, heroic wife".[3] This giant woman seems to have been a personification of earth, whom the old husband carried around locked up in a crystal casket (winter ice?). Shortly after this episode, the elder and younger heroes found, as they journeyed among certain holy mountains, a great coffin in which Svyatogor, now in constant decline, knew it was time to entomb himself. Caught in the tomb, he gave Ilya a huge sword with which to smite the lid of the coffin, not so much in an endeavour to free his old friend as in order to give passage to his death sighs, which Ilya at first eagerly breathed up.

> Yet again spoke Svyatogor: "I die, oh, younger brother! Bend down now to the crevice. Yet once again will I breathe upon thee and give thee all my vast strength."
> But Ilya made answer: "My strength sufficeth me, elder brother; had I more, the earth could not bear me."[4]

But since we are not interested here, except speculatively, with the youth and tutelage of the Falstaff-personae – only with their later adventures as banished sun-kings who, usually at a rather advanced age, have to be recalled from mountain, steppe, or forest exile to substitute for an upstart conqueror at Christmas and teach his son Divine King secrets, let us proceed at once to an examination of Ilya in his Mock-Monarch and Tutor-of-the-Sun-Prince Role.

Before telling this story, however, we should stress the likelihood that Ilya was descended from pre-Christian Slavic deities of fire and hearth as well as from the ancient Slavic sun-god. As I have said, in the northern countries the drunken tutor–saviour is almost bound to be connected with fire, a portion of the sun enkindled on earth to help men survive the months of intolerable darkness and cold. Thus it is impossible not to find an ancestor of Ilya in Domovoy, the god of the hearth who lived behind the peasant's stove. We are told that in art "Domovoy was represented as an old man, dressed either in a long robe tied around his waist, or in a red shirt. Although old, he had a thick head of bushy hair, and his eyes gleamed. His entire body was protected by a coat of soft, thick hair."[5] In such a description we also catch glimpses of old friends like Silenos and Bes. There was nothing, we are told, which Domovoy would not do for a master he loved, protecting him at all times and stealing from others to increase his master's wealth. Ilya seems also to have taken a trait or two from Leshy, the Russian genius of the forest and lord of animals, who was ordinarily represented as an old man with a bestial face set in an aureole of flaming beard and hair, a humorous demi-god somewhat resembling the Celtic or Wodewose, who usually in October, after a period of dangerous pranks, disappeared underground for the winter months.

The great fire-god of the pre-Christian Slavs, the old deity with whom Ilya has perhaps most in common, was Svarozic, a blood-brother of the sun, who fought off demons of darkness and maintained health of body and mind in men. His statues of idols, especially among the Elbe Slavs, were made of gold and showed him as a fearsome warrior associated with a buffalo, whose head was represented on either his shield or breastplate – a sun-animal we have not so far come across in this study. By Christians Svarozic was regarded as an old white-bearded devil; Bruno, the Apostle to the Prussians, called him "Zuarasiz Diabolus".[6] All our solar figures have appeared at one time or another as warriors, but it is only now, here in the north, that we find a heat-god warring fiercely on cold, disease, and injustice, whose presence was customarily detected by making the accused walk on living coals. The Slavs seem to have believed that the souls of their ancestors lived again in the fire of the winter hearth, and that consequently every kind of good could be expected from the flames of the earth–sun. Often they lit the hearth-fire at midnight, the hour when demons of cold raged, to get at men's bodies, souls, and the harvest stored in the barn. Sick people were lifted over bonfires by their families, and well people held above them to be purified of sin. These bonfires were a special feature of the New Year's festival, which among the Slavs was celebrated at the autumn equinox rather than during the shortest days of December. On this day all the old fires on family hearths were extinguished and relit with coals from a great communal bonfire. When we read of the tremendous heat generated by Falstaff and of the way in which his body, tossed in the Thames, made the water boil – "glowing hot, in that surge, like a horse-shoe; think of that – hissing hot – think of that, Master Brook"[7] – we can hardly help seeing in him traces, however attenuated, not only of a sun- but of an old fire-god. Svarozic was also celebrated by a feast of candles, which makes us remember that Falstaff referred to himself as a "wassail candle, my lord, all tallow; if I did say of wax, my growth would approve the truth".[8] In addition, the reference to Falstaff as a burnt-out taper makes us recall that the candles for the Slavic feast were made in human shape and that women, before lighting them, wept and wailed over them as if they were indeed human – another sign which points to Falstaff as, possibly, a predestined victim. Again, it is thought that certain ancient boundary stones found in Prussia, enormous in bulk and each carved with a bearded face and hands holding a drinking-horn and a club, may represent Svarozic, who stood firm against the encroaching demons of cold and darkness – and here it is intensely interesting to recall that Ilya of Murom, in his last fight against the Tartars, did not so much die as turn into a mountain-sized boundary stone which effectually blocked their further progress into Holy Russia.

The Slavic sun god whom Svarozic–Ilya helped in winter was called Dazbog. He is referred to in all the old Russian chronicles as Tsar Sun, and it is impossible not to see in Little Sun Vladimir, the prince for whom Ilya fought, an earthly representative – not particularly worthy – of this pagan deity. We are told that the sacrifice Dazbog liked best was the head of a boar decorated with red ribbons. Vladimir I of history, who is often compared to the Little Sun of the *bilyny*, was in early life a thorough-going heathen and erected at Kiev a great statue of Dazbog. When, later on, he found it desirable to import a religion for his people he rejected Judaism, it is said, because it forbade the eating of boar's flesh and Islam because it rejected alcohol, which he believed indispensable for ice-bound Slavs. He chose, rather, Greek Catholicism because his emissaries reported that Hagia Sophia, the great mother church at Byzantium, shone like the sun in heaven.

In Russia the Divine King needed plenty of assistant rulers or Mock Kings in carrying out his fertility function, for the land was for many months of the year beleaguered by demons, usually called Black Tartars, who roared like monsters and whistled like serpents so that "pebbles were scattered over the plain, the grass withered, the flowerets drooped".[9] Such weather demons, often at the head of vast armies of deadly imps, bear in the *bilyny* such names as Tugarin, Batyg, Bukar, the Nightingale Robber, the Hunter Falcon, or the Black-raven Knight, the three last-named devils being so called because they were comparable to great birds with wings that shut out the sun and storm and with songs that shook cities to rubble. They are counterparts of the various demons of cold and night whom we have so often encountered since first meeting them in this book as the Turkish Knight of the Mummers' Play. Sorely beset by these fierce enemies, it is no wonder that Little Sun Vladimir turned to the Old Cossack Ilya for help, or that Ilya recruited for the king's service an army of fighters, many of uncouth origin – or, rather, of once-royal blood – like himself much as Dunsi Ivanovitch called "the Serf". However humbly born, all of these by fighting for their king became great heroes or *bogatyrs* who, gathered in defence of Vladimir, constituted a sort of unkempt Russian Round Table. The problem, as winter deepened toward the shortest day, was to outmagic this trio of ghastly birds and kill their leader, the infamous Nightingale Robber. The confrontation shaped up with Vladimir heading the forces of light under Ilya's tutelage against the Nightingale Demon.

Many of these heroes seem to be simply lesser Ilyas, distinguished from the Old Cossack chiefly by being able to drink less than he and being accordingly less strong. Ilya's drinking cup, we are told, held six buckets and a half of wine, while that of Dobrynya Nikitch contained but four and a half, and Alyosha Popovich's was unbelievably small, holding but two and a half. Surely, Ilya excels all the drinkers we have so far come across in these pages in the floods of liquor he consumes as he takes his ease in the "imperial pot-house"[10] surrounded by hangers-on, sots of every description, indeed all who can quickly down successive quarts of "good green wine" without choking. These humble–heroic Slavs simply swim in the stuff, and their noisy boasting far excels the clamour that issued from the Boar's Head or any similar powerhouse of solar force encountered in these pages.

Falstaff, you recall, threatens on a famous occasion to depose Hal for not being an apt pupil, for being in fact a coward who is not learning his fertility lessons fast enough, and Ilya reproves Prince Vladimir for neglecting similar counsel in similar scenes.

> *Fal.:*   A plague of all cowards, I say still.
>
> *Prince:*   How now, wool-sack. What mutter you?
>
> *Fal.:*   A king's son! If I do not beat thee out of thy kingdom with a dagger of lath and drive all thy subjects afore thee like a flock of wild geese, I'll never wear hair on my face more. You Prince of Wales! ... Give me a cup of sack. I am a rogue if I drunk today.
>
> *Prince:*   O villain! Thy lips are scarce wip'd since thou drunk'st last.
>
> *Fal.:*   All's one for that. (*He drinketh.*) A plague of all cowards, still say I.[11]

When Vladimir irritates Ilya, the Old Cossack sends him messages like this:

> "Let strict ukases be promulgated through all the towns of Kiev and Charnigraf, that all the pot-houses and drinking places of whatever sort be opened freely for the space of three days, that all the people may drink green wine without price. And whoso drinketh no green wine, let him quaff the sweet mead; that all may know that the Old Cossack Ilya of Murom is come to famous Kiev town. Let this be done, (*he tells his messenger*) and let an honourable banquet be made, or the Prince shall reign no longer than until tomorrow's morn!"[12]

Characteristically, Ilya and his rout, an army of high and low whom he has rallied to Vladimir's standard, not only scorn Vladimir's constables and judges, but never miss a chance to attack the Church. To be sure, it is the Roman Church that they deride, not the Greek Orthodox, but it is hard when "priests" are being ridiculed to remember that there are sheep as well as goats in the pinfold.

As for the gigantic lovemaking of Ilya and the *bogatyrs*, they pour out fructifying fluid in almost exact proportion to the size of the potation. I will pass over their erotic feats except to say that they are usually performed with strong and beautiful *polyanitzas* or warrior-women, magnificent Russian Amazons who well personify Mother Earth and on whom they beget daughters whose yellow hair ripples in the wind like fields of ripening grain, sons who partake transparently of the solar nature of their fathers – "His little legs are silver to the knee, his arms to the elbow are of pure gold; upon his brow gloweth the fair red sun, upon his crown shone countless stars ..."[13]. Not a few of the heroes lie from time to time with the queen herself, Vladimir's wife Apraxia, which suggests that little Vladimir was not merely a young man in search of instruction but – at least, at times – a full-fledged monarch who, like Arthur perhaps, was forced to let his Round Table heroes lie with the queen in order to escape the death decreed for ageing sons of the man. Much fiercer than King Arthur, however, in sacrificing the muscular heroes who had played proxy for him in times of crisis. Vladimir was continually imprisoning them, beheading them, or condemning them to a fate which may have been horribly ritualistic in pagan Russia: "they hewed off his nimble feet to the knee, his white arms to the elbow, plucked his clear eyes from his brow and his tongue from his mouth and buried him to the breast in damp mother earth".[14]

On one occasion when Ilya was threatening the prince – boasting that even as he dragged his mantle of marten over the kitchen floor, "so he would drag Vladimir by his yellow curls"; that even as he poured green wine upon the mantle, "so he would pour out Prince Vladimir's burning heart with his own white hands"[15] – Vladimir incarcerated even the Old Cossack. He did not manage this feat by force, of course – Ilya was too strong – but by threatening, if he did not descend into the pit, to overwhelm Ilya's friends and companions-in-arms with his displeasure. To the imprisoned Old Cossack, however, the Princess Apraxia, more concerned with the good of Holy Russia than with her impetuous husband, dug a passage, apparently with her own hands, carrying him "sugar viands" and mead and giving him to drink of a particularly intoxicating cup of her own mysterious power, which much like that of the Holy Grail, kept the Russian lands in bloom. This secret *connubium*, this subterranean warming and massage of the soil, seems to have worked very well for about three years, but finally a terrible winter attacked Russia in the person of the dragon Tsar of the Tartars, King Kalin. Kalin, having heard that, Ilya being dead or imprisoned "there was none to defend Prince Vladimir",[16] had determined to overthrow once for all the prosperity of the Russian land.

Thus we come to the great battle in which the Little Sun comes of age, and after or during which the powers of the tutor decline quickly toward death. The whole of the episode seems to be contained in two *bilyny*, now presented as separate and unrelated, entitled "Ilya and the Boon Companions" and "Ilya of Nurom and Tsar Kalin". Ilya is freed from confinement, but he is a very old man now, forced to hobble at first with the help of a "crutch of nine fathoms"[17] and a hooked staff. His great beard is sprinkled with grey and his head all white, yet he recruits his energies for the battle by wassailing with his "poor boon companions of the pot-house," swallowing a bucket and a half of green wine "in one breath". After this

> the aged man climbed upon the brick oven and slept. Very early on the morrow, as the warm, red sun arose, he descended to the cellars, burst open the doors with his foot, took a cask of forty [gallons?] under one arm, another of the same under the other, and rolled a third before him with his foot, into ... the marketplace. Then he shouted with all his heroic might in a fearsome, thunderous voice:

"Ho, ye boon companions and ye peasants of the village! Come to the old man's feast! I will give ye all green wine, even to drunkenness, without price."[18]

Much strengthened by the noise and liquor, Ilya is nevertheless loath to help ungrateful Vladimir, saying to his messengers, "In vain do ye disquiet me, brothers! Let the old man sleep." Then, like Falstaff to his sea-coal fire, he turns back to the warm brick. Still, he scrambles down from it at last and passed through Kiev shouting almost in derision at his royal pupil, "I go now to the open plain, to the heroic barriers, to the damp oak."[19] In many of the *bilyny* we hear of the barriers or Barrier of the Nevida Oak, the spot where, apparently, the powers of darkness, having been turned back, were entirely (?) routed at the vernal equinox. Here beneath the great tree Ilya found his recruits, Falstaffian bullcalves now grown into buffaloes, heroes of Holy Russia, banqueting in a white pavilion as they awaited the final Tartar attack.

In some versions of the story it is not Vladimir himself, now king, but his nephew, young Yermak Timofervich, the heir-apparent, who leads the battle against Kalin, Prince of Darkness. Not understanding much of these ritual matters, Yernak was at first vexed that in the teeth of the enemy the heroes kept eating, drinking, and "playing checkers upon a board of gold" while Ilya slept, as unconcernedly as Falstaff when threatened with deadly danger, "upon a couch of fishes' teeth, beneath a coverlet of sables".[20] Unable for all his shouting to stir the heroes from their games or wake the Old Cossack, Yermak himself attacked the army of darkness. It was only after three days, days during which Yermak spent himself in futile attempts to kill Kalin, that Ilya awoke and, with his companions-in-arms, rescued the boy, saying, "Calm thy heroic heart ... we will labour now."[21] Shakespeare, of course, makes Falstaff pretend sleep or death at Shrewsbury and gives him only a mendacious victory over "the spirit Percy", but there is an odd parallel, in this moment of battle crisis, between the actions of Ilya and Falstaff. In other *bilyny* we have seen Ilya vanquish, largely by magic means, the terrible Nightingale Robber and the Hunter Falcon, demons not too unlike "that great magician damn'd Glendower" or "that fiend Douglas", and now in Tsar Kalin he seems to be face to face with an Asiatic Percy, a monstrous Turkish Knight who, however often killed, keeps reviving so that his slaying takes "a long hour [here, days] by Shrewsbury clock". In the end he is vanquished, of course, but most of the famous recruits are now dead, and the only way in which the Old Cossack of the Don can stop the onslaught of Kalin's last troop is to die into a flaming rock of mountainous shape and size which seals off the possibility of even mingling (?) with troops from the Black Tartars.

Now at last Prince Vladimir and the heir-apparent, young Yermak, begin to understand the meaning of all the crude revelry of the recruits. Hot of heart, clear of purpose, brave unto death, they have fought the "Prince of

Ilya of the Slavs

the [Winter] Air" to a standstill, and given the once Little Sun a clear and lovely field in which to perform adult-sized miracles. In some versions only these two regal persons survive the battle – "There's not three of my hundred and fifty left alive".[22] The trenches with which the old companions had scored the bosom of Mother Earth are packed with their bodies – "They'll fill a pit as well as better."[23] When the uncle asks his nephew, "How shall I reward thee? ... Wilt thou have estates or golden treasure?" the percipient prince answers simply, "Grant me only, Uncle, that I may drink beer and wine without price in all the pot-houses."[24]

Such is the chief Slavonic version of the solstice battle, the Agincourt of Russian folklore, from which the sun-prince or king emerges a full-grown hero of irrepressible light and warmth. The seasonal symbolism of the heroic ballads of Russia lies unusually, for such ancient folk productions, near the surface and we cannot fail to see in them the degenerate libretti of old seasonal rites and dramas. True, no folklorists* I know of have interpreted the epic of Ilya and his warriors as I have done here, but no one has ever treated Bes, Silenos, Ganeśa and Co. in this way either. Even the historical heroes of Russia come down to us in clear association with seasonal imagery: Prince Igor in *The Tale of Igor's Argument* held the barrier (not too firmly) against the Polovtsy, while Alexander Nevsky broke the power of encroaching knights in a battle on a frozen lake. In their lives and acts the solar imagery is almost as obvious in those of Little Sun Vladimir or Ilya himself, whose very name means Elijah, and summons up in any reader's mind, as it does in the minds of Russians, the picture of an old bearded prophet who ascended to heaven in a chariot of fire, leaving his mantle to Elisha as Ilya left his scarlet-coloured cloak of marten to Vladimir or his nephew. In fact, the old Cossack is called by many Russians Ilya the Prophet, and in Kacharov, his reputed birthplace, a statue dedicated to him in his vatic capacity was erected over a spring which was said to have burst from this rock beneath the hoofs of his great white war horse. A legend to the effect that fierce bears still come to this spring to drink of its waters and gain heroic strength gives us a hint that perhaps a bear, rather than a horse or buffalo, was really Ilya's favourite sun-animal, just as it seems to have been that of Elijah's heir, Elisha. Not many years ago two or three different tombs in Kiev were still pointed out as Ilya's but, though they received some reverence, no one had much faith in their authenticity since it was well

---

*For Slavic folklore the reader may consult:

(1)   L.A. Magnus, *The Heroic Ballads of Russia* (London, 1921);

(2)   Y.M. Sokolov, *Russian Folklore*, tr. C.R. Smith (New York, 1950);

(3)   L. Leger, *La Mythologie Slave* (Paris, 1901);

(4)   A. Bruckner, *Mythologie Slava* (Bologna, 1923);

(5)   F. Haase, *Volkgelaube und Brauchten des Ostelaven* (Breslau, 1929); and

(6)   R. Loukine, *Mythologie Russe* (Bruxelles, 1946).

known that his enormous figure had turned to stone, or retreated into a rock at the Battle of the Barrier. Besides, no one really believes that he died, and it is expected that he, like so many solar heroes, will again descend to earth in human form, drinking, shouting, and revelling as in the past, to rescue mankind in a season of wintry crisis such as the world has never seen.

The southern Slavs have an Ilya-like hero, Marko Kralyevich*, who rivals Ilya in strength (he boasts that he can overturn Mother Earth with one hand and defeat God Himself in personal combat), in the ability to consume floods of liquor (not only he but his white horse Sharats loves to drink – the first till he becomes red in the eyes, the second till he becomes scarlet to the ears), and in streaming hair and flaring whiskers (his moustache was as large as a year-old lamb). Though he beheads several coal-black Arabs and Turkish knights, the sun-monarch for whom he battles and by whom he is imprisoned is, oddly, the Muslim Sultan himself. Many of the Marko stories seem to have taken their present form at the time when the Yugoslavs lived under Turkish rule, all resistance to which appeared hopeless after the terrible defeat at Kosovo. Like many another Falstaff-figure, Marko swallowed his pride and worked strenuously in the role of a Mock Monarch, accepting all the indignities usually heaped on such characters, in order to keep the soil productive and his oppressed people fed. His name Kralyevich means "the king's son" and we may assume that in his enormous eating, drinking, boasting, loving, robbing, fighting, in his imprisonment and death, he is acting the part of a degraded Divine King solicitous for the good of his stolen land and his fallen people. He does not perish in battle but, good soldier that he is, simply fades away as, his sable cap pulled over his once golden eyes, he lies on a green cloak spread under winter pines. It is not clear what animal he is to be associated with, but much is made of his customary dress of a cloak and cap lined with wolfskin, the fur of which he turns to the outside whenever he battles the powers of darkness. On such fearful occasions while his great golden mare whirs sun-like across the sky, his flowing hair and incredible moustache unite with the wolfskin to surround him completely with a shaggy halo of light. As a ranting boaster, Marko makes one think more of Ancient Pistol than of Falstaff, while his grimaces in battle are even more furious–comic than Pistol's, suggesting the horrid countenances of the Ganas who lead the rout of Indian dances – creatures who might be denominated "very ancient Ancient Pistols."

It is probably Ilya, however, of all the Falstaff-figures we have so far examined, who is most clearly and signally the braggart captain, the *miles*

---

*The reader may find the various tales of Marko translated or described in the following books:

(1)   G.P. Noyes and L. Bacon, *Baltic Ballads of Servia* (Boston, 1913);
(2)   W.W. Petrovich, *Hero Tales and Legends of the Serbians* (London, 1914);
(3)   J. Stojković, *Kralyevic Marko* (Dovi Sad, 1922);
(4)   D.H. Low, *The Ballads of Marko Kraljević* (Cambridge, Mass., 1922);
(5)   C.A. Manning with G.W. Fuller, *Marko the King's Son* (New York, 1932).

gloriosus, to whom Falstaff has been so often compared by critics like E.E. Stoll. Stoll holds that the fat knight is simply a stock comic character whom Shakespeare introduced into the *Henry* plays for one reason only: this type could be relied on to make the Elizabethan audience laugh, and Shakespeare wanted to give comic relief, from time to time, to his grand historical pageantry. Dover Wilson sees in Falstaff not so much the boastful soldier as the old soldier, the survivor of many campaigns; this is a more adequate estimate of him, though (as is to be expected from Wilson) Falstaff is held to have lied about his derring-do and to have survived the wars chiefly by running away from danger. All critics who try to explain the significance of Falstaff – who try, that is, to explain it away – in terms of the theatrical tradition of the braggart soldier, trace his provenience to the *Miles Gloriosus* of Plautus, whose Pyrgopolinices is described by them as an incredibly vain, deceitful, lying, lustful, and at last gullible blackguard, epithets that perfectly hit off, they say, his English descendant. But it is difficult to find so little real significance and such unqualified baseness as this even in the boastful soldier of Plautus. Indeed, there is good reason to think that a play like the *Miles Gloriosus* is itself the direct descendant of a ritualistic drama enacted during the more ancient celebrations of the Saturnalia, and it is not impossible that this play, or plays like it, constituted a regular feature of the later New Year's festivities. Pyrgopolinices has in him not a little, it seems to me, of the Mock King, that regal boaster, shouter, drinker, and whorer who fought winter in his own peculiar way, if only to get severely slapped in the end.

It is amusing to note that Pyrgopolinices boasts that, once in India, he broke with a blow of his fist the foreleg of an elephant. Now in that country Kubera, the Old God who guarded the north, was in later days given an elephant head and made the leader of a boastful, noisy, amorous crew of Indian revellers, a *Gana* array such as Pyrgopolinices is said himself to be recruiting for the benefit of King Seleucis. We can agree with Stoll and Wilson that the Roman braggart boasts of slaying or repulsing an incredible army of men, multiplying the numbers at every fresh count in a way mildly suggestive of Falstaff in the great post-mortem held on the Battle of Gad's Hill at the Boar's Head; but Ilya, the folk-drawn portrait of whom can hardly be traced to an imitation of Plautus, is guilty of the same extravagance, as also is Samson in the Bible and, among the figures we have been considering why not?

> *Ariotrogus:* I do remember this. In Silicia there were a hundred and fifty men, a hundred in Crythiolathronia, thirty in Sardis, sixty of Macedon, whom you slaughtered altogether in one day.
>
> *Pyrg.:* What is the one total of these men?
>
> *Ario.:* Seven thousand.
>
> *Pyrg.:* It must be as much: you keep the reckoning well.[25]

The city in which the Roman play takes place is Ephesus, and those who surround the vain captain are undoubtedly Ephesians of that Dianic allegiance or way of thought which by the day of Falstaff had become "the old school". At one point in the play Pyrgopolinices, being begged by a servant to hurry to his mistress, becomes the centre of chatter not a little reminiscent of that of the Boar's Head:

> *Milphidippa:*   Come, my Achilles, let that be done which I entreat. Save her, charmer, by your charming ways. Call forth your kind disposition, stormer of cities, slayer of kings.
>
> *Pyrg.:*   O, by my troth, 'tis a vexatious thing! (*To Palastrio, his slave.*) How often, whip-scoundrel, have I forbidden you to make promises of my attention thus common?
>
> *Pal.:*   Do you hear that, honey? I have told you already, and now I tell you again, unless a fee is given to this boar-pig, he cannot possibly throw away his attentions in any quarter. ... Of those that become parents by him true warriors are born, and his sons live eight hundred years.
>
> *Mil.:*   (*aside to Palastrio*).   Fie on you for a fibber!
>
> *Pyrg.:*   Why, straight on, from age to age they live for a thousand years.
>
> *Pal.:*   I spoke within limits lest she suppose I was telling lies to her. ...
>
> *Pyrg.:*   Wench, I was born the day after Jupiter was born of Ops.
>
> *Pal.:*   If he had only been born the day before Jupiter, he would have had the realms of heaven.[26]

This is egregious fooling, of course, but it cannot be said that the boastful soldier does not, here and elsewhere, see himself in a distinctly mythic role, that is, as one who just missed the governance of the cosmos, for which trick of fate he is forced to compensate by acting the role of a strutting but doomed Lord of Misrule. This comes through with unmistakable sharpness, it seems to me, when in the last act this Recruiting Sergeant's enemies, after beating and humiliating, set about to kill or at least emasculate this "dear little grandson of Venus".[27] Actually, they spare him finally, but he has come as close as any but unimaginative readers could desire, to paying the symbolical price of a typical Mock King's day of power.

There are many ways of reading plays as well as many of writing them. It has always seemed to me that the great writer and the good reader – that is, those to whom the creation and enjoyment of art are the bread of life – often operate, to the glory of the awesome human psyche, on a level just below the conscious, and that at least one of the functions of criticism is to bring the significance of these subterranean operations to light. It is grotesque to assume that Shakespeare stirs us deeply for the simple reason that he introduced into his plays stock characters that he was sure would please his audience, or that he introduced them merely because that was "as they liked it". Recruiting officers, soldiers, warfaring, Armageddon, have always been words that it is almost impossible to take in a merely literal sense, and I cannot believe that the imagination of mankind created the fat, bestial, weapon-waving, shield-banging, sword-dancing figures from Bes to Falstaff simply to give us a realistic report on a type easily spotted in any summer encampment of the National Guard.

X

"Carry Sir John Falstaff to the Fleet"

Perhaps the most vexing question concerning the relations of Falstaff to Hal is raised by the episode in which the one-time pupil, now become king, denounces his old tutor publicly and incarcerates him in the Fleet, sending all his motley followers, Hal's sometime cronies, into exile:

> But all are banish'd till their conversations
> Appear more wise and modest to the world.[1]

Can Hal be exonerated of ingratitude or heartlessness, impercipience or even brainlessness? The question arises because by the last scene of the last act of *2 Henry IV*, a good many drama-lovers have become pretty well convinced that the worldly wisdom of a stammering politician like Henry IV or a streamlined and bloody prince like John of Lancaster is not real wisdom at all. Indeed, it may look as if the reader will have to place Hal, once "the nimble-footed madcap Prince of Wales / ... that daff'd the world aside / And bid it pass",[2] in this same lamentable category of the unwise worldly-wise:

> *King:* I know thee not, old man; fall to thy prayers.
> How ill white hairs become a fool and jester!
> I have long dreamed of such a kind of man,
> So surfeit-swell'd, so old, and so profane;
> But, being awak'd, I do despise my dream. ...
> Presume not that I am the thing I was;
> For God doth know, so shall the world perceive,
> That I have turn'd away my former self;

So will I those that kept me company.
When thou dost hear that I am as I have been,
Approach me, and thou shalt be as then thou wast,
The tutor and the feeder of my riots;
Till then, I banish thee on pain of death.[3]

Bradley has taught us to think of this episode as the Rejection of Falstaff, and he and other critics from Hazlitt to Masefield have felt that the ungrateful deed definitely proves that Henry, however his blood may have once been warmed to genial sympathy with his fellow-creatures, however clearly his mind may have once been sharpened to distinguish between honour and justice, righteousness and right, has slipped back into the hereditary pattern of the Plantagenets. In the Rejection Scene he seems to have become the unscrupulous politician glad to heed to the dictates of Old Father Antic and the bishops in order that he may bend the institutions they control to serve his appetite for power. Other critics, as we know, and these are more numerous, from Dr Johnson to Dover Wilson, have insisted that Hal did no more than was necessary in sending Falstaff to prison (Wilson points out that the Fleet was really quite a high-class place reserved for aristocratic political offenders, but neglects to mention the scandalous death-rate). They are horrified to have Hal called a cold-blooded opportunist, and insist that in his portrait of him Shakespeare genuinely and sincerely set out to paint the ideal British king. On the basis of any concept of the Rejection so far set forth by criticism, these antagonistic views are irreconcilable.

However, the view of Falstaff which I back, claiming him as the descendant of ancient royalty now depressed but called on in the season of winter crisis to play the role of a temporary Lord of Misrule, goes a considerable way toward reconciling these mutually exclusive views. According to my view of Hal as the prince–pupil of a traditional Mystery Play, it is not only excusable but necessary that, having acquired his old tutor's secrets, he should abandon him, drive him from the city where he has lorded it for a time, and even kill him. This is what happened to the Mock King of the Sacaea, the Interrex of the Saturnalia, and their fellows both east and west. When the seasonal danger had abated, the Mock King was not only banished but frequently scourged from the throne by the reinstated monarch or new instructed prince and often killed for the sake of any little *mana* that remained in his gross body – treatment beside which Hal's tongue-lashing seems comparatively mild. That the prince, now confirmed in kingly office, should acknowledge no kind of debt whatever to the old tutor may itself have been a ritualistic act, and he was surely duty-bound to increase his now growing power by every available means, however cruel, in order that the earth might break into springtime bloom as soon as possible. To our forefathers it was clear enough that the gradual lengthening of the days that followed the winter solstice was far too slow for their purposes; for the good of the fields and herds it was necessary that the daily period of light should exceed that of darkness, a condition that prevailed only after the vernal equinox. The three months between these dates was a period of alternating warmth and coldness, joy and fear, hope and disappointment, though it was fairly certain that the burning New Year babe would grow into a completely victorious warrior by the time of the equinoctial battle that delivered the *coup de grâce* to darkness. Meantime, however, it was necessary to make use of any magic remaining in the now moribund Old Sun or his earthly representative, the Mock King. (The old notion of the symbiotic coexistence of the dying Old Sun and the slowly waxing New Sun is scarcely accessible to reason though it may still be apprehended, perhaps, by intuition.) It was at this point of the story, the period between the two battles, the Campaigns of Winter and Spring, that numbers of the Falstaff-figures, whether largely mythical like Abu Zayd or apparently very real like Li Po, were thrown into prison, clamped into rocky caverns, or crushed under mountains.

We have seen Ilya heartlessly thrown into prison in his later years for boasting that he would surely dethrone, if not kill, the upstart Little Sun, and early men seem to have attempted to trace the ill-treatment of the tutor by his pupil to a kind of feud, in which the teacher only grudgingly imparted his last secrets, his remaining *mana*, to his charge, or was deprived of it by force, though only in the way in which the embryo forces the mother to nourish it. (In the *bilyny* this feud occurred before the winter Battle of the Barrier, at which Ilya was turned to stone, but in most versions of the tutor–pupil story the teacher survives this conflict only to bicker the remainder of his life away in quarrels with the pupil or to suffer imprisonment and death at his hands.)

As I have said, the sun-power in January, February, and March is vacillating and unpredictable, a phenomenon which may have been associated by our fathers with the notion that the Old Sun had not entirely surrendered his warmth and secrets to the New, and led them to believe it was necessary for the young monarch to enchain and torture his old tutor into giving up the very last vestiges of *mana*. In southern countries this version of the myth is rather less common than in northern ones; perhaps because in the south the incandescence of the sun, the burgeoning of leaf and shoot, are more a matter of forward-march than of touch-and-go. Where the triumph of spring is uncertain, especially among people who have been subjected to a gruelling winter, it seems only right that the New Sun or his earthly representative should resort to any measure, however cruel, to bring out the earliest possible growth of the soil. This, as far as I can make out, is the explanation – at once psychological, mythic, and historic – of the rejection and imprisonment of old Falstaff-personae. Perhaps it was in mercy to the playgoer that Shakespeare dropped the curtain on the adventures of Falstaff in the Fleet. We do have accounts, however, of the last months of certain Falstaff-figures, and I shall use the story of Loki, from Teutonic mythology, to throw what light I can on this obscure period in Falstaff's steady decline toward death.

Loki is often, like Ilya, supposed to have been more of a fire- than a sun-god; but he differs from many of his mythic brethren (though not necessarily from Dover Wilson's Falstaff) in being considered not merely naughty but essentially evil, the plotter of Baldr's death and the engineer of Ragnarok, in which most of the famous Teutonic deities perished. Actually, he seems to have been an ancient culture-god, pretty clearly connected with sun-power as well as with fire, and it is obvious from both *The Poetic Edda* and *The Prose Edda* that, though probably an older god than Othin (Odin, Woden, Wotan, etc.) or any of his pantheon, he is not really their foe but helps them more often than not in their battles with Frost Giants and Demons of Darkness. As early as 1911, H. Celander upset the notion that Loki was merely a fire spirit, while E. Mogk later proved, as clearly as such a point can be proved, that Loki had originally nothing to do with Baldr's death at the hands of Hodr, the story having been made up by Snorri Sturluson (1179–1241) in an attempt to rationalise the material of the "Voluspo" or "Wise-Woman's Prophecy".*

In most of the Eddic material Loki appears as a companion and friend of Othin, who cannot do without his instruction and aid. He is also shown as the helpful servant of Thor, a kind of Hermes to the AEsir or Teutonic gods around Othin; this suggests that he was probably a pre-Aryan deity, dethroned but persuaded or forced to bolster with his ancient wisdom the pantheon of invading tribes. It is true that he likes to play tricks on those whom he more or less willingly helps, but the most lethal weapon he uses against them is, as in the famous "Lokasonna" or "Loki's Wrangling", scurrilous invective of "the singing-man of Windsor" type. For the most part, he uses his wit and wisdom – in contrast to Othin, he is a real seer or piercer of the veil of the future, "wise-minded Loki" – to aid the gods in their eternal struggle with the Frost Giants. He has many of the traits of a Falstaffian Lord of Misrule. He is a tremendous eater and drinker, has a

---

*The best works on Loki are:

(1) H. Celander, "Loki's Mystiska Ursprung", *Sprakvetenskapliga Sallskapets i Uppsala Forhandlingar, 1906–1908* (Uppsala, 1911);

(2) E. Mogk, *Lokis Anteil an Baldrs Tode* (Folklore Fellows Communications, no. 57, Helsinki, 1923);

(3) E.J. Gras, *De Noordse Loki-Mythen* (Haarlem, 1931);

(4) J. DeVries, *The Problem of Loki* (Folklore Fellows Communications, no. 110, Helsinki, 1933);

Books, primary and secondary, on general Teutonic mythology are:

(1) *The Poetic Edda*, tr. R.A. Bellows from the Icelandic, 2 vols (Princeton and New York, 1923);

(2) Snorri Sturluson, *The Prose Edda*, tr. A.G. Brodeur from the Icelandic (New York and London, 1916);

(3) J.L.C. Grimm, *Teutonic Mythology*, tr. J.S. Stallybrass from the German, 4 vols (London, 1880–88);

(4) K. Krohn, *Skandinavisk Mytologi* (Helsingfors, 1922);

(5) F. Jostes, *Sonnenwende: Forschungen zur Germanischen Religions-und Sagengeschichte*, 2 vols (Munster im Westphalen, 1926–30);

(6) F. von der Leyen, *Die Gotter der Germanen* (Munchen, 1938).

great following among the motley dwarfs, kobolds, oafs, and elves of the Northland, is famous for his sexual prowess, loves to steal and to break the laws of the gods, and is an irrepressible mocker of the AEsir. His barbs usually draw blood inasmuch as these gods honour their own ideas of goodness almost exclusively in the breach. He loves recreation and fun; the oldest representation of him of which I know is that on the Gosforth Cross in Northumbria, which dates from about the middle of the tenth century and shows him – though in prison – as a plump, dwarfish, jolly, long-haired, and heavily bewhiskered figure. Traditionally, he is said to have been beautiful, in spite of his devilish nature, but we must not assume that the old Teutons meant by this adjective exactly what we do. However, the Gosforth Cross shows a beautiful deity in, perhaps, the same sense that Oberon, the good-natured Fairy King, was always said to be beautiful.

Now it is significant that "Oberon" is widely held to be a form of "Alberich" or "Andvari", names that were applied in Germanic countries to the King of the Dwarfs, those wondrous goldsmiths and jewellers whose underground activities, roaring with flames of sun and fire, undoubtedly defended the Northland against the settled melancholy of winter. Andvari, Alberich, and Oberon may, in fact, all be forms of Loki. If Loki was not indeed the original king of the dwarfs – creatures who recall, perhaps, the pre-Aryan peoples of the north forced "underground" by conquerors who replaced an ancient pantheon with that of their war-god Othin – he certainly lived on good terms with these small creatures. Master smiths frequently persuaded them to perfect for the gods wonderful gifts of gold such as an aureole-wig for Sif, wife of Thor (to be sure, Loki as a practical joke had previously stolen the vain goddess's real hair); the wonderful ship Skidbladnir, an obvious sun symbol which could float on the water or sail through the air, and was so elastic that from a tiny toy it could unfold into a vessel large enough to contain all the deities and their favourite steeds; and finally the boar Gold Bristle or Fearful Tusk, on which Freyr, a pre-AEsir sun-god, rode through the sky. Having joined forces with the AEsirs (when he could no longer resist them) Loki often turned to the dwarfs when devising ways to defend the conquering AEsir from their enemies, as when with the help of nine dwarfs he built the noble abode of the gods called Lyr, meaning the Heat-Holding, as we read in the "Svipdagsmol" or "Ballad of Svipdag". Loki's many associations with dwarfs, smiths, wells, and wisdom link him to still another ancient deity, either as ancestor or descendant, but more probably the latter inasmuch as Loki, though no giant himself, was said to have been the son of a giant, and Mimir (Mimer, Mimi, Mime, etc.), the old god I have in mind, is more often represented as a giant than as a dwarf.

As with Bes, Janus, Kuvera, and other figures we have come across, Mimir is often called the Old One, an epithet that usually points to the chief of the aboriginal gods of a conquered country. His memory is preserved in dozens of place names in Germany and the Scandinavian lands, and a good

Loki from Gosforth Cross, Cumbria

deal of lore which shows him as a less mischievous Loki has come down to us. In the *Edda* Mimir

> has a fountain, in which wisdom and understanding lie hidden: drinking of it every morning, he is the wisest, most intelligent, of men. To Mimir's fountain came Odin, and desired a drink, but did not receive it until he had given one of his eyes in pledge ... Mimir is no Asa [AEsir], but an exalted being with whom the Asas hold converse, of whom they make use – the sum total of wisdom, possibly an older Nature-god. Later fables degraded him into a wood-sprite or clever smith.[4]

One tradition holds that Mimir was the creator of the human race while another affirms that the creator was Loki – a distinction which seems, in the light of their many other similarities, to make them identical.

Other instances of the help which Loki gave the upstart gods who in the end rejected and imprisoned him are numerous. Once he saved them, huddled with fear, from the wrath of the warrior giantess Skadi, who was about to annihilate them for killing her father. She was willing to be reconciled with the AEsir, the members of Othin's pantheon, only if they could do

> a thing she thought they would not be able to accomplish: to make her laugh. Then Loki did this: he tied a cord to the beard of a goat, the other end being around his own genitals, and each gave way in turn, and each of the two screeched loudly; then Loki let himself fall onto Skadi's knee, and she laughed. Thereupon reconciliation was made with her on the part of the AEsir.[5]

On another occasion, described in the "Thrymskvitha" or "Lay of Thrym", one of the most famous ballads in *The Poetic Edda*, Loki saved the gods by devising a clever trick to recover Thor's hammer, stolen by the great King of the Frost Giants, Thrym. On this occasion Loki muffled himself as well as Thor in women's clothes in order to carry out his plan, an incident that reminds me that there are no less than three famous tales in which Loki appears disguised as a female, either woman or mare. Though I have not had occasion to make this point before, many of our long-haired sun-figures from Enkidu onward have appeared disguised from time to time as women – so often that it would have been surprising, perhaps, had not Falstaff, on one occasion at least, been found masquerading as the Witch of Brainford. It is also true, you remember, that the man–woman was a very common figure in the English Mummers' Play. Just what was the significance of the man dressed as a woman is not certain, but it has been suggested that it was simply one more attempt on the part of our essentially self-sacrificing hero to promote fertility. Among certain primitive tribes the custom of the king, or perhaps all the males, adopting female clothing is supposed to double the chances for a good harvest, and the tradition "has even been thought to survive in the Londoner's habit of changing hats with his lady on bank holidays".[6] On the occasion when Loki took the form of a mare, it was in order to save the gods from surrendering Freya, the northern love-goddess, to a giant who had built, apparently according to Loki's blueprint, a great citadel to protect the AEsir from the Hill and Frost Giants.

More often than not this fortress is called Valhall, but sometimes Valhall is said to be the name of another fortified castle. In Valhall Othin, at Loki's advice, gathered together the ghosts of dead warriors who were to help him fight the Battle of Ragnarok. This was an immense recruiting effort, for this army of the dead ran into thousands, who turned the great fortress into a scene of endless eating, drinking, shouting, fighting, and lovemaking. Over the gate of Valhall hung a great boar's head, and the only food served inside, from morning to night and night to morning, was boar's flesh which, washed down with draughts of boar's blood, was thought to make the heroes invincible. These warriors of Valhall were called berserkers, meaning "bare of shirts", not only because they were so anxious to fight that they would not take time to put on armour but because they were something of a ragged crew. In this respect they were not very different from Falstaff's "tatter'd prodigals lately come from swine-keeping".[7] Between bouts of eating, boasting, and fighting, these overstimulated recruits made violent love to the Valkyrs. In a word Valhall, intended to save the world from a new ice-age, was the most stupendous, uproarious, demonic Boar's Head Tavern ever – Loki's most imaginative invention to protect the gods who cared so little for him.

Not a few mythologists think that Othin simply took over traits and powers once enjoyed by Loki, and several stories in the Eddic poems show him doing just this. It is probable, therefore, that at first Loki himself, as *Schimmelreiter*, a Rider of the White Horse, with Othin as a companion or pupil, led the berserkers, howling, foaming at the mouth, biting their shields, and making a most unholy din in the midwinter battle which was fought each year in the sky. Later Othin took over the leadership, and the screaming berserkers, fending off fiends of darkness, came to be known in Germany as *Wodenes Her* or Woden's Army. Still later, in Christian times, when all the pagan gods with their followers had been turned into demons, the phrase was twisted by priests or people who no longer knew what it meant to *Wutendes Heer*, often translated into English as the Raging Rout and used to identify the half-mad recruits with the very fiends they were supposed in the first place to fight. This sky battle came to be known also as the Wild Hunt, led by Othin, Charlemagne, or King Arthur, depending on the country over which it was passing, and its object was said to be the capture either of a great golden boar or of certain small-breasted girls called Moss-maidens, the first representing, perhaps, the sun and the other spring-time greenery. The *recapture* of either or both of these would have been the legitimate object of the winter battle in days when its symbolism was better understood.

The midwinter battle having been successfully won by Othin under Loki's direction, it became high time for the plump, naughty, hard-drinking old deity to pass to his bitter reward. We have seen that modern mythologists reject the notion that Loki killed the sun-god Baldr, and we can see for ourselves that the idea that he could have done so is totally inappropriate. His role was, rather, to help Othin to hold his usurped or ill-gotten power by fighting frost giants and to train Othin's heir-apparent in the land's ancient fertility wisdom. In the oldest versions of the myths there is, indeed, evidence that he played precisely such a role, not for Baldr, of course, but for Vali, the son of Othin who was born the morning after Baldr's death yet grew by evening to such maturity that he was able to avenge Baldr's death by slaying the blind culprit Hodr, an obvious variant of the Turkish Knight or Black Tartar.

A nice problem in Teutonic myth is presented by the fact that not only Othin but Loki himself had a son called Vali – a problem easily solved, perhaps, if we are willing to see these two Valis as one and the same deity, the actual son of Othin and the foster-son or pupil of Loki. Perhaps Vali was even called "son" by Loki, as Hal was by Falstaff in the Mock King Play at the Boar's Head. An equating of Vali with Hal on one side and Loki with Falstaff on the other is further suggested by the way in which Othin – one-eyed, aged, often tottering around in a grey cloak, sometimes sick, and continually complaining about the responsibilities of power – makes an almost perfect Henry IV. *The Poetic Edda* does not tell us much about Vali, either as son of Othin or pupil of Loki, except that after the battle at Ragnarok (the springtime fight?) he became the sun-god of a transfigured heaven and earth. The Frost Giants utterly vanquished, the very Northland itself was turned by Vali into a weeded and well-ordered garden.

Before this blissful consummation, however, it was necessary, as we well know by now, for the mischievous old tutor to be rejected, cast into prison, suffer, and die. It is the imprisonment and torture of the Falstaff-figure that I wish to stress in this chapter, although not very much, as I have indicated, has come down to us on the subject. In the "Lokasonna", one of the best-known parts of *The Poetic Edda*, we have what seems clearly to be the libretto of an old drama or rite in which the Æsir, firmly ensconced in power after the midwinter battle led by Loki, feasting apparently in the very "heat-holding" palace of Lyr which he had built for them – "glittering gold they had in place of firelight; the ale came in of itself; and great was the peace"[8] – seek by howling and shaking their shields at the Old One to drive him "away to the forest".[9] This is a recognisable Rejection Scene but Loki, unlike Falstaff at the end of *2 Henry IV*, will not submit to such ingratitude quietly. He turns on the gods and denounces them in stanza after stanza of choice invective, capping every one of their attempts to silence or refute him with fresh outbursts of "foul mockery".[10] No such denunciation of the gods or the religion presided over by the powers-that-be can be found among Falstaff-like myths anywhere. Stung to madness by his denunciations and threats, the gods pursue Loki to a waterfall under which he tries to hide as a salmon. At last, however, they capture and imprison him, some say in the depths of "wet woods"[11] while others say in the cleft of a mountain, binding him fast to a rock with the bowels of Narfi, one of his own sons. Then an AEsir called Skathi

> took a poison-snake and fastened it up over Loki's face, and the poison dropped thereon. Sigyn, Loki's wife, sat there and held a shell under the poison, but when the shell was full she bore away the poison, and meanwhile the poison dropped on Loki. Then he struggled so hard that the whole earth shook ...[12]

In that frightful prison, we are told in conclusion, Loki must lie bound till the end, that is, perhaps till the springtime battle in which Vali, with whatever fresh sun-secrets he has been able to extract by torture from his now agonised tutor, will conquer the remnants of "the children of darkness" in a walk-over battle.

In Teutonic myth, however, this second seasonal battle, corresponding roughly, I suppose, to Henry V's Agincourt, has, in contrast to other versions, several peculiar features. Usually the sick old father of the prince dies long before it, and the tutor himself also dies of torture or is killed previous to the fight, while most of the new monarch's entourage triumph with him. By the time of Agincourt, for instance, both Henry IV and Falstaff are dead, and in the battle Henry V loses only twenty-nine soldiers as against ten thousand lost by the French. At Ragnarok, however, Loki is still in fighting condition: indeed, he has broken from his prison and is fighting, not with the ungrateful gods, but against them. Indeed, he is said to have organised this battle, while many of the monsters who slay the gods are sometimes said to be his children. All this is not according to Hoyle, especially when all the AEsir, including Othin himself, as well as Loki and his so-called demons, are killed. The end result, however, is just about the same as in most versions of this story, for the crown prince Vali (though sometimes the conqueror is said to be a resurrected form of Baldr) from now on rules in warm and serene majesty over fields which "unsowed bear ripened fruit".[13]

The Teutonic myths were collected too late and tinkered with by writers too sophisticated to allow us to do much more than guess at their original form. One thing seems very clear, however: that Loki was a form of the Mock King who sought to save the land by acting as a substitute for a usurper and educating the illegitimate prince in the fertility wisdom that makes fields, man, and animals increase and live joyfully together. It also seems clear that he was rejected more violently, perhaps, than most Mock Kings, more deeply imprisoned and more viciously tortured, probably because the variability of the weather in northern lands during the first months of the new year suggested that the old tutor had not told all. That he was perhaps searched, burned, or branded, either with poison or with metal, in order to make him reveal his remaining fertility secrets was, however cruel, not inappropriate, for it was the mystery of heat, of solar fire, that he was being forced to unfold. We cannot help remembering that Falstaff himself, antler-crowned under the great oak in Windsor Forest, was burned with candles by a band of mock-fairies.

If Loki is to be identified with any particular animal (and I am not sure that he is), I suppose it would have to be the boar, for he was continually chasing that animal through the sky, making presents of it to the gods, or himself feasting off it. We have seen that it was probably Loki who set the great boar's head over the gate of Valhall, and it is more than likely, as I have indicated, that the ghastly berserkers of the sky fortress, who lived on nothing but boar's flesh and blood, were originally the motley rout of Loki rather than Othin. The wild banqueting in Valhall is, as it were, a perpetual Christmas feast inasmuch as the berserkers are always laying up strength to fight the Frost Giants and have no other function than to prevent their triumph in the midwinter battle. It is probable that the boar's head that presided over the traditional Christmas banquet in many of the northern countries, though most notably perhaps in England – a feast when great supplies of pork were made almost as available to the poor as to the rich – was the representative, at least in pagan times, of the deity who fought and died in giving himself, body and soul, for the heartening of his people in the days of pinching frost and desperation. Perhaps he is to be thought of as the representative or at least royal mount of the sun-god, now giving his very flesh to reinvigorate the sun-god's earthly avatar, the divine king, or to nourish a new sun-prince in the months of danger. The English Father Christmas, the personification probably of the Old Sun, seems more often than not, as we have seen, to have had a bull or stag as his favourite animal, but there is no doubt that he was also closely associated with the boar in the great feasts which his many earthly surrogates, so often encountered in the Mummers' Plays, presided over.

Even if we cannot connect Father Christmas indubitably with Loki, it is possible, it seems to me, to spot the old Teutonic king of the dwarfs or fairies in a Christmas figure, a kind of Swedish Santa Claus, who is still very much alive, and very much pig-associated, in our own day. I refer to Yultomte, a small, often fat, jolly troll who wears a brown, grey, or green costume and lives in the depths of the forest, from which he emerges on Christmas Eve with a fur-lined red cloak thrown over his shoulders and carrying a lighted lantern. On this dramatic occasion he is either riding on the back of an unruly goat (we have seen Loki associated, even if only in obscene fun, with this animal) or in a sleigh full of presents drawn by a goat or goats. The important point for us here is, of course, not Yultomte's goat but the golden pig or boar who always accompanies him, presaging his dramatic appearance from the forest or running under the belly of his furiously prancing goat. In typical icons Yultomte's great beard flares in the wind while he shouts defiance at the darkness and his hair streams behind him in the best Bes-to-Ilya fashion. This latter detail can usually be observed because Yultomte's pointed fur cap has, at least on most Swedish Christmas cards, blown off as he charges against the winter wind, holding his lantern bravely aloft. In this Scandinavian figure we have possibly a direct descendant of Loki in his earliest form of benevolent master of the fire elves or Fairy King – a double of the "handsome" figure on the Gosforth Cross.

Perhaps we should note here that the swine-eating that went on at Christmas time had an economic cause as well as a possibly mythical explanation, inasmuch as it was impossible to keep any considerable number of farm animals alive throughout the northern winter. Lack of provender caused a large-scale slaughter of cows and, more especially, of pigs in November and early December. The ensuing banqueting, when "the Sun-bak'd Peasant" went often "to feast it with a Gentleman", reached climaxes on St Martin's Day, 11 November (Falstaff, you remember was described as a living Martlemas: *"Poins*: How doth the Martlemas, your master?"*)*, St Nicholas' Day, Christmas, and Twelfth Night. In an old Christmas carol Father Christmas describes the duration of his protective winter watch as follows:

> Here have I dwelt with more and less,
> From Hallow-tide till Candlemas!
> And now must I from you hence pass,
> *Now have good day*!

Like Yultomte or any Interrex, he had come from apparent banishment in the forest, and now "To wilderness I must me dight" again. In other words, the Christmas season over which he presided seems to have been thought of by our forefathers as lasting from All Saints' Day, 1 November, to the Presentation of Jesus in the Temple or Candlemas Day, 2 February: that is, a full three months. By the time he returned to the woods, however, the pig supply must have run very low indeed, it having been practically exhausted, as the famous "Boar's Head Carol" suggests, by Twelfth Night. From Christmas to 6 January the eating of the pigs killed in November was carried on at a simply furious rate for the good reason that unsalted meat would not keep well, even in the cool north, for much more than a month. Dover Wilson has pointed out that Spenser in the "Book of Mutability" personified November, the month of butchering, in terms which exactly describe Falstaff:

> Next was November, he full grosse and fat
> As fed with lard, and that right well might seeme,
> For he had been a-fatting hogs of late,
> Yet his browe did sweat and reek and steem,
> And yet the season was full sharp and breem.

Significantly, December and January are personified by Spenser as considerably leaner though, as I have said, the consumption of pigs seems to have reached its apex during the Christmas season when, as the "Boar's Head Carol" affirms, the pig was "chief service in this land". But

> The boar's head, I dare well say,
> Anon after the twelfth day,
> He taketh his leave and goeth away:
>   *Exivit tunc de patria.*

Anyone with considerable imagination and the desire to do so may see in this stanza the libretto-like accompaniment to an ancient enactment of the Rejection of Falstaff.

    To return to Loki, it is not impossible that the great boar Gold Bristle, said in the *Edda* to have been forged at Loki's request to be the steed of Freyr, was once ridden by the naughty god himself. There is such a powerful tradition to the effect that Loki was himself a most beautiful god – though perhaps only in proto-Falstaffian ball-form – that he may have been the predecessor, displaced in the days of the conquering AEsir, of handsome Freyr. It is also possible that Loki was the original lover of the old goddess of springtime and beauty, Freyja, who may have liked to caress his fat little cheeks in some pre-AEsir Boar Hall. There are two or three legends that indicate that Freyja, like Circe, had power to turn men into boars, but it was those she liked whom she treated in this way, and only because she liked them in this shape. Whether Freyja's first lover or not, Loki advised Othin strongly against handing her over to giants in payment for the building of Valhall, and it was only by his deviousness that she was saved from these frost-titans. Loki alone, it seems, knew the true worth of love; only he understood the subtle means by which it operates to make earth and sky, body and soul, coalesce in fruitfulness. Perhaps this was the secret, the ancient wisdom, extracted from him by the agonies of his mountain prison. Wagner was clearly aware of this love-wise aspect of Loki's character, and in *Rhinegold* makes him perhaps the most admirable of all the gods, putting into his mouth a rather beautiful defence of the physically and spiritually fructifying love of man and woman. Loki (Loge) is addressing the gods:

> Thankless is ever
> Loge's lot!
> For thy sake alone,
> Roaming I went.
> I stormily strode
> To the ends of the earth,
> A ransom seeking for Freia
> Such as the giants would suit.
> In vain sought I,
> And now I can see
> That there's naught so rich,
> Naught in the world,

That a man as ransom would hold
For woman's beauty and worth.

(All (the gods) look bewildered and surprised.)

> Where life ebbeth and floweth,
> In water, earth and air,
> There sought I,
> Asked them to tell me
> Where'er there is strength,
> And seeds are seen stirring:
> What could a man
> More mighty deem
Than woman's wonders and worth?
But, where life ebbeth and floweth,
> They laughed aloud
> At my curious zeal:
> In water, earth and air,
> Nothing is dear
> As woman's love.[14]

That Wagner's view of Loki was not a mere invention of the dreaming composer is suggested by the deeds of the Fairy King Oberon, whose name derives from "Alberich", itself a variant of "Andvari", by which the King of the Dwarfs was known in Teutonic myth. Oberon, as we have already seen, had several traits in common with Loki, and the temptation to identify the two is irresistible. In the French *chanson de gestes* called *Huon de Bordeaux* Auberon appears, in spite of his shortness, as a beautiful creature with a morally lovely soul – *"plus biaus que solaus en este"*. Even in the Old Norse and Germanic accounts of Loki, there is a strong tradition, as we have seen, which makes him a plump and kindly deity, protector of the family, lover of children, and lord of the hearth-fire, which should, we are told in *The Prose Edda*, be called the "Sun of houses".[15] On one occasion Loki saved a baby, gambled away by its father in a game of chess, from a giant who was determined to collect his ten pounds of flesh. In fact, he often did his best to protect grown-ups as well as children – why shouldn't he, since the tradition that makes of him a benevolent god affirms that he was also the creator of mankind? Thus the Wagnerian conception of Loki corresponds quite accurately with at least one Teutonic tradition and with the character of the Fairy King revealed in *Huon de Bordeaux*, whose chief interest is to further true love, since the love of woman is an ennobling thing.

> Oberon thus has a distinctly moral nature, is a beneficent character, and ... a king of fairyland only because possessed of magic powers. ... He has moral dignity, and his weaknesses are human, not elfish. ...
> No incident indicates possession of what the world now accepts as a dwarfish nature. Perhaps it was for this reason that he was represented not as a real dwarf, but as one who had ceased to grow when a beautiful child. ... He is never a spiteful elf.[16]

Neither, as we know, is Shakespeare's Oberon, who is also occupied with bringing true lovers together. Nor need we be surprised to note that Falstaff indirectly (no commander of magic ever needs, or tries, to work directly to attain his end) acts to unite Fenton with Mistress Anne Page at the end of *The Merry Wives*, and even, in all likelihood, Henry V with Katharine of France, for it was through this marriage that Henry, as beneficiary of Falstaff's death-bed preoccupation with flowers and green fields, achieved "the world's best garden". Similarly, the protection and education which Auberon gave to Huon of Bordeaux in his various battles with monsters show him in the honourable old role of self-sacrificing friend and tutor, anxious to restore to earth the Fairy Régime or Terrestrial Paradise. And it was precisely a New Eden which, after Auberon's voluntary death, Huon inaugurated on earth, just as Vali, Hal, Horus, Dionysos, and all the rest began a New Age after the last seasonal battle.

But in all this rejoicing we must not forget the old tutor, pushed out, scorned, shoved into darkness, for his suffering was the price of the return to summer glory. While, as Sir Richard Fanshawe wrote,

> 'Tis innocent in the sweet blude
> Of Cherry, Appricocks, and Plumms
>   To be imbru'd,

such bloodshed has often, it seems, like the reaping of all ripeness, to be preceded by heartbreak, by a descent into the prison-house, by suffering, and even at times by a form of bloodshed far less innocent.

XI

Merlin of the Celts,

Who "Went Away As It Had Been Any Christom Child" Rejected by Woman

Throughout the last few chapters we have been coming ever closer in time and place to the England of Shakespeare and his Falstaff. We have also, by this time, discussed nearly all the chief aspects of Falstaff's character and activity except his passing, his death, which we will now examine in relation to a famous character from folklore never before, so far as I know, identified as a possible Falstaff-persona (not that many other of our heroes have been). I mean Merlin. Near the beginning of this book we found in Father Christmas of the English Mummers' Play, in old Hind-before who, disguised in an animal mask, acted as master of ceremonies for the ritual fight between St George and the Turkish Knight and, at least on one occasion, was killed for his pains, a prototype, perhaps of Falstaff and a justification for regarding Shakespeare's great pentalogy, stretching from *Richard II* to *Henry V*, as a Mystery rather than as a Morality Play. The question now is: Can we connect Father Christmas with some old deity of the British Isles who played a clearly Falstaffian role? I think we can.

We know that Father Christmas of the Mummers' Play was wearing a bull mask as late as the nineteenth century, and from the Renaissance have come down to us several pictures of mummers dressed in animal masks. Usually it is impossible to identify these figures with specific character parts played in specific folk plays, but one of them, the stag-antlered figure, is known to have been particularly popular among midwinter mummers. It may well be that Father Christmas of the Renaissance Mummers' Play was just as fond of the stag mask as of the bull one, perhaps fonder; certainly many Christmas and New Year revellers loved the branching headdress, and reindeer are associated with the modern form of Father Christmas. Now if we can imagine Father Christmas dressed as a stag, we can immediately find for him a genealogy reaching back to Palaeolithic times. One of the earliest paintings in Europe, in the Caverne des Trois Frères at Ariège in France, represents a bearded man dressed in a deer's skin and wearing over the upper part of his face an antlered mask. He may be playing the role of the totem father himself, or perhaps only that of a priest of the stag-father now regarded as divine.

The deity which this figure represents has enjoyed a long and honourable iconographical history in western Europe, where he is known chiefly by the name Cernunnos, meaning simply the Horned One. Clearly he was the Kuvera of the old Europeans for in many of his icons he sits cross-legged, practically in the posture of an Indian deity, holding in his arms a great purse or sack from which pours an abundance of gold or grain. This deity is obviously fat and usually heavily bearded, while from his head spring either antlers or short bull's horns. At his feet are often sculptured representations of the two animals most frequently associated with him, the bull and the stag, and on either side of him stands a plump child, a pair of abundance tokens often replaced in Gallo-Roman times by childish forms of Apollo and Mercury. That Cernunnos was an obese, good-natured, usually stag-horned god of wealth and increase is beyond doubt, but no connected account of his activities that I know of has come down to us. When and how – and even whether – he and his earthly representatives were dethroned by conquerors in the usual fashion, the old stag-kings being made to play jolly–sacrificial Mock Monarchs and tutors of upstart royalty, I do not know. However, we have only to remember that certain old Celtic heroes having white-stag souls, that is, souls symbolised by this animal, were tortured and baited, even to death, by red-eared dogs of Hell, to see that a typical dethroned-god past could probably be reconstructed for Cernunnos. The stories of these victims can be read in the *Romance of Pwill, Prince of Dyfed* and the *Romance of Math the Son of Mathonwy*, and a famous victim who fell into this category was Oisin or Ossian, son of the deer-goddess Sadb.

An earlier example of a stag-king or avatar hunted to death is the Aktaion of early Greek myth. In some versions of the story he is said to have been killed by his own dogs or those of Artemis, but these were undoubtedly the hounds of spring, the ravening passions of an earth goddess, anxious after a hard and sterile winter period to regain her beauty and fecundity. Though the story is, and was, often told in a form prettified for children, the old versions tell us that Artemis took Aktaion as her lover after bathing naked in a sacred fountain which refreshed her virginity. After the sacred *connubium* she killed him with her own bow and arrow. The ancient myth of the stag-king betrayed by the goddess in the more usual sense of the word "betrayed" survives in the European convention of representing a cuckold as wearing antlers. This may probably be affirmed: that when this ancient deity re-emerged in Europe, in the art and poetry of the Middle Ages, he began at once to play the Mock King, the lover who was sacrificed, the tutor who was finally rejected. I refer to the career of the stag-riding and sometimes antler-crowned Merlin.

That Merlin was, if not the oldest, at least a very old god or avatar-figure of the Celts, perhaps even of the pre- or proto-Celts, who corresponded in his nature and function to Egyptian Bes, Enkidu of Sumer, Kuvera–Ganeśa of India, Domovoy–Ilya of the Slavs, and Mimir–Loki of the Teutons seems reasonably certain. In *Celtic Myth and Arthurian Romance* R.S. Loomis traces him back to Irish Curoi, and affirms that his essential divinity was never forgotten.

> Not only does a Welsh triad call Britain Merlin's Close, not only does *Claris and Laris* refer to Merlin as he "who knows all, does all, and sees all." But also the *Vulgate Lancelot* states that he "knew all the wisdom that can descend from the devils, and therefore he was so feared of the Britons and so honoured that all called him the holy prophet and all the lesser folk their god."[1]

Merlin, famous as a shape-shifter, loved a metamorphosis we are now well acquainted with: that from boyhood to age or vice versa.

> Right so came by him Merlin like a child of fourteen year of age and saluted the king and asked him why he was so pensive [but did not wait for his answer] ... That know I well, said Merlin, as well as thyself and all thy thoughts, but thou art a fool to take thought for it will not amend thee. Also I know what thou art, who was thy father and of whom thou wert begotten; King Uther Pendragon was thy father and begot thee on Igraine. That is false, said King Arthur, how shouldst thou know it, for thou art not so old of years to know my father? Yes, said Merlin, I know it better than ye or any man living. I will not believe thee, said Arthur, and was wroth with the child. So departed Merlin, and came again in the likeness of an old man of fourscore year of age, whereof the king was right glad for he seemed to be right wise. ... Yes, said the old man, the child told you truth and more would he have told you and ye would have suffered him.[2]

In the *Morte d'Arthur*, from which this episode comes, we see a Bes-like deity, or rather his earthly representative, taking a potential prince in hand, grooming, enlightening, and instructing him from childhood with a view to making of him a monarch capable of bringing peace and abundance to the world. In the Merlin story (as perhaps in that of many another tutor-persona whom we have studied, though the specific information has been lost) the young–old teacher is represented not only as being concerned with the education of a prince but as having been concerned, from long before his birth, with finding good pupil-material. With the help of his magic Merlin is said to have arranged for Uther Pendragon to beget Arthur upon the wife of another, perhaps in order to make sure that, at least through the mother, his

Merlin of the Celts (Ms. Douce 178, fol. 249).

pupil-to-be would inherit the blood of an ancient dynasty of Divine Kings recently replaced. There is a tradition, also, that Arthur was actually the son of Merlin himself, and it has been shown that the phrase which identifies him as the son of Uther, that is *mab uter*, may just as well have meant "the terrible or wondrous youth".[3] *Le Livre d'Artus* affirms that Merlin carried off Arthur's mother to the Chastel de la Merveille, while in *Die Krone* she was abducted to the same castle by Gansguoter, a figure who, according to Loomis, resembles Merlin and is probably identical with him in being an avatar of Curoi.[4] Like so many Falstaff-personae Merlin, in accord with the principle that the god of the old religion becomes the devil of the new, is often called in the Arthurian romances a demon or Satan himself, though it is perfectly clear that he is a great love-god, the lord of fruitful fields and king of abundant animal life. As we have indicated, he is associated with an animal himself, more particularly the stag, and appears in the stories either as a great white buck or as a wild man mounted on one. As a wild man he is called a Carl or Churl (*bachlach*) or the Man of the Wood (*Fer Caille*) in the description of whom, especially as he appears in the Old-French *Livre d'Artus*, we cannot help recognising one more manifestation of "that bolting-hutch of beastliness" whom, in so many of his metamorphoses, we ·have already considered:

> he transformed himself into such a shape as no man ever saw or heard of before. He was a herdsman, a great club in his hand, clad in a great hide, the fur of which was longer than the breadth of the largest hand known. ... He had eyes in his head, large and black, and a head as big as a buffalo's and hair so long that it brushed his girdle, all bristly, stiff, and black as ink. His mouth was as large and wide as a dragon's, and gaped up to the ears; his teeth were white; and his thick lips were always open so that the teeth showed all around. He had a hump behind on his spine as big as a mortar. ... He was so hideous and ugly to see that no man living would not be seized with great dread. ... When Merlin had turned himself into this shape ... he caused by his art stags, hinds, bucks, and all manner of wild beasts to come and graze around him.[5]

Needless to say, in this shape Merlin is "old with a great age" and corresponds quite perfectly to any of the Old Sun figures which we have come across with the exception that in this medieval incarnation he has, while keeping his hump behind, lost his hump before, perhaps in answer to the thirteenth century's fondness for artistic elongation.

Malory says that Arthur once found three churls chasing Merlin, and would have slain him. Arthur drove off the grim villains exclaiming,

> O Merlin, ... here hadst thou been slain for all thy crafts had I not been. Nay, said Merlin, not so for I could save myself and I would; and thou art more near thy death than I am.[6]

It is important to note that Arthur won his first encounter with any enemy only with the help of a great body of churls who were undoubtedly part of Merlin's tatterdemalion train of recruits:

> And then the commons of Carlion arose with clubs and staves and slew
> many knights ... [so that Arthur's enemies] fled and departed. And
> Merlin came unto Arthur and counselled him that he follow them no
> further.[7]

There is an old analogy with Mimir–Loki's smithy in the way in which
Merlin by his "subtle craft" (in metallurgy?) made

> twelve images of laton and copper, and overgilt it with gold, in the sign
> of twelve kings, and each one of them held a taper of wax that burnt day
> and night; and King Arthur was made in sign of a figure standing above
> them with a sword drawn in his hand, and still the twelve figures had
> countenance like unto men that were overcome.[8]

These conquered kings represented, pretty clearly, the frigid forces of
darkness, perhaps the twelve crucial nights of Christmas, which Arthur
battled and beat, as we know, to his own sun-will. In fact, all his education
by Merlin was directed precisely toward winning the battle with these
stubborn and rebellious kings, at which Merlin acted as master of ceremonies quite in the spirit of Father Christmas of the later Mummers' Play
backing Arthur–George against all comers, protecting him from wounds,
and helping him, at last, to overcome the equivalent of a dozen Turkish
Knights.

It is interesting that Merlin decreed that the great seasonal battle should be
joined just at the stroke of midnight, the hour at which witches and
magicians still enjoy, it is said, their greatest power (we could, if we had
space here, write an essay on the important part played by the witching hour
in the careers of Bes, Silenos, Kuvera, and other Old Sun figures who dance
or fight or otherwise die back into youth – on the longest night of the year –
in the persons of their shining and triumphant pupils). In Arthurian romance
the ritual contest, fought near Arthur's castle in Sherwood Forest, was called
the Battle of Bedegraine, a word in which it is impossible not to recognise a
corruption of French *blés des graines*, spikes of wheat. Some time after the
battle, to wit on Candlemas Day (2 February), Merlin appeared to Arthur in
his form of enormous Churl or hairy Man of the Wood and pointed out that
beneath the Wasteland over which the great battle had been fought were
hidden stores of gold which would in due time come to light, though Merlin
himself would not live to see the recovery of the treasure. This prediction
forecasts nothing, of course, but the unfolding of routine "fertility magic".
Merlin did not participate in the equinoctial Battle of Badon against the
Saxons, the walk-over Agincourt which the king, now firmly initiated into
the seasonal rites required of the monarch, was easily able to win by himself.
It is of interest, however, to note in passing that this battle is traditionally
located in the neighbourhood of Uffington Castle, Berkshire, where a
prehistoric white horse carved in the chalky hillside overlooks a perfectly
shaped but decapitated knoll long held to be the spot on which St George
killed the dragon. Thus far evil, and no farther. ...

More willingly than Loki, Merlin embraces a fate involving imprisonment and at least so-called death. There is little evidence in the medieval romances (but these are exceedingly sophisticated treatments of the ancient material) that Arthur had anything to do with the imprisonment and death of his old saviour and tutor. In all available accounts Merlin appears to have arranged his own passing.

In the favourite version of the imprisonment and passing of Merlin, it is a beautiful girl Nimue (Niniane, Viviane, Vivien, etc.), not his famous pupil, who undoes the old enchanter. It is quite true that in many of the romances Merlin shows a weakness for beautiful girls. In the *Lestoire de Merlin*, on which nearly all the Middle English romances of Merlin are based, Merlin in his white-stag form reveals to Arthur that only a wild man or churl can explain the king's dreams, leaving instructions as to how this wild man, himself of course, may be caught. Then he vanishes into the forest where he eludes capture by all except the maiden Grisandoles, to whom he willingly surrenders. Of her he says jokingly to Arthur's heroes: "A woman took me through her cunning and power, something which none of you men could have done with all your strength".[9] Grisandoles was famous for her beauty, but Nimue's loveliness was incomparable. By becoming Merlin's mistress, Nimue wormed from him magic secrets that enabled her to enchain him forever without fetters or prison bars, simply in the mist-walls or perhaps merely the unbreakable nothingness of love, in the Forest of Broceliande. This Nimue or Viviane is said to have been the daughter of Diana (Artemis) who did the Stag-king Aktaion to death. Other versions of their love story, such as that followed by Malory, affirm that

> by her subtle working she made Merlin to go under that stone to let her
> wit of the marvels there, but she wrought so there for him that he came
> never out for all the craft he could do,[10]

a proper punishment, Malory says, for one so assotted of love in the days of his dotage. Elsewhere he is said to have been confined by Nimue in a giant oak tree.

Any of these strongholds will serve for the performance of the rites that I think were performed in Merlin's prison. Here I differ from most of the traditions and follow the lead given by the story of Ilya's incarceration or by the tales of Chinese Hsien who, whether legendary figures or real poets, seldom went into mountain exile – usually voluntary banishment – without one or two beautiful concubines. The probabilities are, it seems to me, that Merlin and Nimue simply slipped into a fairy hill or forest glade to work together to revive the waste with whatever energy was still left in the Old Sun persona after the midwinter battle. Hardly any of the versions of their love affair say that Nimue simply shut the old wizard up in a mist-tower, tree-trunk, or underground cavern and went off for ever. She went away, many times over, but always returned, and always returned, we may suppose, to tackle the slow thawing-out of the soil. That it would bloom

Merlin of the Celts (Ms Douce 178, fol. 299).

again had been assured by the Battle of Bedegraine, but spring had still by no means arrived. Possibly the torture of the imprisoned tutor (and one likes, when thinking of Falstaff, to believe this may have been true for him too) consisted in nothing worse than the extraction, the love-robbery of his remaining energies in magic if fatal *connubium*. Such love-deaths among Chinese Hsien, kings, and even businessmen are well authenticated – in Chinese literature! Thus, willingly or unwillingly – though usually willingly – the last flame of the Old Sun's warmth, the last sparkle of his corona, were extracted in lovemaking. Though he died banished by his king and persecuted (if that is the word) by an Ishtar, a Nimue, or a Quickly, the Falstaff-persona perished in the full consciousness of a life well-spent, of indispensable service performed for king, woman, and country.

According to Dame Quickly, Falstaff died as happy and pure as a child in its first innocence, playing with flowers, babbling of the fields which were sure to grow green soon after, and at least in part because of, his death.

> *Hostess.* 'A made a finer end and went away and it had been any christom child: 'a parted ev'n just between twelve and one, ev'n at the turning o' th' tide: for after I saw him fumble with the sheets, and play with flowers, and smile upon his fingers' ends, I knew there was but one way, for his nose was as sharp as a pen and 'a babbled of green fields. "How now, Sir John!" quoth I: "what, man! be o' good cheer." So 'a cried out, "God, God, God!" three or four times. Now I, to comfort him, bid him 'a should not think of God ... So 'a bade me lay more clothes on his feet: I put my hand into the bed and felt them, and they were as cold as any stone; then I felt to his knee, and so upward and upward, and all was as cold as any stone.[11]

Shakespeare could hardly have suggested more clearly how Falstaff came by his end – a consummation in strict accordance with his life and habits, the appropriate climax of an extraordinary career.

Perhaps the death of Falstaff deserves to be compared at more length with what we can find out about the passing of Merlin. First of all, it should be noted that Dame Quickly probably mistook the significance of Falstaff's cry of "God, God, God!" She herself had just said that he passed away as if he had been any christom child, that is, as pure and uncorrupted as any baby in its "christom" or "chrisom", the white robe in which an infant, in token of its innocence, was arrayed for baptism and which it wore throughout the first month of life. It is not likely the dying figure could have been stricken by pangs of conscience at the very moment before he passed away in childlike sanctity. There is evidence, however, that French and English witches, both before and after Shakespeare, prayed to their deity – probably some form of Cernunnos the Horned One, often called Mamilion (I shan't try to derive the name from Merlin or from a portmanteau version of Merlin and Mammon)

– with the words "My God, my God" in order to avoid naming One whose overt worship would have brought persecution.

> At Edmonton in 1621 Elizabeth Sawyer confessed that "he charged me to pray no more to Jesus Christ but to him the Devil." In Lancastershire in 1633 Margaret Johnson "met a spirit or devil ... [who] instructed her to call him Mamilion, and in all her talk and conference she called the said Mamilion her god." ... Of the Essex and Suffolk witches, whose trials made such a stir in 1646, Rebecca West "confessed that her mother prayed constantly (and as the world thought, very seriously) but she said it was to the Devil, using these words *Oh my God, my God,* meaning him and not the Lord."[12]

One of the most interesting problems connected with Falstaff's death lies in Dame Quickly's answer to Bardolph's "Would I were with him, wheresome'er he is, either in heaven or in hell!": "Nay, sure, he's not in hell: he's in Arthur's bosom, if ever man went to Arthur's bosom." From the beginning of Shakespeare criticism it has been dogmatically asserted that the ignorant hostess really meant to say "Abraham's bosom". However, we are entitled to suppose that a woman who did so well as Quickly did in the Fairy Queen role in *The Merry Wives of Windsor* is not likely to have made fundamental mistakes about any form of midnight rite. The fairy folk danced and played their pranks just between the hours of twelve and one and also chose this time to return occasionally to their Other-World home. Falstaff's passing at this hour must have come within the domain of Dame Quickly's special competence. When she said Arthur, she meant Arthur. In the course of time all New Suns like Arthur in his prime become Old Suns and, after in their turn bringing up an ungrateful heir, as Arthur brought up Modred, undergo a fate not unlike their tutor's. In order to understand why Falstaff went to Arthur's bosom, we must answer the question: What actually happened to Merlin when he gave up the ghost in Nimue's arms, or to Arthur when he "passed" in a boat ferried by weeping queens?

The old romances suggest that Merlin, and tell us that Arthur, was carried to Avalon or some other heaven in the west, an island or islands famous for eternal summer, where no lightning strikes or hailstorm, where it is never too hot or too cold. This island, we are told, is inhabited by a veritable fraternity of wondrous creatures who can be no other than shimmering shades of departed sun-kings and their surrogates, great Falstaff-personae now associating pleasantly with their ungrateful pupils. In *Perlevaus* the knight Percival, his ship driven beyond all known seas and stars, had a chance to visit the Islands of the Blest, where he found the very gravel made of gold and precious stones, and where handsome men, "their beards and hair whiter than the driven snow, albeit they seemed young of visage",[13] treated him to a feast at which wine flowed like water among the "Masters clad in long white robes" and drinking from cups of gold. It is not too fantastic, I think, to imagine that one of these brothers, the greatest of all perhaps, may have been Arthur arrived at journey's end; not too fantastic to see in the dying Falstaff, dressed in his bed-sheet as in the white christening robe of a plump-bellied child and playing with flowers, a figure setting out just between twelve and one, even at the turning of the tide, to join this crew of majestic revellers. On his extraordinary death-bed Falstaff is arrayed in the very uniform, thinking the very thoughts of retired figures who had held the beleaguered fortress of the sun, even to death, against the eternally encroaching demons of darkness and distress.

There is a strong tradition that Arthur in the Isle of Avalon, or in some other island of the west, lies on a golden couch. Once, it is told, a groom of the Bishop of Catania caught a glimpse of him dazzlingly couched in a marvellous palace in the wilds of Sicily. That handsome old men lying on golden beds are sun-gods is expressly stated in the Middle English *Wars of Alexander*, and Pseudo-Calisthenes' fourth-century *Romance of Alexander* tells how Alexander the Great, the pupil of Khadir – often compared to Dionysos the pupil of Silenos or thought of, at least by Fluellen, as a prototype of Henry V, the pupil of Falstaff – came upon an island city with twelve towers of gold and emeralds, whence he ascended a high mountain, discovering on its top beautiful houses of gold and silver and a round temple.

> "Inside and outside were images of demi-gods, bacchantes, satyrs, and of others initiated into the sacred mysteries. ... A couch was placed in the middle of the temple: on this couch lay a man clothed in silk. I could not see his face, for it was veiled; but I saw strength and greatness."[14]

In his *Otia Imperialia*, written in 1212, Gervase of Tilbury describes the Temple of the Sun in Ethiopia in similar terms. Near the limit of the ocean, he says,

> is the Land of the Sun in the form of an island. ... There is the couch of the Sun made of refined gold and ivory, studded with most precious stones, and the splendour of the couch shines throughout the palace.[15]

It was probably, then, this magnificent sun-palace, in which beautiful if broken sun-gods nest under white silk sheets around an eternal feast in a land of unbroken warmth and radiance, that Dame Quickly had in mind when she referred to the destined heaven of Falstaff. For the British, Arthur, not Alexander, was the greatest of sun-kings and probably thought of as the master of post-mortem solar ceremonials. It was he who clasped the new arrival to his bosom. It was to that bosom, and that bosom alone, that Falstaff went, if ever man did. "Nay, sure, he's not in Hell!"

Not infrequently Falstaff had Arthur on his mind. In one of the great Boar's Head scenes we find him singing snatches from an old ballad in praise of the most famous of pupils.

> *Fal.:* (*Singing.*) "When Arthur first in court" – Empty the jordan. (*Exit l. Drawer.*) – (*Singing.*) "And was a worthy king." How now, Mistress Doll?[16]

Mistress Doll, as we know, thought Falstaff far superior to Arthur himself, at least "ten times better than the Nine Worthies",[17] one of whom was the British hero, rolled into one. Arthur again fills a niche in these plays when Justice Shallow reminisces of the time when he was "Sir Dagonet in Arthur's show"[18] – an archery contest which reminds us that there existed in Shakespeare's London a club of bowmen known as "The Auncient Order, Society, and Unitie Laudable of Prince Arthure and his Knightly Armory of the Round Table", the members of which called themselves after the characters in the romances.[19] In the *Morte d'Arthur*, Sir Dagonet was the fool. We have no idea who played Arthur to Shallow's Dagonet or who played Merlin to that Arthur. If anyone, it may have been Falstaff himself in those days when he and the man "like a forked radish" lay at Clement's Inn "in Mile-end Green", "heard the chimes at midnight", and passed the time from then till sun-up with Jane Nightwork "in the windmill in St George's field". When Falstaff tells us that the sexual feats of Shallow's youth, boasted to have been "done about Turnbull Street", are bigger lies than "the Turk's tribute" in the Mummers' Play, we are overwhelmed with the seasonal symbolism of Arthur's archery show. Clement's Inn, Mile-end Green, St George's field, Turnbull Street, the Turk – surely Falstaff had trained for his role as fertility teacher in an unusual college of mummers under the name of Merlin!

More on Falstaff's mind than the memory of King Arthur (Merlin?) is that of Robin Hood and his merry men. Even in the black of night, he recognises in the "highjackers" of Gad's Hill "knaves in Kendal green",[20] the suiting for which Robin Hood's outlaws were famous (though in a few of the old plays and ballads the colour is given as Lincoln green), and he has a tendency to identify Dame Quickly with Maid Marian. Also, he loves to order about his pot-house companions, red-nosed Bardolph and the sturdy pickpocket Nym, by the names of "Scarlet" and "John",[21] i.e., Will Scarlet and Little John, a pair of Robin's most famous fellows, so high in the outlaws' ranks that they took orders only from the chieftain himself. In *2 Henry IV* the mere presence of Falstaff sets Justice Silence, not ordinarily represented as a man of imagination, to singing ballads of "Robin Hood, Scarlet, and John",[22] while in *The Merry Wives of Windsor* we find Falstaff and his crew treating Shallow as if he were the outlaw-bedevilled Sheriff of Nottingham:

> *Shal.:* Knight, you have beaten my men, kill'd my deer, and broke open my lodge.
>
> *Fal.:* But not kiss'd your keeper's daughter?
>
> *Shal.:* Tut, a pin! This shall be answer'd.
>
> *Fal.:* I will answer it straight; I have done all this. That is now answer'd.[23]

The fat knight's tone here, while Falstaffian enough, is also the very tone used by Robin Hood when defying Old Father Antic the Sheriff of Nottingham to put an end to the rowdy feasting of his band on the King's deer in Sherwood Forest. It should be remembered, too, that this forest, the scene of many successful exploits against the dead hand of the law, was also the seat of one of Arthur's castles and the site of the victory of Bedegraine. Almost the first words that we hear Falstaff utter show his affinity for the forest and outlawry – "Let us be Diana's foresters, gentlemen of the shade, minions of the moon"[24] – and he would probably have fitted nicely (if noisily) into the shoes of the exiled Old Duke who lived with his merry followers in the forest of Arden: "There they live like the old Robin Hood of England ... and fleet the time carelessly, as they did in the golden world."[25]

In *The Merry Wives* Falstaff enjoys playing the role of Herne the Hunter, sometimes identified as a certain Richard Herne who hunted unlawfully in one of Henry VIII's forest preserves, a latter-day Robin Hood who, after his death, became associated with an antlered fertility-god called Horne or the Horned One, pretty clearly a descendant of Cernunnos–Merlin and naturally identified by Christians with Old Hornie or the Devil.

> *Mistress Page*:   There is an old tale goes that Herne the hunter,
> Sometime a keeper here in Windsor Forest,
> Doth all the winter-time, at still midnight,
> Walk round about an oak, with great ragg'd horns ...
> You have heard of such a spirit,
> And well you know
> The superstitious, idle-headed eld
> Receiv'd and did deliver to our age
> This tale of Herne the hunter for a truth.
>
> *Page*:   Why, yet there want not, many that do fear
> In deep of night to walk by this Herne's oak.[26]

In fact, Falstaff leaps at the chance of impersonating Herne in order, ostensibly, to further his amours with Mistress Page and Mistress Ford, his "doe with the black scut", but even more, perhaps, for the purpose of perpetuating old forest-rites descended from Cernunnos through Merlin and Robin Hood to Henry VIII's outlaw, only lately dead. Who can tell what really took place in a brain warmed in its affections, dried of all crudy vapours, and sharpened and deepened by sack into insights denied prosaic and sober minds? To be sure, Falstaff in the great midnight scene in the forest is made a fool of, as he is, ostensibly, at the battle of Gad's Hill; but just as he came off with final honours in the latter episode, he triumphs here too, if the promotion of true love, between Mistress Anne Page and Fenton, between country couples who have come to take each other for granted, can be considered a triumph.

> *Fal.*:   I am glad, though you have ta'en a special stand to strike at me, that your arrow hath glanc'd.
>
> *Mistress Page*:   Good husband, let us everyone go home, and laugh this sport o'er by a country fire; Sir John and all.[27]

That Robin Hood, haunter of forests in the neighbourhood of the Battle of Bedegraine, self-appointed lord of the royal bucks and does, some wild man and animal-headed masker, is to be thought of as a descendant or avatar of Cernunnos–Merlin is now a commonplace of folklore. The miniature epic called "A Gest of Robyn Hode" and the dozens of Robin Hood ballads that have come down to us follow much too closely the pattern that we have seen unfold so often in this book, to be thought of as mere records of reality or creations of folk *sentiment*.

To begin with, the England of Robin Hood had fallen on evil days – a fact indispensable to any comic–tragic Falstaff success-story. Richard the Lion-hearted had gone to the Crusades, and under the cold, calculating tyranny of John, buttressed though he was by the authority of Holy Church personified in the Bishop of Nottingham, and of Old Father Antic personi-fied either in the Sheriff of Nottingham or Sir Roger of Doncaster, justice and fertility had begun to decline together. The legend insists that Robin was a wronged and persecuted nobleman related to a once-royal house. In the forest he set about the usual Mock King's work of fighting the forces of blight by spreading great feasts of wine and ale, presiding, perhaps in a stag mask (*Little John*: "Lo, sir, here is the mayster-herte"[28]) over dancing, revelry, lovemaking, and archery contests conducted by drunken competi-. tors, which are strangely reminiscent of the ritual shooting in the Ming T'ang by which the Emperor of China once chose soldiers to aid him in the seasonal battle.

> A stately banquet the [y] had full soon,
>   All in a shaded bower,
> Where venison sweet they had to eat,
>   And were merry that present hour.
>
> Great flaggons of wine were set on the board
>   And merrily they drunk round
> Their boules of sack, to strengthen the back,
>   Whilst their knees did touch the ground.
>
> First Robin Hood began a health
>   To Marian his onely dear,
> And his yeomen all, both comly and tall,
>   Did quickly bring up the rear.
>
> For in a brave veine they tost off the [ir] bouls,
>   Whilst thus they did remain,
> And every cup, as they drunk up,
>   They filled with speed again.[29]

Robin Hood's men, frequently referred to as his forest herd, may themselves have cavorted in stag masks or antlers; the famous horn dance of Abbots Bromley in Staffordshire, performed to this day on the first Monday after 4 September, is believed by some to commemorate an ancient ritual once presided over by the great outlaw. The dancing deer of Abbots Bromley, men who carry in their hands great reindeer antlers arching high over their heads, are supposed to be hunted by a group of revellers led by Robin Hood and are made up of a hobby horse, Maid Marian, a jester, a drunkard, and other figures typical of the Mock King's motley rout.

With the exception of the famous Maid Marian, we do not hear much of women in Sherwood Forest, but medieval Christmas and May Day celebrations, often led by local incarnations of Robin and Marian, Little John and Marian, or Friar Tuck and Marian, are thought by a perceptive poet of our time to have helped keep the population of England steady in those days of devastating sickness and plague.

> It is probably because each year, by old custom, the tallest and toughest village lad was chosen to be Little John (or "Jenkin"), Robin's deputy in the Merry Men masque, that Johnson, Jackson and Jenkinson are now among the commonest English names – Little John's merry-begots. But Robin did as merrily with Robson, Hobson, Dobson (all short for Robin), Robinson, Hodson, Judson and Hood; Greenwood and Merriman were of doubtful paternity. The Christmas "merrimake" (as Sir James Frazer mentions in *The Golden Bough*) also produced its crop of children. Who knows how many of the Morrises and Morrisons derive their patronymics from the amorous "morrice-men", Marian's "merry-weathers"? Or how many "Princes", "Lords" and "Kings" from the Christmas King, or Prince, or Lord, of Misrule?[30]

Such seasonal celebrations (the May Day one was called in the fifteenth century and even later Robin Hood's Festival) constituted defiance of law, both civil and ecclesiastical. Like a typical Lord of Misrule, Robin never abated the feud which he carried on against church and state, seeming, as Ritson says, "to have held bishops, abbots, priests, and monks, in a word all the clergy, regular and secular, in decided aversion".[31]

Not, to be sure, that Robin Hood was an irreligious man. By the people his day was observed as a religious feast over which he presided as both king and abbot, or, indeed, the founder of what has been called "the Robin Hood religion".[32] This, I imagine, was simply a late form of the old Cernunnos–Merlin–Arthur faith. Indeed, Merlin, under the name of Merddin, is said to have been "Christianised as 'Robin Hood,' apparently a variant of Merddin's Saxon name"[33] – a suggestion of some interest, though the word "Christianised" does not seem to make much sense here. Moreover, the witches of Somerset are known to have called their god Robin; Dame Alice Kyteler, the early fourteenth-century witch of Kilkenny, confessed that her deity was "Robin son of Art".[34] It is not surprising, then, that the Scottish Parliament asked the King to prohibit plays of Robin Hood, King of May, on the Sabbath, but it is surprising to note that they made this official request as late as 1577. That a mythic Bishop of Nottingham had trouble with a mythic Robin Hood in the twelfth century is credible enough, but it is surprising to learn that

Bishop Latimer, in his sixth sermon before King Edward VI, stated that he had given notice of his intention to preach at a certain church on the following day, being a holy day, but when he came there found the door of the church locked, and one of the parish said to him, "Sir, this is a busy day, we cannot hear you; it is Robin Hood's day. The parish are gone abroad to gather for Robin Hood, I pray you let them not."[35]

In spite of his unremitting opposition to the Church and churchmen, Robin Hood loved the Virgin Mary dearly, and

Ffor the loffe of owre ladey,
  All women werschepyd he ...[36]

Many a solemn oath he swore "by Mary free", especially when threatening to punish some churchman who had been preying upon the poor. There is great reason to think, however, that the Mary by whom Robin swore was not the Mother of Christ but the sweet Earth Mother, whose place his own Maid Marian took as Divine Queen when they performed ritual *connubia* at the May Day and Christmas festivals. There is evidence in the Mummers' Plays that these feasts were accompanied by drama in which the roles of Robin, Little John, Friar Tuck, Scarlet, and Marian were played by mummers who seem clearly to have been performing a rite, while "A New Ballad of Old Robin Hood, showing His Birth, Breeding, Valour and Marriage",[37] one of the most curious and interesting of the Robin Hood poems, is obviously the libretto for a Christmas ceremonial performed by Robin, Little John, and Marian, here called Gloriana.

To fit perfectly into the rule of Substitute King, it was necessary finally for Robin Hood to educate a prince or ruler of the reigning family of his fertility vision. Reminiscences of this initiation rite can still be found in the ballads, chiefly "A Gest of Robyn Hode", where King Richard or some other monarch, often called "Edwarde our kynge",[38], returned from the Crusades and went to the forest to subdue the outlaw against whom Old Father Antic of Nottingham was powerless but stayed, having fallen in love with the free life of the forest, long enough to master Robin's wisdom and learn to love the rough, common folk who helped to make up his band of outlaws. Often the king is said, on leaving the forest, to have forgiven Robin, but the forces of Church and State, the former led by a certain "pryoresse of Kyrkasly/That nye hwas of his kynne" and the latter, not by the much discomfited Sheriff of Nottingham but by "Syr Roger of Doncastere",[39] combined to bring about his death.

It is not impossible, of course, to see in this mysterious prioress a form of Nimue who extracts the last ounce of the ageing sun-king's energy. The story is that Robin Hood, when ill, visited her for medical treatment, but the priory is described as much more like a prison than a religious house, Robin finding it quite impossible to escape from the upper room in which he was confined. There he was slowly bled to death by the crafty prioress. In other

accounts, notably the ballad called "Robin Hood's Death", he was treacherously stabbed to death by Sir Roger of Doncaster, here called Red Roger,
as he tried to break from "a shot-wyndowe" of the tower.[40] Buried with his
bright sword at his head and golden arrows at his feet, we can only imagine
that he did not so much die as simply go to join Arthur and Merlin in the Isles
of Eternal Summer.

It is possible that ancient Cernunnos enjoyed, in addition to Merlin,
Robin, and Herne the Hunter, several other incarnations. As we all know,
he turned up in a striking tableau in *The Merry Wives of Windsor* performed, we are told, on a Christmas night around 1599. Internal evidence in
the Henry plays shows, perhaps, that Falstaff was sometimes imitating still
another avatar or form of the old god. "In northern Europe the ancient Neck
or Nick, meaning a spirit, had such a hold on the affections of the people
that the Church was forced to accept him, and he was canonised as
St Nicholas, who in Cornwall still retains his horns."[41] Now certainly the fat,
stag-riding St Nicholas whom we know as Santa Claus has nothing in
common with St Nicholas the wonder-worker who was Bishop of Myra in
Licia in the fourth century. This patron of schoolboys, sailors,
pawnbrokers, and dowerless virgins, whose feast day is 6 December, and
who in Holland and elsewhere is always represented as a thin old gentleman
dressed in robes, wearing the mitre, and carrying the crozier of a bishop of
the Catholic Church, is definitely not Santa Claus.

It is unfortunate that while the story of St Nicholas of Myra can be read at
length in the *Golden Legend*, that of St Nicholas the Neck can only be pieced
together from fragments of pagan poetry and folklore. Before he was
adopted by the Church his whole career was that of a demon, perhaps a
descendant or incarnation of Merlin, who was sometimes called Old Nick
and may be the original of the power disparaged or deprecated by this name.
When Old Nick became St Nicholas, however, there arose within the
community of Christians themselves and among those only tangentially
attached to it the possibility of practising a very equivocal form of
hagiolatry in the season of December. Gadshill's characterisation of Falstaff
and his robber band as "Saint Nicholas' clerks"[42] is wittily apt, since he is
thinking not of the sainted bishop, but of the sanctified Nick or Neck who
had once presided over a Saturnalia of topsy-turvy morals and ritual
robbery. Gadshill's speech about the clerks or priests of St Nicholas gave
Shakespeare, or so I suppose, a fine chance for ironical word play, punning,
and a disguised reference, perhaps, to the loosely organised worship of a
pre-Christian British deity.

> *Gads.:* Sirrah, if they [the company of the rich franklin from Kent]
> meet not with Saint Nicholas' clerks, I'll give thee this neck.

> *Chamberlain:* No, I'll none of it. I pray thee keep that for the
> hangman; for I know that thou worshipp'st Saint Nicholas as truly as a
> man of falsehood may.

> *Gads.:*   What talkest thou to me of the hangman? If I hang, I'll make a
> fat pair of gallows; for if I hang, old Sir John hangs with me, and thou
> know'st he is no starveling. Tut! there are other Troyans [rogues] that
> thou dream'st not of, the which for sport sake are content to do the
> profession [of thievery] some grace ... I am joined with no foot
> landrakers, no longstaff sixpenny strikers, none of these mad mustachio
> purple-hued malt-worms [who cluster around Falstaff at the Boar's
> Head; not with these merely] but with nobility and tranquillity, Burgo-
> masters and great oneyers [owners]; such as can hold in, such as will
> strike sooner than speak, and speak sooner than drink, and drink sooner
> than pray ...[43]

In other words, Gadshill, Falstaff, and here the Prince himself are clearly
said to be practising "for sport sake" robbery considered as a symbolic act in
the ritual of some secret lodge, perhaps affiliated to a non- or anti-Christian
form of faith, in which men of high standing who loved drink better than the
conventional prayers of the established Church were the true leaders. This
speech of Gadshill's has never been satisfactorily explained, but is it too
fantastic to suppose that he is referring to an underground religious movement dedicated to the old antlered god of peace and plenty? Historians and
folklorists are continually unearthing fresh examples of such movements all
over Europe, and certain medieval and Renaissance revolts against the
Church may be interpreted as having been, essentially, of this character.

In this connection, I would like to suggest a remaining twig for Falstaff's
family tree (not that I intimate for a moment that Falstaff's lineage included
in any but a contingent or homomorphous sense the blood or spirit of Bes
and the dozens of fat creatures we have found hanging like ripe fruit from
every bough). What I have to say here is pure speculation, and it is this: that
a missing link in the lineage leading from Cernunnos through Merlin, Robin,
Nicholas, and Herne to Falstaff may have been one Sir John Oldcastle.
Certainly a real man, he "was historically a friend and fellow-soldier of
Prince Hal in the reign of Henry IV, but was burnt as a heretic by the same
prince when he became King Henry V".[44] As everyone knows, Shakespeare's
Falstaff originally bore this name, it having been adopted by the dramatist
both from history and from the play known as *The Famous Victories of
Henry V*, of which he makes a little use in his own work. Shakespeare was
forced to abandon the name, we are told, because the wife of his "old lad of
the castle" was the ancestress of the Cobhams, who were powerful nobles at
Elizabeth's court. In addition, one of the Cobhams, as Lord Chamberlain,
was Shakespeare's official controller, and hasty changes in the prompt-book
were made soon after the play was first produced.

The original Sir John Oldcastle – far from being a fat fertility wizard –
was, we are told, a famous Lollard leader, but we know too little of Lollardy
to be able to say with assurance that the term was not used as a catch-all to

denote various forms of heresy, one of which may have been an underground movement devoted to "the oldest religion". All that we know,
practically, of the purpose, beliefs, and functioning of the Lollard movement was that it was opposed to the Church in the name of justice for the
common people of England and that it operated largely above ground in the
days of Sir John Oldcastle; it appears that Sir John attempted to convert
Prince Hal to his belief (whatever that really was), only to be "rejected" in a
most fearful way when his one-time friend and, it would seem, pupil became
king. Some critics believe that "traces of Lollardy may still be detected in
Falstaff's frequent resort to scriptural phraseology and in his affectation of
an uneasy conscience".[45]

Now it is true that Falstaff's digs at ritual, as in his swearing by the mass
and in the *ecce signum* episode, may be interpreted as attacks on the Church
in keeping with those known Lollard tenets that condemned sacraments,
images, prayers for the dead, auricular confession, and a celibate clergy (in
fact, all clergy). "The use of the Bible [by Lollards] is probably to be taken
for granted",[46] but what they believed on the positive side in matters
religious is not clear. Economically they attacked the Church's ownership of
great properties, and politically denounced the State as a cat's-paw of
priestly oppression. They denounced economic injustice, caste, war, and the
armaments industry of their day so vigorously that in 1401 a statute, *De
Haeretico Comburendo* (*On the Burning of Heretics*), was passed by Parliament in order to bring the movement to an end. At first, however, the
frightful punishment at the stake was applied only to the lower classes and
certain merchants who belonged to this elusive socio-religious organisation.
But there were among the Lollards a few nobles, notably Sir John Oldcastle,
who sought, in defiance of the statute, to give active expression to the
widespread English dissatisfaction with Church and State. Oldcastle was
quickly imprisoned, however, and the petty rebellion provoked in his behalf
was quickly put down; he himself was executed at the command of his
ex-friend, now Henry V. These seem to be all the facts we have to go by
when trying to estimate the significance of Sir John's life and death.

There is not enough here to enable us to prove or disprove anything about
the real-life activities of Oldcastle. We do not know to what he may have
tried to convert the prince: whether to a return to early-Christian commun-
ism or a pre-Christian economy of peace and plenty, a crusade for a purely
Biblical Christ, or the revival of a still older deity represented on earth by a
line of self-sacrificing priests or Mock Kings of whom Sir John considered
himself a scion. One thing does seem fairly clear: that he rejected the ideals
of power and honour which all Lollards thought were poisoning England
with poverty and hatred and ruining it with expensive civil war. Let me say
again that there is nothing to prove that Sir John, the acknowledged leader
of a band of rebels, many of whom may have been somewhat down-at-heel,

was not the heir of a pagan faith rather than the founder of an early form of Protestantism; Wyclif was the latter but Sir John, a man so highly connected that he had been for years the close associate and mentor of the crown prince himself, was not necessarily so. Burning, before being adopted as the appropriate penalty for heresy, had long been practised as a favourite form of punishment for witchcraft. In spite of the Church's campaign to liquidate paganism, we know of many, even of hundreds of, noble European families who held out for centuries against conversion to Christianity, doing their best to keep alive the old faith in sun and spirit, in fertility of body leading to grace of soul.[47] Sometimes they suffered death for their pains. It is not, therefore, hard to imagine an intransigent yet self-sacrificing nobleman, anxious to help his country in its time of troubles, stepping forward and attaching himself to the child of a usurping father for the purpose of instructing him in the tenets of a purified faith, or even a pre-Christian one. Whether such an education included training in drinking and whoring, I do not know; that it included scoffing at the beliefs and practices of the received religion is clear from the Lollards' own Memorial to Parliament, while its attitude toward law is amply shown by the open rebellion that broke out on the imprisonment of Oldcastle. That Oldcastle, at some point in their relationship, actually brought Hal to the point of slapping the face of the Chief Justice is one detail of their legend which seems to me quite credible.

All I wish to do here is to suggest that Falstaff may not have been called, by the author of *The Famous Victories* and Shakespeare, Oldcastle for nothing. Oldcastle, whose very name is reminiscent of ancient lineage – perhaps of an actual place where the rites of the Grail, the pagan Grail, were performed – may just possibly have been a genuine Interrex or Mock King working in his own chosen way for the good of his country. As with all Mock Kings and tutors of would-be sun-princes, it was necessary finally for him to die a martyr's death. Perhaps no one understood this better than his quondam friend and pupil, who in condemning his old tutor to imprisonment in the Tower and finally to a wizard's death may simply have been adding the last touches to a preconceived and preconcerted plan. At any rate, no one would have known better, I suppose, than Henry V just how heretical was the heretical Lollard leader.

I hold no brief for Henry V's action in the so-called Rejection of Falstaff. The scene is, perhaps, just as repugnant to the morals of good-fellowship, just as much the act of a heartless schemer, as it has been made out. I certainly do not glory in it with Wilson as the wise act of a reformed prodigal who has undergone a "solemn self-dedication" to a life of peace with honour – meaning, as usual, war without honour – and who in Old Father Antic

> has found a friend and a counsellor and a father at last; and he promises to be guided in all things by his advice. What chance has Falstaff with such a Prince? The young man has already made his choice between Justice and Vanity. The fat knight is rejected before he can have sight of his sweet boy.[48]

... Shakespeare himself has been busy ever since Shrewsbury manoeuvring these former friends into different universes, between which conversation is impossible. And if the language of the speech sounds formal and homiletic, that is because Hal is learning to speak, not as Bradley complains "like a clergyman", but like the Chief Justice ... and the only speech the regenerate Harry can now have with his old Adam is a public one.[49]

Such an analysis of the Rejection scene is perilously close to nonsense, yet we know that Hal simply has to renounce, imprison, and even kill his old friend if he is to become an invincible sun-king and win the springtime battle which will give England "the world's best garden". Henry V is neither such a crass ingrate as Bradley would make him out nor such a pious ass as Wilson suggests. In this scene he is simply but fully a king, that is, a vessel who can do no wrong, especially when, as the result of a sound education at the Boar's Head, he is filled with *mana* and carrying out the last ceremonial rite connected with a coronation that will turn him into an irresistible force of nature.

The Magnificent Relevance of Falstaff

In the light of what has gone before, it is not necessary for me even to sum up the relevance of Falstaff to the dramatic unfolding of the plays in which he appears. Obviously, he is a prepotent tutor who spends his declining energies helping his royal pupil fight the forces of sickness, evil, darkness, and division that had been undermining the happiness and greatness of England since the days of Richard II. The untended garden wrested from Richard by Henry IV had grown still weedier under the neglect of that faint-hearted, chilly-minded power-politician, sick in body and soul, a mere singing eunuch of Windsor. Civil strife, conspiracy, and treason had broken out on every side, and it seems that the very earth itself had responded to Richard's despairing prayer to her to starve his enemies. To a group of religious dissidents (I am still talking of Shakespeare's play though I may seem to have switched to history – actually, there is little history to speak of in all this: only the hieratic myth) – to a group of dissidents, then, including noblemen and "great oneyers" and led perhaps by one Sir John Oldcastle, it appeared high time that the crown prince be taken in hand and instructed in a wisdom that did not come naturally to his dank-blooded, lank-limbed stock. The prince, it seems, did not have even the shape of a true king, and Sir John Falstaff, if not Sir John Oldcastle, felt forced to shame him into a more regal figure.

> *Fal.* 'Sblod, you starveling, you elf-skin [eel-skin?], you dried neat's tongue, you bull's pizzle, you stockfish [dried cod]! O for breath to utter

what is like thee! You tailor's-yard, you sheath, you bow-case, you vile standing-tuck [small rapier] ...[1]

Elsewhere Falstaff calls Hal a pint-pot and explains to the Chief Justice that so long as Henry's shape does not improve he, Falstaff, will have to do what he can to save the realm: "I am the fellow with the great belly and he is my [scrawny?] dog."[2] Though Hal does not know exactly what is happening to him, he is being groomed for kingship – that is the deep theme of the plays – by a figure who is indispensable if the deadening effects of Bolingbroke's usurpation are to be countervailed for so much as one king's reign. Perhaps Shakespeare himself was not entirely aware of Falstaff's complete relevance to the dramas. After all, he had inherited a tradition about Hal and his tutor, some scraps of their history, a poor play which sloppily stitched them together, and some vivid memories, perhaps, of the Stratford-on-Avon folk plays – the legend of Merlin and Arthur, the story of Herne of Windsor – elements enough, it may be, to have enabled his fertile brain to devise the great series of dramas in the form in which they have come down to us. Whether Shakespeare was or was not conscious of what he was achieving – rapt from his ordinary self (if he had one) by his memories – these plays are quite capable of bearing the full weight of the construction I have laid on them. I think the passages which I have quoted liberally drive this home. Again, why shouldn't Shakespeare have understood exactly what he was trying to do? After all, the author of *A Midsummer Night's Dream* was a considerable folklorist, and he could hardly have failed to sense in his material the full folk meaning with all its upthrusting symbolism on every plane of body and spirit. The brilliant insights into human nature and destiny which he added could hardly have been interwoven, no matter how great a poet he was, out of apprehensions and cognitions he had never had.

Actually, the Falstaff–Henry plays are a rather tight-knit unit, not at all the "ill-constructed ... monstrosity" they have been called. Hal may talk patronisingly of the crew at the Boar's Head, but from association with them he gains, time after playful time, the common touch which is to stand him in good stead on his two battlefields, while with the help of sack and sherris his affections are warmed and his mind cleared to the point where he can see the hollowness in at least certain forms of the world's wisdom. Having learned to rob, as it were, his own exchequer for the good of his people, he is guided by Oldcastle–Falstaff through a successful battle against three mighty demons at Shrewsbury, and prepared to receive the sun-corona which his father had disgraced so miserably.

At this point it becomes necessary, according to the traditional unfolding of the ancient rite, for Oldcastle–Falstaff to be deposed from his inter-regnum, humiliated, cast into prison, and finally killed. These are the fixed conditions by which the last ounce of his magic energy may be syphoned into his pupil, who is now, and now only, prepared to win on his own the miraculous springtime battle of Agincourt.

That history and myth should have been inextricably intertwined by
Shakespeare is nothing to wonder at. Every country, as we have seen, has
identified its historical enemies with powers of cold and infertility, and has
hailed its historical victories as a form of symbolical ploughing and
fertilising destined to make it once again flourish. Thus it is perfectly clear
that the presence of Falstaff is not only relevant but absolutely indispensable
to everything that happens from beginning to end of the three Henry plays,
while his significance as a fertility power is underscored, for any who may
have missed it, in the doings of the *Merry Wives of Windsor*. To insist with
Wilson on setting up a Falstaff canon from which *The Merry Wives of
Windsor* must be dropped and also the account of Falstaff's death in *Henry V*
is certainly a purposeless procedure. Further to cramp the discussion of the
significance of Falstaff by ignoring his relations, open or covert, with
Glendower, Hotspur, Prince John, Quickly, and others in the Henry IV
plays, as Wilson does, is suicidal for a critic who is attempting to find out
what the myriad-minded poet, sympathetic and subtle beyond parallel, has
poured into this bombard. "I am attempting to discover," says Wilson,
"what Professor Charlton has called 'the deliberate plan of Shakespeare's
play' and, if such a plan existed, how far he succeeded in carrying it into
execution."[3] For this purpose Wilson could not possibly have adopted a
procedure more inadequate. Falstaff's presence, whether in body or spirit, is
not only relevant to the overall plan and moral of the plays, but that
relevance can be thoroughly understood only by examining his relations
with all the characters in all the plays. In a word, Falstaff's role in the
magnificent Mystery is precisely the opposite of what it has been termed. It
is magnificently relevant!

But it is a deeper relevance that I wish to discuss in this concluding chapter
– the relevance of the Falstaff-persona not to a cycle of plays by
Shakespeare, not even to a ritual pattern which emerged millenia ago from
the myth-making minds of our ancestors for the purpose of fighting winter's
sadness, but to the operation of our own minds here, now, today. Why do
we continue to cherish Falstaff and Falstaffian figures like Santa Claus in the
West, Ganeśa in India, Ts'ai Shen in China? Why do we not let these fat old
daimons, often the possessors of widely disapproved, not to say bestial,
characteristics, quietly die, as the pattern decrees they must, in the dark
prisons to which they are at last condemned? Why does Falstaff possess our
imaginations as a towering, health-giving, sanity-restoring figure of whom
it is absolutely impossible to say with Dr Johnson or his sedulous ape that he

> is a character loaded with faults and with those faults which naturally
> produce contempt. He is a thief, and a glutton, a coward, and a boaster,
> always ready to cheat the weak, and prey upon the poor; to terrify the
> timorous and insult the defenceless. At once obsequious and malignant,
> he satirises in their absence those whom he lives by flattering. He is
> familiar with the prince only as an agent of vice.[4]

To attempt an answer to this question that will not be altogether superficial I feel it necessary, at this point, to resort to the aid of that fascinating school of psychological thought headed by Dr Carl Jung, who has discovered in the dreams of his patients continual occurrences of Falstaff-personae – figures indispensable to what he calls the integration of the personality, figures that stand for a wisdom crucial for all who would live in warmly aerated blessedness. Jung, I imagine, would have congratulated Hal on the fact that he was long "haunted" by a devil in the likeness of a white-bearded brute, that he

> long dream'd of such a kind of man,
> So surfeit-swell'd, so old, and so profane ...[5]

Certainly he would have advised him not to "despise" his dream. He would have pointed out to Hal that his ability to win wars against demons, his facility in gaining the affection of his soldiers and the love of Kate herself – his integration into a regal human being – were all achieved not in spite, but because, of the ubiquitous dream-presence of Falstaff. The fumes of the Boar's Head surrounded Hal with a protective aura, clothed him in an eyeletted robe of fresh-air health naturally not appreciated in the sick court at the other end of London.

As well as I can understand this matter, the Falstaff-persona, a figure which as we have seen has haunted the imagination not only of Hal but of mankind in every country and throughout recorded time, is what Carl Jung calls an archetypal familiar of the psyche, that is, an image burned into the human mind so long ago and throughout so many centuries that it lives on in us, carrying still its ancient significance as a touchstone or symbol by which the psyche, working unconsciously, seeks to understand and evaluate the actual experiences of life or, when deprived of these, to catalyse and precipitate them. In Jung's theory these archetypes, symbolic figures of high antiquity with the help of which ancient man came consciously to terms with the frightening world into which he had been born, exist in modern man only on an unconscious level because modern man seeks, however unsuccessfully, to make himself at home in the world merely by understanding it intellectually. In an attempt to relate ourselves to the physical universe and to our fellow-creatures by sheer ratiocination, by science or social science, we have rejected the wisdom so painfully learned over thousands of years and crystallised in the archetypes. For centuries now we have beaten these holy pictures, these archaic icons, these fabulous forms into unconsciousness. We have hunted them underground with a kind of insane savagery. Fortunately we have not been able entirely to destroy them for they remain even in our time, or so it seems, our most valuable symbols.

Of course, we would never call their operation in our dreams and daydreams, thinkings. I say the most valuable symbols because it is by means of these that we come to terms with life's deepest demands. It is by means of them that we do make the maximal use when building strong, balanced, crystalline personalities. According to Jung and others, the impoverishment of symbolism in our time, our rejection and suppression of the towering figures of myth and fable, have reduced our ability to understand, enjoy, endure, and even feel life to the point where experience has become a colourless waste, a void which strikes us down from behind, as Melville might say, with thoughts of annihilation and fear of death. As Jung puts it,

> While our intellect has been achieving colossal things, our spiritual dwelling has fallen to pieces. We are thoroughly convinced that even with the latest and largest reflecting telescopes, now being built in America, we will discover behind the farthest nebulae no empyrean ... and we know that our might will wander despairingly through the emptiness of immeasurable extension. Nor are matters improved when mathematical physics reveals to us the world of the infinitely small – swarms of electrons into all eternity! In the end we dig up the wishes of all times and peoples and find that everything most dear and precious has already been said in the most winning and lovely words.[6]

But we cannot possess this wisdom merely by reaching out for it. Through a peevish but persistent misunderstanding of the difference between facts and science, between knowledge and wisdom, we have created in the psyche a deep cleft which will not soon be healed, though no problem is as important for us as that it should be. Otherwise, we will, in our loneliness and craving, our despair and self-accusation, destroy ourselves and each other. As another thinker puts it,

> A philosophy that knows only deductive or inductive logic as reason, and classes all other human functions as "emotive", irrational and animalian ... can show us as the approach to Parnassus [only] the way of factual data, hypothesis, trial, judgment, and generalisation. All other things our minds do are dismissed as irrelevant to intellectual progress; they are residues, emotional disturbances, and throwbacks to animal estate.
>
> But a theory of mind whose keynote is the symbolic function, whose problem is the methodology of significance, is not obliged to draw that bifurcating line between science and folly ...
>
> The continual pursuit of meanings – wider, clearer, more negotiable, more articulate meanings – ... permeates all mental life: sometimes in the conscious form of metaphysical thought, sometimes in the free, confident manipulation of established ideas ... and sometimes – in the greatest creative periods – in the form of passionate mythical, ritual, and devotional expression.

Only the recovery of myth and rite, of vast ancient icons and moving symbols, can help us heal the spirit in the modern psyche, can refill the springs of thought and imagination which have so obviously run dry, reducing us, in spite of all our boasted science, reason, and progress from the healthy animalian into blind, despairing, and vicious animals not infrequently more murderous, certainly much less adapted and effective, than the beautiful beasts of the jungle.

Fortunately, the means of our cure lies within us, though so completely submerged that we have no notion at all that it is there until the archetypes, those submerged touchstones of vital values, begin to force themselves upon our notice in what Emerson called "the strange masquerade of dreams". Now these archetypal images or icons are so common to the human race at all times and in all places that Jung calls them communal or collective, and speaks of the unconscious level or layer or world in which they exist as the Collective Unconscious. It appears to him that they do not derive from personal experience or achievement but are, definitely, inborn. "I have chosen the term 'collective' because this part of the unconscious is not individual but universal; in contrast to the personal psyche, it has contents and modes of behaviour that are more or less the same everywhere and in all individuals." We can see that the Swiss psychologist has given up the notion that the mind of the newborn child is a *tabula rasa* or that there is nothing in the individual's psyche which was not first in that individual's senses. As Jung, speaking of the archetypes which he calls the Anima and Animus, says:

> they bring into our ephemeral consciousness an unknown psychic life belonging to a remote time. This psychic life is the mind of our ancient ancestors, the way in which they conceived of life and the world, of gods and human beings. The existence of these historical layers is presumably the source of the belief in reincarnation and in memories of past lives. As the body is a sort of museum of its phylogenetic history, so is the mind. There is no reason for believing that the psyche, with its peculiar structure, is the only thing in the world that has no history beyond its individual manifestation. ... But the unconscious psyche is not only immensely old, it is also able to grow unceasingly into an equally remote future. It forms, and is part of, the human species just as much as the body, which is also individually ephemeral, yet collectively of immeasurable duration.

Jung tells us very little about how the archetypes which the human species has inherited got into the mind in the first place. His system implies, however, and I think it may be safely said, that there is nothing in the collective psyche that was not at some time in the collective senses of men.

I mean simply that the basic facts of life, the forces of generation, love, growth, sun and rain, summer and winter, matriarchy and patriarchy, animals, healing, and death, furnished the early mind with images or combinations of naively related images – such as those in which mother, earth, and queen were equated with goddess, or those in which beast, sun, and king were equated with god – which the human race lived with so long that they have come down to us in the shape of ineffaceable thought-forms, relatively unchanged over thousands of years. The universal diffusion of such imagery is perhaps to be accounted for by the universal diffusion of the prehistoric experiences out of which they were fashioned. Of course, the uniformity with which primitive men in all parts of the world hit upon icons, rites, and myths to symbolise their perceptions and values is uncanny, and validates, to a degree at least, Jung's hypothesis of a Collective Psyche which insists on organising the material of experience in such a way as to strengthen mental health instead of sheepishly following at all times the lead of facts. These latter can be, *per se*, either neutral or hostile to psychic life.

The problem for disoriented modern man, as Jung sees it, is how success-fully to dredge up from the deep waters of the unconscious those potent images called archetypes, which can still, in the midst of our self-inflicted chaos, support the mind in its search for the deep joy, the pulsing awe, the integration with mystery which make life worth living. This is where Falstaff can help us, as he once helped Hal and so many other would-be lords of life, for he is, curiously, one of Jung's archetypes. This figure is called by the psychologist the archetype of the Wise Old Man.

Dreams, according to Jung, work for us – seek to bring to our attention things we need to know, disagreeable truths that we will not admit, wisdom which, because it is not the wisdom of this world, has been denied us by our parents, teachers, and so-called peer groups. Like Hal, most of us, it seems, are "essentially mad without seeming so". Astray in a world where honour- and power-mad men like Hotspur and Henry IV seek to purchase success by the subjugation of natural instinct, humane feeling, and personal affection; where faith, love, joy, and self-sacrifice are considered mere words; where honour, which is indeed a mere word, is valued above faith, love, joy, and self-sacrifice – so derailed, we need to return to the life-nourishing wisdom of the past. We need to recover the great symbols which made it great to live, and can make it great again if we can free these giants from the prison into which we have thrown them. Fortunately, says Jung, "there is not a single important idea or view that does not possess historical antecedents", and some of the most important, the most life-sustaining, are among the oldest. All are represented by, "all founded upon archetypal, primordial forms, whose sensuous nature dates from a time when consciousness did not yet think, but merely perceived".[7] Now, the archetypal figure that can open the way for us out of the dark forest of the meaningless, purposeless waste of spirit which this world calls honour and enterprise is precisely that of the Wise Old Man – the undying Falstaff of dreams. It is just this archetype which Jung singles out as perhaps the most important "authority" operative in the unconscious psyche. It is interesting that one of the titles of Indian Ganeśa is Opener of the Way, a title which could be justly applied, it seems, to all the figures we have been studying in this work.

An old Greek work, Δφόιον'Iηoo'ν, represents the way to the Kingdom of Heaven as being pointed out to man by animals, and Jung tells us that the

Wise Old Man of dreams is often associated with animals or even, on occasion, takes their forms. These animals represent, perhaps, the soundness, trustworthiness, of our instincts when left untroubled by conscious attempts to explain them, or rather to explain them away. This archetypal figure associated with animals sheds a bright light, but it is not the light of ratiocination; "he is an immortal demon, and he penetrates the chaotic darkness of mere life with the light of meaning".[8] He is himself the symbol of "the pre-existent meaning concealed in chaotic life", and it is this meaning that he illuminates, to which, as the master, the teacher, the enlightener, he points the way. He is the ancestor of all prophets and "the father of the soul". When he speaks to us in dreams – and he sometimes conveys his ideas in pronouncements as direct as those of the skin-clad prophet who left the wilderness of Tekoa in order to bring warning and light to the Hebrews – his tone is that of authority and solemnity, even if what he is saying may seem to be, according to the wisdom of this world, nonsense. To experience this archetype in the strange masquerade of dreams is to enjoy an experience which is, says Jung, essentially religious. Though this "demon of wisdom" may appear as a handsome old man dressed in white in whom we easily recognise a conventional icon of Zeus or God or Arthur in Avalon, he comes to us more often accompanied by the animals, sometimes enormous and dangerously wild, which represent the natural instincts that underpin successful daily living but only when used and directed by the bearded master of life. Jung says that had the name Lucifer not been prejudicial, he would have adopted it for this archetype, for this word not only means "light-bringer" but calls up the picture of a bearded creature accompanied by animals or himself possessing horns and hoofs. "But I have been content to call it," concludes this pioneering psychologist, "the *archetype of the wise old man or of meaning.*"

A typical dream in which this wise old "mana personality" appeared to a male patient is reported by Jung as follows:

> He [the patient] is in a primeval forest. An elephant is somewhat threatening; then [appears] a large ape-man or bear or cave-man with a club, who threatens to attack the dreamer. Suddenly he of the "pointed beard" is there and fixes the assailant with his gaze in such a way that the latter is held off by his spell. But the dreamer is in great fear. A voice says, "Everything must be ruled by the light."[9]

It would be whimsical of me to attempt to add anything to Jung's analysis of this dream, but it is odd to find in it so many of our Falstaff figures. Ganeśa the elephant, Bes the ape, and Merlin the wild man or Wodewose, not to mention the Devil himself, who is a more humanised form of the bestial gods who here seem to be his attendants. It must be the Devil's voice speaking in the role of Lucifer that says, "Everything must be ruled by the light." The sun, Jung points out, "is a symbol of the wellspring of life and of the final wholeness of man ... a classic symbol that even yet stands very close to us."

Sometimes the Wise Old Man appears as a "miraculous fellow traveller" encountered, much to the relief of the dreamer, on a journey where he opens the way to untold spiritual treasure. Outstanding examples of this archetype guiding famous dreamers are to be found, says Jung, in Krishna instructing Arjuna in the *Bhagavad-Gita*, in Khadir leading Moses in the Koran. Sometimes this archetype appears – surely this will not surprise us – as a plump dwarf or bearded child. Always the master of life, in whatever shape, praises brilliance, pointing to "a spot on the ground with red light on it"[10] or presiding over the construction and operation of a complicated orrery, but the attainment of the light in question is often made conditional upon what the dreams call "the reconstruction of the gibbon". This has no other meaning, says Jung, than that the anthropoid – man as an archaic fact – must be reconstituted and the rightness and importance of his animal instincts, properly understood and heartily embraced, recognised as the basis of all deep and high human existence. To these teacher–pupil pairs we might add all those we have encountered in the preceding chapters, with Virgil–Dante and Mephistopheles–Faust for good measure.

> The regressive identification [of the dreamer] with the human and animal ancestors means psychologically an integration of the unconscious, actually a bath of renewal in the source of life ...
> If it is taken seriously, the symbolism of the rites of renewal points beyond the affairs of childhood to the innate psychic disposition that is the result and deposit of the whole ancestral life reaching back to the animal level: hence ancestral and animal symbolism. It is a question of attempts to annul the separation of consciousness from the unconscious, this being the actual source of life, and to bring about a reunion of the individual with the maternal soil of the inherited, instinctive disposition. ... The autonomy and autarchy of consciousness ... spell the danger of isolation and barrenness in that they produce, by splitting off the unconscious, an unbearable *remoteness from the instincts*, and the loss of instinct is the well-known source of endless errors and confusion.

Such renewal and integration of unconscious forces, resulting in a deepening and strengthening of the personality, may be promoted not only by sleep and its dreams, especially if the Wise Old Man presides over their "work", but also by drunkenness, especially if the revels at the Boar's Head are presided over by a Falstaff. "We are confronted, therefore," says Jung, "with a Dionysiac mystery" involving a Socratic questioning and reversal of the values of this world, a consecration or apotheosis of the drunkard and a ritualistic death to worldliness. Jung is referring here not so much to actual as to dream-symbolic intoxication. In addition to Falstaff, the Boar's Head Tavern itself is, it seems, a construct of dreams, a rather shabby form of an archetypal image called the *temonus* or sacred place. That the Boar's Head Tavern may be aptly compared to a sacred enclosure suitable for initiation, maturation, and consecration is suggested by the drinking that went on in Valhall and that goes on continually in Christian churches in the form of

Holy Communion. Here the wine represents, it would seem, the deep spring of unadulterated life force.

A typical dream recorded by Jung, one from which, we may be sure, the Wise Old Man with his prophetic pronouncements was not far distant, runs as follows:

> Immense Gothic cathedral almost completely dark; High Mass is being celebrated. Suddenly the whole wall of the transept collapses. Blinding sunlight streams into the interior of the church, and with it a large herd of bulls and cows.

Jung assures us that in these dreams in which light and animals play so important a part the unconscious, the Collective Unconscious, is not playing tricks or craftily seeking to lead the dreamer still further astray, but is working desperately to revive, to resurrect, in him divine truths distorted by convention or blanked out by the pale cast of thought. The unconscious, he says, "is simply trying to restore to the world of religion the lost Dionysos, who is somehow lacking to modern man". "Everything must be ruled by the light" was the utterance that summed up the dream commanding "the reconstruction of the gibbon" – the oracular pronouncement of one whom Christians call "the Lord of Darkness with horns and goats' feet" but who is "actually a Dionysiac corybant who has rather unexpectedly attained the honours of a grand duke".

The soul's need of Silenos–Satan is likewise, according to Jung, the true meaning of a dream in which the dreamer found himself in a large gathering in a great mosque-like temple bare of ornament:

> Many jovial and solid people are there. We all go back and forth, speak together, greet one another, and wine (*from an Episcopal seminary for priests*) and refreshments are handed around. ... A *priest* explains to me: "These somewhat trivial pleasures are officially approved and permitted. We must adapt ourselves to the American methods. That is unavoidable with large-scale operation as we have it. But we distinguish ourselves fundamentally from the American churches by an outspoken anti-ascetic tendency." Then I awoke. Feeling of great relief.

Jung stresses the point that it is one of the functions of this type of dream to convince the dreamer that the return to the deep sources of life and light has a strictly sacramental character. Such a dream "brings the church into immediate relation with the sanctuary of Dionysos, as indeed the historic process has done, though in the reverse direction. ... It is not a backsliding but ... a psychological *nekuia*"[11] or guiding back of the dead to the flowing sources of life. And the guide, the opener of the way, the tutor, the master, the enlightener, is – need we say it again? – precisely the Falstaff-persona with whom we have been dealing throughout this book.

Before summing up the utmost range of this archetype's "authority", it will be useful to refer to one more dream in which his appearance is reported.

> I came into a particular, *hallowed house*, the "house of the gathering".
> In the background are numerous candles that are arranged in a peculiar
> form with four points running upward. Outside, at the door of the
> house, stands an old man. People go in. They do not talk, and stand
> motionless in order to collect themselves inwardly. The man at the door
> says of the visitants of the house, "As soon as they come out again, they
> are clean." Now I go into the house myself and am able to concentrate
> fully. Then a voice speaks: "What you do is dangerous. Religion is not a
> tax that you can pay to enable you to dispense with the image of the
> woman, for this image is indispensable. Woe to them who use religion as
> a substitute for another side of the life of the soul; they are in error and
> will be accursed. Religion is no substitute, but is to be added to the other
> activity of the soul as a completion. *Out of the fullness of life shall you
> bring forth your religion: only then will you be blessed!*" While the last
> sentence is being spoken in especially loud tones, I hear distant music,
> simple harmonies upon an organ. Something about it recalls the "fire
> magic" theme of Wagner. As I now go out of the house I see a burning
> mountain and feel: "The fire that is not quenched is a holy fire."

It is not clear just whence the oracular voice issues, but it may be assumed
that it comes from the light-associated Wise Old Man who stands outside
guiding people into the temple, and who reappears at the end, somewhat
like the Old Cossack of Murom after the seasonal battle, as "a burning
mountain". It is hardly necessary to remind the reader of Falstaff's association with candles, either when he is compared directly to a great taper or
when, in the Christmas forest, he is made the centre of a drama of
candle-crowned fairies whose headdress is described as resembling precisely
that of the Lucia Queens of modern Sweden, long recognised as descendants
of pagan witches. As Jung says of this dream: "the view ... that religion may
not be a substitute for 'another side of the life of the soul' merely spells for
any persona a striking innovation. According to this conception, religion is
equated with completeness; it even appears to express the integration of the
self in the 'fullness of life'." Such fullness of life, at least for modern man, is
hardly possible, Jung seems to think, without the help of the Falstaff-
persona, visiting us either from the unconscious or through great creations
of art, and he therefore finds that in this dream "the soft chiming in of the fire
magic, the Loki theme, is not inappropriate".[12]

These dreams dominated by the Wise Old Man and his authoritative
pronouncements are then, according to Jung, forms of genuine religious
experience, which he tends to define as "that kind of experience which is
characterised by the highest appreciation", by a kind of ecstasy deriving
from the individual's realisation that his psychic contents are of a supra-
personal order and the attendant conviction that "in man God is accom-
plishing his own transformation. The changes to which man is subject, his
whole evolution, are in the last resort nothing less than a reflection of the
Becoming of God – a pattern of emergent Deity." Jung insists that the term
"religion" is not to be identified with a confession of faith or the codified and

dogmatised forms of any so-called religious organisation, but is essentially "an experience of the numinous" characterised by a blissful sense of meaning, significance, purpose – a conviction that we were there when God laid the foundations of the earth, that we know what he had in mind, that in a mysterious way we are one with him, that our whole duty is to co-operate with his will to emerge.

> I must point out that religion is not a question of faith at all but of experience. Religious experience is absolute and cannot be disputed. ... It makes no difference what the world thinks about religious experience; those who have had it possess a great store of something that can be a source of life, meaning, and beauty for them; something that sheds a new radiance on the world and all men. Such people have *pistis* and peace.

Experience of this kind is both the seed and the flower of the whole – that is, the wholly alert or integrated – personality for the achievement of which all the weirdly glorious pageantry of the unconscious is summoned up, marshalled, and set in action by the Wise Old Man. We have seen how men have at all times identified real battles with struggles against seasonal force, but the true and continuing significance of all the Shrewsburys and Agincourts is that they symbolise an inward struggle for spiritual rebirth. Every man who wishes to live at peace with himself and be a blessing to others needs a Falstaffian tutor to help him see through the mirages of honour, power, money, and bowdlerisation of values which cannot nourish, which may even destroy, the life of the spirit. The only true water of life is love of life, the only true growth of the spirit is growth in love. Beginning perhaps on what is called the animal plane ("the image of the woman ... is indispensable") and slowly raying out from there to include the creation, love is the only cure of souls. Nothing less than this completeness in love can give the individual psychic rest, for the individual soul, according to Jung, is but a fragment of a Collective Psyche, an Emersonian Oversoul, in which it lives and moves and has its being.

If it is objected that this Oversoul is merely an under- or inner-soul, that the God whom the dreamer is helping to emerge is merely a portion of the individual himself, that the hieratic pronouncements of the Wise Old Man are simply the hidden vision of the individual talking to himself, Jung will not really object. The one thing needful is to *experience* in the heart's depths the valour and glory of an emotion so mysteriously shot through with gleams of omnipotence, omniscience, and conscientiousness that, for the time of its duration, we feel a blessed release from our customary irksome mediocrity, an immersion in what we tend to call, perhaps for want of a more precise word, Godhead.

> Unfortunately we live in a modern setting, where ultimate things are doubtful ... and where people are fully aware of the fact that if there is any numinous experience at all, it is the experience of the psyche. We can no longer imagine an empyrean world revolving round the throne of

> God, and we would not dream of making for him somewhere beyond
> the Galactic system. But the human soul seems to harbour mysteries ...
> [and the mind in search of wholeness will be grateful for religious
> experience, from whatever source] for if it means anything, it means
> everything, to those who have it. ... Through the spiritual need of my
> patients I have been forced to make a serious attempt at least to
> understand some of the extraordinary implications of the symbolism
> produced by the unconscious mind.

The greatest of these implications is that we, all of us everywhere, are
literally, even if on an unconscious level, parts one of another, those deepest
but hidden values – if they are not those of the world – are essentially the
same. Though an aberrant desire for honour, wealth, and cultural con-
formism has taught us, at shattering cost to our mental health and physical
survival, to repress this fundamental psychic fact, the strange phenomenon
of bad conscience and the commandments of dreams are always trying to
force us to acknowledge our true oneness in and through the Collective
Psyche. This Psyche is as mysterious, as omnipotent, as omnipresent, and as
omniscient a deity as any ever described, seizing upon and reducing to
misery and madness the human soul that denies the commandments to love
and thereby be fruitful.

Our whole study of the Falstaff-persona, the archetype of the Wise Old
Man, in this book is itself considerable evidence, it seems to me, for Jung's
claim that the human psyche in every time and country is full of collective
material which, in the mythology and folklore of different peoples, repeats
itself in almost identical form. Indeed, we are all parts one of another, in
token of a common parent, "the eldest god", who "haunts [us] in the likeness
of an old fat man", and seems from the evidence assembled in this book to be

> an universal and common Spirit to the whole world. ...
> If there be a common nature that ... ties the scattered and divided
> individuals into one species, why may there not be one that unites them
> all? However, I am sure that there is a common spirit that plays within
> us ... and that is the Spirit of God, the fire and scintillation of that noble
> and mighty essence which is the life and radical heat of spirits. ... This is
> that gentle heat that brooded on the waters and in six days hatched the
> world: this is that irradiation that dispels the mists of Hell, the clouds of
> horror, fear, sorrow, despair; and preserves the region of the mind in
> serenity.

God reveals himself to us in strange ways, and the Falstaff-epiphany may
seem to us the strangest of all, but it is possibly the oldest and certainly the
most irrepressible. This is the end to which our globe-encircling journey has
led us, an unveiling and a revelation somewhat unexpected, perhaps, but
not too unforeseen in a study which has carried us back again and again to
"the eldest god". What we did not foresee was that the white-bearded baby
whom we magi have found lying among his animals in the manger of a
tavern was *the* God. But here we are, it seems. Everything ideal springs

organically from a sensuous basis – the highest flight of good government and constructive imagination from dancing, drinking (of one intoxicant or another), coupling with "the female", questioning law and religion – everything considered sacrosanct – and Falstaff is the spirit that negates convention in behalf of the "elder world", a sturdier truth. This is the significant relevance of Falstaff.

Fortunately Falstaff stands, like Ilya, a mountain of fire against his critical blasphemers from Johnson to Wilson, and in his latest incarnation as reindeered Santa Claus he stands fast still – the Mock King of mankind's latest version of the Sacaea, of man's continuing brave attempt through jollity and equality, hilarity and love, to recapture the Golden Age – against all ill-natured attempts to overthrow the dream. In 1950 the Dutch Reformed Church of South Africa, spurred by ex-pastor Malan, the Prime Minister of the country, "denounced Christmas celebrations as 'heathen rites' and ... condemned Freemasonry, the equality of the sexes, and the U.N. Declaration of Human Rights", while in December 1952 the Rev. J.S. Bonnell of the Fifth Avenue Presbyterian Church of New York City denounced Christmas parties in offices as often "nothing more than old Roman Saturnalias", recalling with horror that in the original Saturnalia "masters mingled freely with their slaves in an orgy of feasting, drunkenness, and immorality" and imploring Americans to combat the Falstaff-hot "wave of secularism which is sweeping across the nation like a sea of lava". Also in December 1952, the Roman Catholic Church of Spain issued through its organ *Ecclesia* a solemn episcopal warning against "the increasing popularity of Santa Claus and of 'profane' Christmas cards. ... *Ecclesia* charged that 'the impudent appearance of Father Christmas in the dreamland of our children' concealed 'a sectarian sin, hidden under the red garb of an Old Man, who seems naive but who has spent many hours of his life as a knave'." Every year, in fact, churchmen attack this figure, "so surfeit-swell'd, so old, and so profane", whom they, at least, do not confuse with Bishop Nicholas of Myra. In December 1951, the Roman clergy and lay organisations in Mexico formally denounced the Christmas tree and Santa Claus as "pagan and Anglo-Saxon", while during that same season of good will to all men we read that

> Through the streets of Dijon, France ... two days before Christmas paraded a troupe of boys and girls bearing an eight-foot effigy of the French Santa Claus, *Père Noël*. Before Dijon's cathedral the marchers halted, and one of their number stepped out and addressed the others:
> "What shall we do with *Père Noël*?"
> "Burn him at the stake!" piped the children.
> They hung the straw-filled effigy on the cathedral fence and set it afire. Over the smoking embers they posted a notice: "This is not a sporting boast nor a publicity stunt, but a loud and strong protest against a lie which is incapable of awakening religious sentiment in children ... *Père Noël* is the son of minds empty of God."

> The auto-da-fé was part of a campaign by Roman Catholic clergy
> against the "paganisation" of Christmas. It drew an approving ... nod
> from the West Reverenurice Feltin, Archbishop of Paris: "the Christian
> significance of Christmas is debased by this legend [of Santa Claus]
> originating in the dense Saxon forests."

In tracing the lineage of Santa Claus, these ecclesiastics are perhaps not
too far off the track, but I offer this whole book as evidence that they
misunderstand the significance and power of the legend. His avatars and
followers, the witches of the Middle Ages, the Oldcastles of the Renaissance,
have been burned in fact as well as in effigy, but the divine force which alone
can reconcile body and soul, heaven and earth – presiding over a realm of
mental summer, hope, and sanity – lives on and will continue to unless
mankind, gone collectively mad through its stubborn denial of the Collective Psyche in which we are one, chooses to liquidate its very existence,
now considered so hopelessly torn, tense, and miserable that suicide is
clearly to be preferred.

I did not write this book to prove that there is still a Santa Claus, but I am
willing to predict that he will be around for a long time. For thousands of
years before the appearance on earth of any church now surviving and in a
truly catholic, that is, a worldwide sense, this old, white-bearded figure
came to life in the human mind. In one global form or another he led the
attack on the wisdom of this world, on man's inhumanity to man, on
heartless power-seeking, cold-blooded ambition, murderous honour, and
wars that violate the central divine commandment to couple, preserve, and
multiply. It sometimes seems as if this old mentor of mankind, though
tortured, derided, and thrust into the black prison of the unconscious, were
still our most vocal and trustworthy Opener of the Only Way that can
preserve the human race from insane and self-inflicted destruction. If this be
so, we can only pray that he strengthen us nightly in dreams, daily in the
world's drama, especially the plays of Shakespeare, and as many times a
year as possible in Saturnalian holidays intended to combat all that contracts, constricts, and freezes up the spirit of man, making it impossible for
him to "foot it fleetly as in the Golden Time".

Notes

Preface

1   J. Dover Wilson, *The Fortunes of Falstaff* (Cambridge and New York, 1944), p. 13.

2   H.B. Charlton, *Shakespearean Comedy* (New York, 1940), p. 163.

3   H.C. Goddard, *The Meaning of Shakespeare* (Chicago, 1951), p. 178.

4   Lord Raglan, *The Hero* (London, 1949), p. 216.

Chapter I   The "Magnificent Irrelevance" of Falstaff?

1   J. Dover Wilson, *The Fortunes of Falstaff* (Cambridge and New York, 1944), p. 17.

2   Ibid., p. 18.

3   Loc. cit.

4   *Henry IV*, II, iv.

5   F.L. Lucas, *Tragedy in Relation to Aristotle's "Poetics"* (New York, 1928), p. 77.

6   E.E. Stoll, "Falstaff", *Modern Philology*, October 1944, *passim*.

7   T.W. Spargo, *An Interpretation of Falstaff* (St Louis, 1922), *passim*.

8   Lord Raglan, *The Hero* (London, 1949), p. 214.

9   Sir Charles Oman, *History of England* (London, 1936), pp. 219–20.

10   Raglan, op. cit., p. 213.

11   Introduction to *The Labyrinth* (London, 1935), pp. 213–14.

12   *Kamasastra*, quoted by E. Wellsford in *The Fool* (New York, 1935), pp. 63–4.

13   *Julius Caesar*, I, iii.

14   *Macbeth*, II, iv.

15   *Troilus and Cressida*, I, iii.

16   *Richard II*, III, iii.

17   Loc. cit.

18   Ibid., III, ii.

19   John Harding, *Chronicle*, quoted in M.A. Murray, *The God of the Witches* (London, 1951), p. 153.

20   H.B. Charlton, *Shakespearean Comedy* (New York, 1940), p. 174.

21   Loc. cit.

Chapter II   Presenter of the English Folk Plays as Shakespeare's Model

1   Page 70.

2   Ibid., pp. 170, 174, 188, 219, etc.

3   Ibid., p. 189.

4   Ibid., p. 248.

5   Ibid., p. 157.

6   Ibid., p. 248.

7   Ibid., p. 113.

8   *1 Henry IV*, II, iv.

9   Tiddy, op. cit., p. 229 and *passim*.

10   Ibid., p. 192.

11   Ibid., p. 257.

12   Ibid., p. 256.

13   *The English Drama*, ed. E.W. Parks and R.C. Beatty (New York, 1935), p. 47.

14   Tiddy, op. cit., p. 149.

15   Ibid., p. 185.

16   Ibid., p. 204.

17   IV, i.

18   *English and Scottish Popular Ballads*, col. F.J. Child, ed. G.L. Kittredge (Boston, etc., 1904), p. 402.

19 Loc. cit.

20 Quoted in Tiddy, op. cit., p. 134.

21 Ibid., p. 157.

Chapter III Silenos, a Greek "Bolting-Hutch of Beastliness"

1 Quoted by H.A. Guerber, *Myths of Greece and Rome* (New York, etc., 1893), p. 300.

2 *2 Henry IV*, I, ii.

3 *1 Henry IV*, II, ii.

4 Mayura, *The Sanskrit Poems*, tr. G.P. Quackenbos (New York, 1917), p. 127.

5 *Dionysiaca*, tr. W.H.D. Rouse, Loeb Classical Library (Cambridge, Mass. and London, 1940–42), ii, 111–13.

6 Ibid., ii, 161.

7 Ibid., ii, 163.

8 *1 Henry IV*, II, iv.

9 Ibid., II, iii.

10 *2 Henry IV*, II, ii.

11 Loc. cit.

12 Ibid., II, iv.

13 *Merry Wives of Windsor*, II, i.

14 *1 Henry IV*, II, iv.

15 *2 Henry IV*, II, ii.

16 Ibid., II, iv.

17 Ibid., I, ii.

18 *1 Henry IV*, V, iv.

19 *Merry Wives of Windsor*, V, v.

20 *1 Henry IV*, II, i.

21 Rabindranath Tagore, *Autobiography* (London, 1914), pp. 35–6.

22 *2 Henry IV*, I, ii.

23 Mayura, op. cit., p. 224.

24 Euripides' *Bacchae*, tr. Gilbert Murray (London, 1904), p. 61.

25 Cf. H. Frankfort, *Kingship and the Gods* (Chicago, 1948), pp. 313–33 for a fine account of the Akitu festival.

26 Plato, *The Symposium*, tr. B. Jowett.

27 Ibid., tr. P.B. Shelley.

28   *Crito*, tr. F.M. Stawell in *Socratic Discourses by Plato and Xenophon* (Everyman Library, 1910), p. 364.

29   Epilogue to *Henry V*.

Chapter IV   Bes of Egypt, Who Was "Born with a White Head and Something a Round Belly"

1   A.E. Wallace Budge, *The Gods of the Egyptians* (Chicago and London, 1904), ii, 285.

2   *1 Henry IV*, II, ii.

3   *2 Henry IV*, I, ii.

4   *Henry V*, II, iii.

5   Budge, op. cit., ii, 286.

6   Ibid., II, pp. 287–8.

7   Enid Wellsford, *The Fool: His Social and Literary History* (London, 1935), p. 56.

8   Ibid., p. 57.

9   Quoted in ibid., p. 57.

10   Henri Frankfort, *Kingship and the Gods* (Chicago, 1948), pp. 79–88.

11   Ibid., p. 86.

12   Adapted from *Ancient Records of Egypt*, ed. and tr. J.H. Breasted (New York, 1906–07) i, 352–3.

13   Sir James Frazer, *The Golden Bough*, abridged ed., (New York, 1922), p. 584.

Chapter V   Enkidu, "the Town Bull" of Mesopotamia

1   *Gilgamesh: Epic of Old Babylonia*, tr. W.E. Leonard (New York, 1934), p. 5.

2   Ibid., p. 3.

3   Ibid., p. 8.

4   Ibid., p. 9.

5   Ibid., pp. 12–13.

6   Ibid., p. 10.

7   Ibid., pp. 10–11.

8   Sir James Frazer, *The Golden Bough*, abridged ed., (New York, 1922), pp. 281–2.

9   *Gilgamesh*, op. cit., p. 9.

10   Ibid., p. 33.

11 Loc. cit.

12 Ibid., pp. 34–5.

13 Ibid., pp. 36–7.

14 V.H. Steinthal, *The Legend of Samson*, repr. entire in I. Goldziher, *Mythology Among the Hebrews and Its Historical Development*, tr. R. Martineau (London, 1877).

15 Ibid., p. 415.

16 *2 Henry IV*, II, ii.

17 Ibid., II, iv.

18 *Merry Wives of Windsor*, V, v.

19 Ibid., II, i.

Chapter VI Abu Zayd of Islam, Who Thumbed His Nose at "Old Father Antic the Law"

1 *1 Henry IV*, I, ii.

2 Loc. cit.

3 *Koran*, tr. J.M. Rodwell (Everyman Library, 1909), pp. 187–8.

4 *The Dialogue or Communing between the Wise King Solomon and Marcolphus*, ed. E.G. Duff (London, 1892) with an introduction on the history of the legend, on which I have drawn heavily in my discussion of the figure, and a bibliography of various early versions of the dialogue. In her book *The Fool* E. Wellsford has also made considerable use of Duff.

5 E. Wellsford, *The Fool* (New York, 1935), p. 39.

6 *1 Henry IV*, I, ii.

7 E. Wellsford, op. cit., p. 81, from which much of the account of Buhlul is adapted.

8 Summarised by D.B. Macdonald, *The Religious Attitude and Life in Islam* (Chicago, 1909), pp. 103–4.

9 R.A. Nicholson, *A Literary History of the Arabs* (Cambridge, 1907), p. 293.

10 Adapted from DeSlane's translation, quoted by Nicholson, p. 295.

11 Ibid., p. 293.

12 Ibid., p. 295.

13 *The Book of the Thousand Nights and One Night*, tr. by Powys Mathers from French tr. of J.C. Mardrus (London, 1937), ii, 242–3.

14 Ibid., p. 535.

15 Hisham Ibn-al-Kalbi, *The Book of Idols*, tr. N.A. Faris (Princeton, 1952), p. 21.

16   Cf. Sir Harry Luke, *An Eastern Chequer Board* (London, 1934).

17   Cf. E. Wellsford, op. cit., p. 32; some of the stories of Si-djoha are summarised here.

18   R.A. Nicholson, *Eastern Poetry and Prose* (Cambridge, 1922), p. 115.

19   Ibid., pp. 122–4.

20   Al-Hariri, *The Assemblies*, tr. T. Chenery (London and Edinburgh, 1867), p. 113.

21   Ibid., i, 222.

22   *1 Henry IV*, II, iv.

23   *2 Henry IV*, II, i.

24   Loc. cit.

25   Al-Hariri, ii, 26.

26   Ibid., ii, 30.

27   Ibid., i, 35–6.

28   P. Villari, *Life and Times of Savonarola* (London, 1888), p. 124.

29   *2 Henry IV*, III, ii.

30   J.L. Ross, *Philosophy in Literature* (Syracuse, 1949), p. 36.

31   J.H. Greenstone, *The Messiah Idea in Jewish History* (Philadelphia, 1906), p. 117.

32   Ibid., p. 119.

33   Ibid., pp. 102–3.

34   Ibid., pp. 224–5.

Chapter VII   From Kuvera to Ganeśa: Indian Falstaffs Who "Forgot What the Inside of a Church is Made Of"

1   *1 Henry IV*, III, iii.

2   A.K. Coomaraswamy, *Yaksas* (Washington, 1928), pp. 36–7.

3   *1 Henry IV*, II, iii.

4   Ibid., III, ii.

5   *The Prema-Sagara or Ocean of Love*, tr. F. Pincott (Westminster, 1897), pp. 88–9.

6   Ibid., pp. 285–6.

7   *2 Henry IV*, II, ii.

8   *1 Henry IV*, II, iv.

9   Loc. cit.

10 Loc. cit.

11 *2 Henry IV*, I, ii.

12 *1 Henry IV*, II, iv.

13 *Merry Wives of Windsor*, I, iv.

14 *Twelfth Night*, I, iii.

15 *2 Henry IV*, II, ii.

16 E. Wellsford, *The Fool* (New York, 1935), p. 199.

17 N. Macnicol, *Hymns of the Maratha Saints* (Calcutta and London, 1919), p. 37.

18 Macnicol, op. cit., p. 35. I have changed Macnicol's word "Bhakti" to "love-work".

19 This story, but told in different words, is available in English in C.A. Kincaid, *Tales of the Saints of Pandharpur* (Bombay and Madras, 1919), pp. 77–80.

20 A. Getty, *Ganeśa* (Oxford, 1936), p. 1.

21 Ibid., pp. 7–8.

22 Quoted in Getty, p. 2.

23 *1 Henry IV*, II, iv.

24 Getty, op. cit., p. 24.

Chapter VIII Ts'ai Shen of China, Who Had a Philosophy of "Good Sherris-sack"

1 V.M. Alexeiev, *The Chinese Gods of Wealth* (Hartford, 1928), p. 4.

2 Ibid., p. 10.

3 R. Patai, *Man and Temple* (London, 1947), p. 174.

4 W.E. Soothill, *The Hall of Light: A Study of Early Chinese Kingship* (London, 1951), p. xviii.

5 The first is translated by J. Legge in *The Sacred Books of the East*, vols. 27–8 (Oxford, 1885) and the second by J. Steele, 2 vols., (London, 1917).

6 Soothill, op. cit., p. 129.

7 Ibid., p. 130.

8 Steele, op. cit., i, 137.

9 Ibid., i, 144.

10 Alexeiev, op. cit., p. 3.

11 *The Texts of Confucianism*, Part I, tr. J. Legge (Oxford, 1879), pp. 128–9, being *The Sacred Books of the East*, vol. 3.

12 Ibid., p. 91.

13   Lionel Giles, *Gallery of Chinese Immortals* (London, 1948), pp. 32–3.

14   *1 Henry IV*, II, iv.

15   Ibid., I, iii.

16   Ibid., III, i.

17   Ibid., III, iii.

18   Loc. cit.

19   Cf. *"The Three Taoist Demons in the Cart-Slow Kingdom"* and *"The Three Demons of the Lion-Camel Mountain"*, the first of which is translated in *Monkey* (New York, 1943).

20   Giles, op. cit., p. 47.

21   Ibid., p. 48.

22   Ibid., p. 50.

23   Ibid., pp. 55–6.

24   Ibid., p. 58.

25   Ibid., p. 86.

26   Ibid., p. 91.

27   H.A. Giles, *History of Chinese Literature* (London, 1901), p. 181.

28   L. Giles, op. cit., p. 92.

29   Ibid., p. 92.

30   Loc. cit.

31   Ibid., p. 118.

32   Loc. cit.

33   Ibid., p. 121.

34   Loc. cit.

35   Loc. cit.

36   Ibid., p. 126.

37   W. Acker, *T'ao the Hermit: Sixty Poems by T'ao Ch'ien (365–427)* (London and New York, 1952), p. 23.

38   Loc. cit.

39   Quoted ibid., p. 24.

40   Quoted loc. cit.

41   *1 Henry IV*, II, iv.

42   Quoted by Acker, op. cit., p. 25.

43   Quoted loc. cit.

44   Quoted ibid., p. 26.

45 "Lu Ki's 'Rhymeprose on Literature'," tr. Achilles Fang, *New Mexico Quarterly*, vol. 22, no. 3 (Autumn 1952), p. 273.

46 Ibid., p. 281.

47 *The Temple and Other Poems*, tr. Arthur Waley (New York, 1923), p. 65.

48 Ibid., p. 72.

49 *1 Henry IV*, I, ii.

50 *Merry Wives of Windsor*, V, v.

51 *2 Henry IV*, IV, iii.

52 A. Waley, *The Poetry and Career of Li Po, 701–762 A.D.* (London and New York, 1950), p. x.

53 Ibid., p. vii.

54 Loc. cit.

55 Ibid., p. 103.

56 Ibid., p. 19.

57 Ibid., p. 20.

58 Ibid., p. 19.

59 Ibid., p. 86.

60 Quoted ibid., p. 59.

61 Ibid., p. 82.

62 Ibid., p. 81.

63 Ibid., p. 88.

64 Ibid., p. 89.

65 Quoted in "Preface" to *The Works of Li-Po*, tr. Shigeyoshi Obata (London, 1923), p. 17.

Chapter IX Ilya of the Slavs, Who "Fought a Long Hour By Shrewsbury Clock"

1 I.F. Hapgood, *The Epic Songs of Russia* (New York and London, 1885), p. 40.

2 Ibid., p. 45.

3 Ibid., p. 43.

4 Ibid., p. 47.

5 H.S. Robinson and K. Wilson, *Myths and Legends of All Nations* (Garden City, 1950), p. 178.

6 J. Machal, *Slavic Mythology* (Boston, 1918), p. 286.

7 *Merry Wives of Windsor*, III, v.

8   *2 Henry IV*, I, ii.

9   Hapgood, op. cit., p. 60.

10 Ibid., p. 110.

11 *1 Henry IV*, II, iv.

12 Hapgood, op. cit., p. 114.

13 Ibid., p. 63.

14 Ibid., p. 106.

15 Ibid., pp. 269–70.

16 Ibid., p. 272.

17 Ibid., p. 148.

18 Ibid., p. 149.

19 Ibid., p. 150.

20 Ibid., p. 273.

21 Ibid., p. 276.

22 *1 Henry IV*, V, iii.

23 Ibid., IV, ii.

24 Hapgood, op. cit., p. 281.

25 Plautus, *Miles Gloriosus*, tr. in *The English Drama*, ed. E.W. Parks and R.C. Beatty (New York, 1935), p. 1425.

26 Ibid., pp. 1454–5.

27 Ibid., p. 1466.

Chapter X   "Carry Sir John Falstaff to the Fleet"

1   *2 Henry IV*, V, v.

2   *1 Henry IV*, IV, i.

3   *2 Henry IV*, V, v.

4   J.L.C. Grimm, *Teutonic Mythology*, tr. J.S. Stallybrass, 4th ed. (London, 1880), i, 379.

5   S.Sturluson, *The Prose Edda*, tr. A.G. Brodeur from the Icelandic (New York and London, 1916), p. 92.

6   R.J.E. Tiddy, *The Mummers' Play* (London, 1923), p. 77.

7   *1 Henry IV*, IV, ii.

8   *The Poetic Edda*, tr. H.A. Bellows (Princeton and New York, 1923), p. 153.

9   Loc. cit.

10   Ibid., p. 158.

11   Ibid., p. 15.

12   Loc. cit.

13   Ibid., p. 25.

14   R. Wagner, *Das Rheingold*, tr. C.H. Meltzer (New York, n.d.), p. 21.

15   S. Sturluson, *The Prose Edda*, tr. A.G. Brodeur (New York and London, 1916), p. 141.

16   C.H.C. Wright, *A History of French Literature* (New York etc., 1912), pp. 26–27.

Chapter XI   Merlin of the Celts, Who "Went Away as It Had Been Any Christom Child" Rejected by Women

1   R.S. Loomis, *Celtic Myth and Arthurian Romance* (New York, 1927), p. 136.

2   Sir T. Malory, *Le Morte d'Arthur* (a title mistakenly given by the printer Caxton to a work which was to have been called *A Book of Arthur and His Knights*), Everyman Library (London and New York, 1906), I, 36–7.

3   V.G. Schoepperle, *Vassar Medieval Studies*, p. 4f. and Loomis, op. cit., p. 352.

4   Loomis, op. cit., p. 135.

5   Ibid., p. 131–2.

6   Malory, op. cit., i, 40.

7   Ibid., i, 17.

8   Ibid., i, 59.

9   Cf. R. Bernheimer, *Wild Man in the Middle Ages* (Cambridge, 1952), p. 142.

10   Malory, op. cit., i, 91.

11   *Henry V*, II, iii.

12   M.A. Murray, *The God of the Witches* (London, 1931), pp. 32–3.

13   Loomis, op. cit., p. 202.

14   Ibid., p. 195.

15   Loc. cit.

16   *2 Henry IV*, II, iv.

17   Loc. cit.

18   *2 Henry IV*, III, ii.

19   For the nature and practices of this order cf. C.B. Millican, *Spenser and the Round Table* (Cambridge, 1932), pp. 61ff.

20   *1 Henry IV*, II, iv.

21   *Merry Wives of Windsor*, I, i.

22   *2 Henry IV*, V, iii.

23   *Merry Wives of Windsor*, I, i.

24   *1 Henry IV*, I, ii.

25   *As You Like It*, I, i.

26   *Merry Wives of Windsor*, IV, iv.

27   Ibid., V, v.

28   *English and Scottish Popular Ballads*, collected F.J. Child, ed. G.L. Kittredge (Boston, etc., 1904), p. 265.

29   Ibid., p. 355.

30   R. Graves, *The White Goddess* (New York, 1948), p. 331.

31   J. Ritson, *Robin Hood* (London, 1823), p. x.

32   Graves, op. cit., p. 330.

33   Ibid., p. 329.

34   Loc. cit.

35   Lord Raglan, *The Hero* (London, 1949), p. 50.

36   *English and Scottish Popular Ballads*, p. 289.

37   Ibid., pp. 352–4.

38   Ibid., p. 278.

39   Loc. cit.

40   Cf. ibid., p. 288.

41   Murray, op. cit., p. 38.

42   *1 Henry IV*, II, i.

43   Ibid., II, ii.

44   J.D. Wilson, *The Fortunes of Falstaff* (Cambridge and New York, 1944), p. 16.

45   Loc. cit.

46   *Columbia Encyclopaedia*, ed. C.F. Ansley (New York, 1941), p. 1059

47   Cf. Murray, op. cit., *passim*.

48   Wilson, op. cit., p. 117.

49   Ibid., p. 121.

Chapter XII   The Magnificent Relevance of Falstaff

1   *1 Henry IV*, II, iv.

2   *2 Henry IV*, I, ii.

3   J.D. Wilson, *The Fortunes of Falstaff* (Cambridge and New York, 1944), p. 15.

4   *Shakespeare*, ed. S. Johnson (London, 1765) iv, 356.

5   *2 Henry IV*, V, v.

6   C.G. Jung, *The Integration of the Personality*, tr. S. Dell (London, 1940), p. 64.

7   Ibid., p. 83.

8   Ibid., p. 87.

9   Ibid., p. 124.

10   Ibid., p. 181.

11   Ibid., p. 150.

12   Ibid., p. 187.

Index

Names of characters and mythological figures are given as written eg Dame Quickly.
Names of real people, authors etc are inverted eg Frazer, Sir James

Lakśmi 102
  Krishna as husband 109
Lame Jane 12, 16
Lan Ts' si-ho 134
laws
  civil-religious of Muslims 79
  controversion by Lord of Misrule 77
  controversion in the name of justice 77
  disregard by fools 91–2
  Islamic and jesters 83
  Moses and Khadir 79
  overturning by Mock Kings 94
Le Livre d'Artus 176
learned fool 8, 82–3, 99
legends viii, ix
Leonard, William E 61
Lestoire de Merlin 179
Li Chi 125
Li Po 128, 139
  at Cha'ng-an 140
  as Banished Immortal 140
  death 142–3
  drinking 140, 141, 142
  sword 142
life force imagery 199
Little Devil Don't 14
Little Twing Twang 21
Little Wits 14
Liu Ken 131–2
Loki 160–171
  animal association 168
  family protector 171
  in form of mare 164
  imprisonment 167
  love of Freyr 170
  as Mock King 167
  Oberon as form 162
  rejection 166
  riding Gold Bristle 170
  similarities to Falstaff 166
  as son of Mimir 162
  trick to recover Thor's hammer 164
Lollard movement 191–2
Loomis R S 175
Lord of Misrule
  controversion of laws in name of real
    justice 77
  Falstaff as 159
  Loki as 161–2
  Robin Hood as 187
love, completeness and psychic rest 205
love-death 181

Lu Ki 136
Lucia Queens (Sweden) 204
Lucifer 201
Lucretius 34
Luke, Sir Harry 87

Ma Hsiang 133
Macbeth 59
Mahabharata 111, 114
  Ganesa's description 118
Maid Marian 16, 184
  as Divine queen 188
Malory 179
*Man and Temple in Ancient Jewish Myth
  and Ritual* 97
Maqamat 80, 87, 88
Marcolf 81–2
Marko Kralyevich 154
Marsyas 30
Martlemas 169
Mayura 30–1, 37–8
Meghaduta 103
Mephistopheles-Faust 202
Merlin 105–10, 173–184
  antler-crowned 175
  carried to Avelon 182
  fertility magic 178
  imprisonment 179
  love affair with Nimue 179
  metamorphosis 175
  seasonal battle 178
  stag association 177
Mesopotamia 61
Messiah 37
  disguised as dwarf 97
  false 97
Metternich stele 51
Michelangelo 34
midwinter ceremony in China 124
Miles Gloriosus 154–5
Milton, John 34
Mimir 162–3
Ming T'ang 124
  ceremonies 135
  first built 136
  Li Po's poem 140
  seasonal ceremonies 127
Minotaur 67
Miracle Plays 2
Mock King 6–8
  Absalom as 41–3
  banishment after seasonal danger 159